MW01013928

UNFINISHED BUSINESS

On and Off the Court
with the 1990–91
Boston Celtics

JACK MCCALLUM

SUMMIT BOOKS
New York London Toronto Sydney Tokyo Singapore

SUMMIT BOOKS
Simon & Schuster Building
Rockefeller Center
1230 Avenue of the Americas
New York, New York 10020

SUMMIT BOOKS and colophon are trademarks of
Simon & Schuster Inc.

Designed by Irving Perkins Associates
Manufactured in the United States of America

10 9 8 7 6 5 4 3 2 1

Library of Congress Cataloging-in-Publication Data

McCallum, Jack, date.
    Unfinished business : on and off the court with the 1990–91 Boston
Celtics / Jack McCallum.
        p. cm.
    Includes index.
    1. Boston Celtics (Basketball team)   I. Title.
GV885.52.B67M33   1992
796.54—dc20   91-41880
                                                     CIP

ISBN: 0-671-73374-5

Photo nine by Nathaniel Butler/NBA Photos
All other photos by Steve Lipofsky

To my father, Jack McCallum, who first took me
to Convention Hall in Philadelphia,
where the air was filled with smoke and magic.

Acknowledgments

One does not enter a project involving the Boston Celtics without trepidation. So much has been written about this celebrated franchise by so many talented writers that one feels the crushing weight of history simply by typing the words "Red Auerbach." Furthermore, the Celtics are covered—and, boy, are they covered—on a daily basis by some of America's best sports journalists. Their constant competitive presence, at home and on the road, made this a better book. I *had* to make that game-day shootaround, ride that early team bus to the arena, collar that stray player when no one else was looking. And for that I thank, in alphabetical order: Mike Arace, Steve Bulpett, owner and proprietor of "Chez Bulpett," Mike Fine, Jackie MacMullen (Boyle), Peter May, Mark Murphy, and Bob "The Commissioner" Ryan.

Thanks also to: Patricia Moran Starner, Barry Isenman, and Stephen Cannella, Boston College wunderkind, for clerical assistance; to four of my (many) bosses at *Sports Illustrated*, Mark Mulvoy, John Papanek, Peter Carry, and Sandy Padwe; to my editor at Summit Books, Dominick Anfuso; and to my agent and friend, not in that order, Reid Boates.

As an organization, the Celtics do not particularly reward their employees for cooperating with the press. Therefore, I won't single out any players, coaches, executives, trainers, doctors, broadcasters, wives, or public relations people, and will merely say thanks to all those who gave me their time. Really, no one dodged me. All right, maybe Dave Gavitt. But he did it so *nicely*.

All my love and appreciation, finally, to Donna, Jamie, and Chris, who, as usual, hardly knew I was gone.

Contents

Introduction

MAY 17, 1991

Like a congregation of lost souls, various members of the Boston Celtics hierarchy drifted aimlessly outside the visiting team locker room in the cavernous Palace of Auburn Hills, the suburban home of the defending NBA champion Detroit Pistons. A long, exceptionally difficult, and ultimately ambivalent Celtics season had ended a half hour earlier with a heartbreaking 117–113 overtime loss to the Pistons in Game 6 of the Eastern Conference semifinal playoffs, and now there was so much to say and no way to say it.

Alan Cohen, the team owner most intimately involved with basketball matters, looked like he was sucking on a lemon. An offensive goaltending call on the Celtics' Kevin McHale made by referee Jack Madden—later revealed through instant replay to be clearly incorrect—had quite possibly cost the Celtics the game; Cohen, who earlier in the season had been fined by the league for criticizing referees after a defeat, was trying, and not succeeding, to get Jack Madden out of his mind. Cohen's partner, Don Gaston, an easygoing fellow who bears an uncanny, and sometimes unfortunate, resemblance to slapstick-comedian Benny Hill, brought his wife, Paula, a diet Pepsi from the locker room. It's a kind of private ceremony they share when they travel on the road together, but this time it was steeped in gloom.

Chris Ford tried to smile from time to time but just couldn't get the corners of his mouth to move upward very well. The rookie head coach had taken his club further than most preseason prognosticators thought he would, but now, as the Pistons celebrated down the hall and the Celtics packed their bags for the last time, that was little consolation. Ford's assistants, Don Casey and Jon Jennings, looked dazed and confused. Generally, they are the ones supplying the behind-the-scenes interpretation of the game to reporters and fans, but now they

11

had very little to say. The playoffs were a new experience for both Casey, who had labored for eight years in the NBA with remarkably unsuccessful teams, and Jennings, a rookie coach. Later Jennings remarked how empty he felt inside.

One can only imagine what club president Red Auerbach was doing in the sitting room of his home in Washington, D.C. Auerbach hardly ever travels to away games anymore, but he viewed this ulcerous pageant live on Ted Turner's superstation, TNT, complete with endless replays of the maddening Madden mistake. It was safe to reach two conclusions about Arnold Auerbach in those terrible moments right after the game: he was smoking a cigar, and he was cursing the absolute living hell out of Jack Madden.

Dave Gavitt, who was in his first year as senior executive vice president of the Celtics, a position created for him right below Auerbach, looked ambassadorial, even in this, the worst of times. He always does. Gavitt whispered words of shared condolence to Ford and his assistants, exchanged sympathetic pats and handshakes with the owners, nodded and smiled and stayed away from Boston reporters, who already had questions about postseason matters. After a few moments Gavitt headed to the Piston locker room to congratulate Detroit coach Chuck Daly and general manager Jack McCloskey. That is the correct thing to do, though Auerbach never did it. The opposition always came to Auerbach; Auerbach did not go to the opposition. In the past, Gavitt and Daly had shared a weekend of golf in North Carolina, an annual event that brings together the crème de la crème of the basketball world, people like legendary North Carolina University coach Dean Smith and superstar Michael Jordan. That was the company that Dave Gavitt kept.

Inside the Celtics locker room, there was a sense of . . . of what? It wasn't anger. It wasn't gloom exactly. And we can safely eliminate joy. It was the emptiness that Jennings was feeling, the experience of losing a game that had been all but won having anesthetized everyone to emotion. Still, there had to be a small sense of relief within each player. The year had been a long, long roller-coaster ride of dizzying highs and stomach-turning lows. For the first three months of the season the Celtics were as good as any team in the league. Then Larry Bird's back turned cranky and they treaded water for a while. Then Bird came back and they were good again. Then Bird went out and they were downright bad. Then Bird came back on kind of a part-time basis, and they were kind of a part-time team, sometimes good, sometimes bad, sometimes mediocre. Along the way, McHale, Reggie Lewis, and Robert Parish had, like Bird, played bravely through pain. It was just no way to go through a season.

A year earlier the Celtics had bowed out in a much more disappointing, and embarrassing, fashion in a Game 5 first-round playoff loss to the New York Knicks at Boston Garden. It was one of the more ignominious defeats in the history of this proud franchise, and no one would compare that to the effort extended on this spring evening at The Palace. Yet . . . the more things change, the more they remain the same. The questions that were asked after the loss to the Knicks were now, one year later, being pondered again. A professional team, particularly one in the spotlight like the Celtics, does not really have an offseason, you see. The endless continuum that is sports demands that the next season begins as soon as the curtain descends on the season before. What changes will be made? Who will be there next year? What has to be done to move you closer to a championship?

At the center of these questions were, predictably, the Celtics' veteran Big Three: Bird, McHale, and Parish. They had been mentioned so often together during the season, usually to compare and contrast them with "The Kids" (Brian Shaw, Reggie Lewis, Dee Brown, and Kevin Gamble), that they now went by one long name: LarryKevinandRobert. That's how they were known, and almost always in that order. LarryKevinandRobert. Last year it was widely assumed that Auerbach and the owners had to trade one of them while their value was still high in order to get a fresh and invigorated team that could challenge for the championship. Over my dead body, was Auerbach's basic response, and his faith in the Big Three proved to be justified. Each had an excellent season, and, in fact, on more than a few winter evenings, each was as good as any of his NBA counterparts—Bird as the do-everything forward, McHale as the prolific off-the-bench scorer, Parish as the indomitable presence in the pivot. But still, no matter how much one praised their valor, the fact remained that by the end of the season they were broken down. All of them.

Parish, the NBA's oldest player at thirty-seven, had been the healthiest of the Big Three through the season, but, ironically, a badly sprained ankle had forced him to miss the final game against Detroit. Dressed impeccably (as usual) in a gray suit, he had nothing to say to the press and was quietly talking to friends near the Celtics' team bus.

McHale's performance in Game 6 had been nothing less than miraculous. Playing on badly damaged feet and ankles, he had squirmed and twisted his way to a game-high 34 points, at times single-handedly keeping the Celtics close. As soon as the final buzzer had sounded, Isiah Thomas, the captain of the Pistons, ran through the crowd to seek out McHale. "I just wanted to tell him what a pleasure it was to play against men like him," Thomas later explained. "People don't realize how infrequently players like Larry, Kevin, and Robert come

along, and I wanted to make sure he knew that it makes me feel proud
to be an athlete at times like this." Thomas bristled when asked if he
made the gesture because he thought that he'd never again be facing
LarryKevinandRobert on the same team. "Now there you are trying to
stir up some shit," said Thomas to a reporter.

McHale, though, touched on exactly that theme as he sat on a stool
in the locker room, speaking slowly and rather sadly, looking a hundred
years old. Dr. Arnie Scheller, the Celtics' team physician, had already
indicated his desire to operate on McHale's left foot in the offseason.

"A great team will find ways to win," McHale said, referring to the
Pistons. "We have to get back to that here . . . whoever of us *is* here."
Someone asked him about the controversial goaltending call and he
just shrugged his shoulders—he didn't even have the energy to go
after Madden. "It just croaked us" was all he said. (McHale often uses
verbs that nobody else thinks of. A few days earlier, when talking about
Detroit's rebounding dominance, McHale said the Pistons "gang-
banged" the boards.) Another reporter asked him to summarize his
feelings. He shrugged his shoulders again. "It's very, very disappointing. And the older you get, the more disappointed you get, because you
never know. This might be your last chance." He sighed deeply. "It's
been a long, hard year, particularly since February 14 [the date he first
sprained his ankle]. I've spent more time with [Celtics trainer] Ed
Lacerte than I have with my wife and kids. It's been a very, very
fatiguing year, one of the more mentally fatiguing of my career. If it
was my team, I'd quit right now."

Now *that* was one bummed-out player. Someone tried to be uplifting
and mentioned the strong Celtics comeback, which had erased a
Pistons lead that reached as much as 17 points in the third period.
"Yeah," he said, "and the patient *almost* lived." Then McHale got up
and hobbled away, his eleventh season, and in many ways his most
difficult, now officially complete.

The final piece of the LarryKevinandRobert puzzle was in hiding.
The visiting team locker room at The Palace is divided into two sec-
tions, separated by the shower room, and theoretically both are open to
the press. But the Celtics—being the Celtics—had closed off half of it
and posted a sign barring the media. Bird was over there, receiving
postgame treatment for his back, as he had been doing for the last four
months of the season. It is literally impossible to overestimate the
degree to which Bird's back problems had dominated the last half of
the season. Either (a) the press was asking about it, and team officials
were being elusive; or (b) Bird was being asked about it, and he was
saying he didn't want to talk about it; or (c) Gavitt was calling an

official press conference to make a statement about Bird's back while never fully addressing all the issues; or (d) no one was talking about it, but everyone was *thinking* about it. It was truly the big, pink elephant hiding in the broom closet. Bird's impressions of Game 6, during which he played bravely but largely ineffectively because of the pain and stiffness, were relatively unimportant. Three weeks earlier, Jackie MacMullen of *The Boston Globe* had broken the story that Bird and his medical advisers had decided that he should have postseason surgery, and the press wanted to confirm whether or not a date had been set.

But word finally filtered down that neither Bird, nor Gavitt, nor any other Celtics official, would have anything to say about a back, a Bird, or a Bird's back. Suddenly the locker room door burst open, and out came McHale, followed closely by Bird, who put his head down and started walking briskly toward the bus almost before anyone could react. MacMullen had stationed herself down the hallway and stepped in toward Bird as he approached. This is known in journalistic circles as "taking the charge," and sometimes it's the only way to get an athlete to answer a question. (Its counterpart in political journalism occurs when desperate White House reporters, cordoned off from the President, scream a few quick questions that invariably get lost in the whirr of propeller blades.) Their exchange lasted about ten seconds.

"In kind of a hurry, aren't you?" said MacMullen.

"I just wanna get the fuck outta here," answered Bird.

"Have you made a decision on the surgery?"

"Not yet," said Bird.

And then he was gone, leaving behind hopes, dreams, memories, and questions, lots of questions.

Walking a few feet behind the throng, assistant coach Jennings paused to look around one last time. His first season on an NBA bench had been eventful and eye-opening—after all, at the age of twenty-eight he had given instructions to legends like Bird and even coached non-Celtics superstars like Michael Jordan and Charles Barkley in the All-Star game—but now it was over, and the emptiness had already begun to set in. Jennings halfheartedly objects when the adjective "bookish" is ascribed to him, but it seems appropriate. Who else in the NBA would be found reading *The New York Times* in the locker room?

"What are you thinking, Jon?" someone asked him.

"I'm thinking that it was a great season," said Jennings. "But, in the end, it was all unfinished business."

* * *

The 1990–91 Boston Celtics season was one of change for the NBA's most tradition-steeped franchise. Not that the Celtics would ever herald it as such, of course. Phrases like "A New Beginning!" and "There's No Stopping Us Now!" are for the Los Angeles Clippers and Sacramento Kings of the world, the mongrels that desperately scramble for scraps of food season after season. But—make no mistake about it— the Boston Celtics were, and still are, a team in transition.

And with good reason. For the better part of three decades they dominated the NBA, winning sixteen championships between 1957 and 1986 and suffering only three losing seasons in that span. At times, the entire league seemed to be engulfed in the smog of Auerbach's cigar smoke as the Celtics set a standard of excellence—and arrogance—that seemingly no one could even approach.

But over the last few years things started happening. Maybe it was plain bad luck or just the worm's inevitable turn, but suddenly it was the Celtics who couldn't buy a break. It started after they won the championship in 1986 with one of the strongest teams in NBA history. Boston's record was 67–15, and McHale, among others, was convinced that they could've gone 82–0 except for lapses of concentration and pure boredom. And in the college draft that followed the Finals, the Celtics appeared to be getting even stronger with the acquisition of Len Bias, the second choice (behind Brad Daugherty) in the 1986 draft. At six feet eight, Bias was a strong yet graceful player, something like Michael Jordan in a bigger, less spectacular package, and the perfect frontcourtman to substitute for both Bird and McHale. Indeed, versatility had been one of the keys to the Celtics' success. Bird was both a small and a power forward, and his passing ability made him, in effect, a guard also. McHale was both a forward and a center. The backcourt starters, Dennis Johnson and Danny Ainge, were nearly interchangeable too. Bias would fit right in.

But less than forty-eight hours after Bias was selected, he was dead. A party back at the University of Maryland to celebrate his good fortune had ended in his snorting a lethal dose of cocaine. To this day it remains unclear whether or not Bias had been a steady drug user, but certainly no one in the Celtics organization had any reason to believe that he was. The loss was devastating. Perennially successful teams rarely get the chance at a blue-chip college player like Bias because the draft is scaled for weaker teams to pick first; the Celtics had moved up to No. 2 through an earlier trade with the Seattle SuperSonics, a typical Auerbach stratagem. "People don't realize we lost Lenny Bias not just for the next season or the season after that," Auerbach would say. "We lost him for the nineties! That's how good this kid was." Shortly before the tip-off of the 1986–87 season at Boston Garden, Celtics general manager Jan Volk noticed something under the couch in his office. He bent over and picked up an unused portion of a plane ticket issued to Lenny Bias—Volk figured that it had slipped out of Bias's pocket during his postdraft visit to the Celtics offices. "It gave me the chills," said Volk. And the tragedy cast a pall over seasons to come.

The Celtics did manage to make the Finals again in 1986–87, but it was a terribly difficult season as injuries all but negated the contributions of backup center Bill Walton, who had been such a pivotal figure in the championship season the year before, and limited those of McHale, who eventually had postseason foot surgery. The Lakers beat them in six games for the title. By 1987–88, the Celtics had clearly been passed by the young, brash, and muscular Pistons, who eliminated them in six games in the Eastern Conference finals. The 1988–89 season was an unmitigated disaster by Celtics standards. Bird, who underwent surgery to both heels in November, played only six games, and Boston barely made the playoffs, where it was promptly swept by the Pistons in the first round. And though the Celtics rebounded to win fifty-two games in 1989–90, they still fell to the Knicks in that infamous Game 5 at Boston Garden.

Nobody announced it. Nobody pounded his fist on the table and said, "That's it!" But clearly it was time for change.

The hiring of Gavitt just a few weeks after the shocking defeat to the Knicks was the first and strongest indication that things would be different. To suggest that Auerbach fought the move, or in any way feared the diminution of his power with Gavitt in charge of the day-to-day operation, is ridiculous. By this stage in his life Auerbach, who was seventy-two, desperately wanted someone like Gavitt, the ultimate man-for-all-seasons in the basketball world, to shoulder the major part of the Celtics responsibility. Volk was supposed to have done that when Auerbach made him general manager in 1984, but Volk, a longtime family friend of Auerbach's who had worked his way steadily up the Celtics administrative ladder, never really had the full respect and cooperation of the players or the owners. Gavitt, who had been a successful player, coach, and administrator, had clout and interpersonal skills that Volk did not possess.

Though it appeared to follow the "Celtics' way of doing things," the hiring of Ford, a former Celtics player and assistant coach, resulted in another major change for the organization. For most of the decade of the eighties, the Celtics' playing style roughly paralleled the organization's management style—it was slow and old-fashioned, as opposed to energetic and fast-breaking. Of course, it was also precise, efficient, entirely apropos for its personnel and, above all, very, very successful. But that playing style, too, had grown shopworn. In his two seasons as head coach (1988–89 and 1989–90) Jimmy Rodgers struggled with the problem of changing the style. He said he wanted to install an up-tempo game but couldn't quite bring himself to do it, and his indecisiveness helped tear the team apart. That was not the only reason that Rodgers was fired two days after the Game 6 loss to the Knicks, but it had a lot to do with it. Ford, however, did more than pay lip service to the idea of running. He *insisted* on it. He screamed for it. He challenged LarryKevinandRobert to follow it. And it brought results.

That playing style was helped, of course, by a decision the Celtics made on the evening of June 27, 1990, when they chose Dee Brown, a relative unknown from Jacksonville University, as their first-round draft pick (and No. 19 overall). Like most teams, the Celtics plan for the draft with several roundtable discussions that include owners, executives, coaches, and scouts. Eventually a consensus is reached, and individuals outside the organization cannot be exactly sure who made the decision and who was against it. (Later, when a draft pick has proven to be boom or bust, the principals either take subtle credit for the decision or subtly distance themselves from it.) The coaching staff loved Brown, who was only six feet one and a skinny 160 pounds but probably the quickest player in the rookie class, and Gavitt came to love him too. Auerbach, as is his wont, had his eye on big centers, however. That is understandable for someone who drafted Bill Russell, placed him in the pivot, and watched the Celtics win eleven championships in thirteen years.

"Look, how about this kid Schintzius?" Auerbach would say during the roundtables, referring to a seven-foot-one center from the University of Florida named Dwayne Schintzius. Or he'd blow some cigar smoke into the air and say: "Shouldn't we be thinking about this Causwell kid?" talking about a seven-foot center from Temple named Duane Causwell. Finally, Gavitt, in his stately manner, turned to Auerbach and said: "Red, if you have your way, we'd have all seven footers on this team. Only trouble is, there wouldn't be anyone to pass the ball to them." Everyone laughed. And the Celtics picked Dee Brown.

They had no way of knowing it at the time, but Brown's selection proved to have a profound sociological impact on the franchise. At the All-Star game in February Brown won the Slam-Dunk Contest, an irony that cut deep into the fabric of the NBA. For the better part of their forty-four years in the league, the Celtics had been identified as the big, slow, white team bound by the laws of gravity, and here came a small, young, black jumping jack to claim the ultimate showtime prize in the ultimate showtime sport. Largely because of Brown, the Celtics telecasts and radio broadcasts started to look and sound different. "I bet this year we've called more slam dunks, spectacular plays, dramatic plays with flair, and things like that than collectively in the last ten years," said Glenn Ordway, the Celtics' respected radio commentator. "That doesn't mean it wasn't great basketball before. But it tended to be guys whipping the ball around in a halfcourt game, or Larry hitting one of his little scoop shots, or Kevin somehow wriggling his way around two defenders to hit a layup. This was clearly different."

At the same time, two other young black players, Lewis and Shaw, were getting more of an identity in Boston too. The net result was that the Celtics started to look and feel more truly "urban." Ordway's production crew started to feed on that also, using rap music to lead into the pregame shows. Young black fans in Boston actually started to wear Celtics green, an anathema in years past when the Chicago colors of Michael Jordan or the L.A. Lakers colors of Magic Johnson would dominate, even in Boston. "I think the black fan who is in Boston, or who kind of liked Boston but didn't want to be perceived as liking an all-white team, now has a reason to pull for Boston," said Jerome Stanley, the young, black Los Angeles–based agent who represents Lewis and Shaw and who himself caused quite a stir in Beantown during the season.

There were other little changes. The hiring of Casey as an assistant coach helped the Celtics, in some small way, to a new identity. A loosey-goosey, high-energy fellow, Casey is the archetypal career coach who has a drill for every situation, a situation for every drill, and a humorous comment for every situation and every drill. He is a long way from the buttoned-down organization types the Celtics customarily favored as assistants, and Case's outgoing personality and off-the-wall manner helped the franchise's public relations immensely.

This was also the season that the Celtics stepped ever so gingerly into the area of halftime promotions. While other clubs around the NBA have for years unleashed a numbing volume of sales pitches on their arena patrons, the joke around Boston Garden was that the most intriguing halftime entertainment was the ball rack. But on a few evenings fans were called out of the stands to shoot baskets for a chance at free trips from Northwest Airlines. That was big news in Boston.

The 1990–91 season was the one in which the hallowed Boston Garden, a foul-smelling, sixty-three-year-old edifice that is, depending on one's perspective, either an antiquated temple of doom or the grandest basketball palace on the face of the earth, seemed to say: enough is enough. During an early season game against Atlanta, players suddenly started slipping and sliding like the Three Stooges on skates. The temperature was unseasonably mild on that day and the Garden's "cooling system," such as it is, could not reduce the condensation that turned the famed parquet floor into a series of small puddles. The game was postponed. That kind of thing happens in high school once in a while but rarely at the professional level.

Another change that cut deeply into the soul of the Celtics was the retirement of legendary radio announcer Johnny Most, who, at the age of sixty-seven, became too ill to continue behind the mike. As Auerbach slipped into the shadows, Most became the most obvious sword carrier of Celtics tradition. Night after night, in arena after arena, smoking cigarette after cigarette, Most viewed the world as one big morality play, with the Celtics dressed in white and everybody else in black. In Most's cockeyed view, his beloved Celtics were never wrong—NEVER, NEVER, NEVER—and who knows how many fans in the Greater Boston area bought into his downright surrealistic homerism. Hundreds? Thousands? Millions perhaps? After all, Most had been around for thirty-eight seasons, just a couple fewer than Auerbach, who was hired as coach in 1950. There was absolutely no one like Most behind a microphone, but he could not properly be called an anachronism because, against all logic, he still had clout. People *bought* him. No other retirement, including Auerbach's, could so drastically alter the public perception of the Celtics. One cannot measure that, of course, but it is significant that fans will no longer get their Celtics news from a propagandist's bully pulpit.

That was the thematic basis, then, for *Unfinished Business*—a look at a professional sports franchise, a uniquely important and interesting one, in flux. But as research and the Celtics' season progressed, themes somewhat gave way to people. As they should. The players, coaches, wives, front office people, announcers, fans, league officials, even the reporters that follow a team, comprise the soul of a daily comic-drama (more comedy than drama) that, in the case of the 1990–91 Celtics, covered almost a full year, from their elimination in the 1990 playoffs to their elimination in the 1991 playoffs. That is the major part of this book.

A professional sports team is rather like the cast of a traveling road show. The actors have three distinct lives, the most obvious spent under the scrutiny of a demanding audience that builds and shatters reputations in the wink of an eye. Basketball is unique among our major sports in that it is so unremittingly *public*. Without the shields of protective equipment and very great audience distance, the pro basketball player is like the stage actor symbolically stripped naked on the court. If one listens and looks carefully, he can see how players react to pressure, how closely they listen to the coach during time-outs, how violently they react to a bad call by an official or abuse from the crowd, how angrily they glance at a teammate for a bonehead play.

A second life goes on when the team is together but away from the public stage, at practices, on bus rides to the game, relaxing on a road trip, kibitzing and trying to chase away the butterflies in the locker room before the game. The book deals heavily with that aspect, for it is in those moments that the true character and chemistry of a team is forged. There is no better place to see a loose and jocular Larry Bird, for example, than when he is kidding his teammates, or "bustin' 'em," as Bird likes to call it. The most accurate way to have taken the temperature of the 1990–91 Celtics was to observe Bird at practice or on the team bus. If he was bustin' his mates, one could be sure that the team was playing well and he was feeling good. If his back was hurting, and the team was doing badly, Bird could brood with the best of them. Fortunately, there were long stretches of the season when Bird was bustin'. There were the friendly but fiercely contested postpractice competitions among McHale and the other big men, who, try as they might, rarely got the best of him, either on the court or in the barrage of insults that followed hard upon the game. There were Dee Brown's experimentations with the dunk before his winning effort in the All-Star game. There were Yugoslavian center Stojko Vrankovic's bilingual workouts with Celtics legend Dave Cowens that bore no fruit, at least not in this season. There was the booming laughter of Parish, a surprisingly enthusiastic practice cheerleader, the nonstop shooting games of reserve Michael Smith, who expended most of his energy during practice, and the endless inventions of Casey, who, at one point, had his big men running from one side of the court to the other, picking up magic markers.

The third life of the players is the private one that they have away from the court and their teammates. McHale jokes with his wife about their childhood days in Hibbing, Minnesota. Lewis and Shaw hand out Thanksgiving turkeys to disadvantaged families in Roxbury, the poorest section of Boston. Dee Brown and his wife, Jill, struggle to come to grips with his sudden celebrity and the rash of ugly, hateful letters about their racially mixed marriage. Kevin Gamble, a shy young man who suddenly found himself in the Celtics spotlight by being promoted to a starter, visits youngsters at a children's hospital at Christmastime. Chris Ford tries to remain outwardly calm as he watches his oldest son play in a varsity basketball game. Don Casey drives, utterly lost, through the streets of north Boston as the time for a pregame meeting with his fellow coaches comes and goes. There are those Celtics, Bird and Parish in particular, who treasure their privacy and guard it with a bulldog tenacity. That is their right and it was respected. But in the extraordinarily public profession that they have chosen, or that has been chosen for them, the public and private man are often

indistinguishable. In the way they approach their art, and the manner
in which they interact with their colleagues, they reveal themselves.

To a lesser extent, finally, the book is about the National Basketball
Association at large. If the NBA has not exactly gone unexplored in
book form, it has most assuredly not been the subject of extended
rapture and wonder, as has, say, major league baseball (or even minor
league baseball). Though pro basketball is uniquely American, it has
never worked itself into our mythic framework. No one ever said, as
Jacques Barzun said of baseball, "To understand the American mind,
you must understand basketball"; pundit/baseball zealot George Will
wouldn't touch the game with a pair of rubber gloves. No, pro hoops
has always appealed, at least relative to football and baseball, to a cult
audience. Yet the popularity of the game keeps growing, almost at an
exponential rate. Baseball offers strategy and serenity and football
offers mayhem and muscle, but pro basketball has speed, sweat, sex
appeal. More than any other sport with the possible exception of
boxing, pro basketball has elevated itself through a cult of personality.
Bird, Magic Johnson, Michael Jordan, and the retired Dr. J, Julius
Erving—these are the people around which the game has grown in the
decade of the eighties and into the nineties. The last major book-length
look at the NBA, David Halberstam's 1981 classic, *The Breaks of the
Game*, chronicled a league in desperate trouble from drug use, indif-
ferent and inconsistent play, embarrassing television revenues, and
ignorant ownership. It was accurate but is now hopelessly outdated.
The NBA under its current commissioner, David Stern, is strong and
vital, not without problems certainly, but much more in the main-
stream of American pop culture than at any time in its forty-four-year
history. Years ago, the Celtics were the exception that proved the rule,
the one NBA team that *was* recognizable to that large segment of a
populace that didn't know, say, Connie Hawkins from Connie Francis.
Now, like so many things about the organization, that status has
changed. The Chicago Bulls are sexier. The Los Angeles Lakers are
more successful. The Detroit Pistons are more arrogant. Imagine that.

It would be ridiculous to claim that the 1990–91 season was the
most eventful in Celtics history. It did not, after all, produce a championship, as sixteen before. But it was an unusual season of great hope
and wrenching despair, of heroic performances and disappointing,
public failures, of change going one-on-one with tradition at every
turn. Those moments are frozen in time. As for the Celtics as a whole,
they are a work in progress.

CHAPTER 1

The Summer of Their Discontent

SUMMER 1990

WASHINGTON, D.C.

Even to a man as well traveled along Trouble's Highway as Arnold "Red" Auerbach, the offseason months of June, July, and August had turned into extraordinarily trying ones. The Celtics' 1989–90 season had ended abruptly and disastrously three months earlier, with a 121–114 loss to the New York Knicks in Game 5 of the Eastern Conference playoffs. Worse for the franchise, the loss had occurred at Boston Garden, the ancient artifact that was at one time a torture chamber for visiting teams in crucial playoff games.

Oh, the questions that swirled around this seventy-two-year-old man as he sat in his office, surrounded by the photos and mementoes of a glorious past. Dave Gavitt, a former Providence College coach and commissioner of the Big East Conference, had been hired to run the basketball operation with the title of "senior executive vice president." That put him directly under Auerbach, who was simply listed as "president" on the Celtics' masthead. When the Celtics brought Gavitt aboard in June, it was truly the equivalent of a white flag, a signal that the franchise needed help, and, oh, how the proud Celtics hated to make that admission. Just how, exactly, did Gavitt's elevation change Auerbach's status?

Days after that loss, Auerbach and the team's two primary owners, Alan Cohen and Don Gaston, had fired head coach Jimmy Rodgers. Auerbach prided himself on taking care of the members of the so-

23

called "Celtics family," and the decision to fire Rodgers, who had been
with the organization since 1979, weighed heavily on his mind. In
keeping with tradition, Auerbach wanted to elevate one of "his boys,"
Celtics assistant Chris Ford, to the head job, but one of Gavitt's first
moves had been to solicit the services of Duke University's Mike
Krzyzewski, the 1988 United States Olympic coach. The Celtics had
finally promoted Ford to the head job, but only after Krzyzewski had
turned them down. How bad did the organization, Auerbach in particular, look by chasing a college coach who ultimately spurned them?

Young point guard Brian Shaw, who after a contract squabble had
skipped out on the Celtics to play the 1989–90 season for Il Messaggero of the Italian Pro League, had spent most of the summer de-
nouncing a signed Celtics contract and stating that he wanted to
remain in Italy for another year. The same Italian team had just signed
another potential property, Yugoslav Dino Radja, a big center with lots
of potential who the Celtics believed was coming to back up Robert
Parish. Christ, what was going on? Auerbach had to be wondering. A
few decades ago, when he started to make trips abroad to run clinics
for the State Department, these people didn't know man-to-man defense from manicotti. And now they're stealing *my players*?

There was trade talk in the summer air too, most of it involving the
possibility—some said the inevitability—of breaking up the Celtics'
aging frontcourt trio of Bird, McHale, and Parish. None of that talk
came from Auerbach, however. Immediately after the loss to the
Knicks, Auerbach flatly stated that his three veterans were not the
problem and would not be traded. What if Gavitt felt differently?

Last but not least, the franchise was being positively bedeviled by a
player-agent, Auerbach's least favorite breed of humanity to begin
with. Jerome Stanley—young, black, outspoken, and relatively unknown (though becoming less so day by day)—was fighting not only to
keep his client, Shaw, in Italy, but also had raised the possibility that
Reggie Lewis, a new client, was not blissful in Beantown and might be
looking to move elsewhere unless he was given a better contract.

"Look, I don't want to talk about specific people and personalities,"
said Auerbach, when asked about Stanley. "It's not my bag."

Well, it is his bag, of course, and a few weeks later he ripped Stanley
to an old friend, *Boston Globe* columnist Will McDonough, wondering,
among other things, what kind of "spell" Stanley had over his two
Celtics clients and ruing the greed and disloyalty that in his opinion
have damaged pro basketball, his life for the last forty-five years.

But how could he not feel otherwise? For years, Walter Brown, the
first and still most beloved of Celtics owners, would steer Auerbach

down one of Boston Garden's musty hallways, shake his hand, and welcome him back as Celtics coach for another year. That's the way contracts were drawn up, that's the way dynasties were created. Agents? Bill Russell didn't have an agent. Bob Cousy didn't have an agent. Hell, Red Auerbach, who commands thousands for a speaking engagement these days, doesn't have an agent.

"I remember Larry Fleisher [the late head of the NBA Players' Association and one of the first player-agents] called me one year, and said, 'I represent [John] Havlicek.'

"So I said, 'I don't believe it. He can't be that goddamned dumb. You musta sold him a bill of goods.' And he said, 'No, I represent him.' And I said, 'I gotta hear that from him.'

"So he puts Havlicek on the phone and I ask him about it, and John says, 'Yeah, it's true. I gotta have representation.'

"And I said, 'Look, what do you want?' And he named a figure. And I said, 'You got it. Now get the hell out of that guy's office and come home.'"

Who knows if it really went down that way—Bob Wolff, who later handled Havlicek, says flatly that it did not—but the point is that Red Auerbach remembers it that way. That's the way Auerbach did business. Obviously, it would be a major part of Gavitt's job description to deal with the Stanleys of the world—Auerbach needed that aggravation like he needed no-smoking laws—but what else was Gavitt hired to do? Who would have the final say? In the old, glory days Auerbach ran what seemed like a one-man ship, but now he was surrounded on all sides by Cohen, Gaston, Gavitt, and Jan Volk, whose title of executive vice president and general manager put him right below Gavitt. The Celtics were starting to sound like General Motors.

"First of all, it was my idea to get Dave Gavitt," said Auerbach, peeling the foil off a Hershey's kiss. "Hell, I wanted a guy like that years ago, but I couldn't find the right person. Here you got Gavitt, a basketball man, experienced in administration, organization, negotiation. Plus on top of it all he was a former player and coach. Ideal."

The idea of another executive to fit in between Auerbach and Volk had been discussed a number of times over the years, but the troublesome 1989–90 season crystallized the matter for Cohen and Gaston. Someone was desperately needed, but that someone would have to have a depth of basketball knowledge and a reputation worthy of the Celtics organization.

"That sounds like we're talking about only one man," said Auerbach.

"Who?" said Cohen.

"Dave Gavitt," said Auerbach.

"There's the phone," said Cohen.

And Auerbach made the call that ultimately brought Gavitt to Boston.

Gavitt was widely considered the most powerful basketball administrator in the world because of his (a) brilliant stewardship of the Big East, one of the best known and most lucrative conferences in collegiate sports; (b) his work in negotiating the billion-dollar NCAA television package; and (c) his involvement with the international game through his position on the Olympic Committee and his work with USA Basketball, the group specifically concerned with amateur basketball. Though the party line on the pursuit of Krzyzewski held that everyone in the Celtics hierarchy was interested in him, there was no doubt that the impetus came from Gavitt. "Chris Ford was our first choice from the get-go," Auerbach had said at a June 12 press conference that presented Ford as the head coach, but such, of course, was not the case. That was Auerbach simply trying to rewrite history. Still, the old man did not step in to pull rank on Gavitt, not, at any rate, with the drama in mid-act. Had Krzyzewski not taken himself out of the running, it would have been interesting to see who would have prevailed, the new franchise saviour or the cigar-smoking eternal presence.

Several weeks earlier Auerbach had seemed to slight Gavitt in a live television interview when he struggled to remember his name. Asked by a local TV broadcaster about the Celtics' then-unresolved coaching situation, Auerbach responded: "I'll hear from What's His Name—Dave—about it." Jim Baker, the television sports critic for the *Boston Herald*, picked up on it. "So if they're such bosom buddies as we've been led to believe," wrote Baker, "how come Auerbach can't even remember Gavitt's name on live TV?" But that was simply Red being Red. The general rule around the Celtics offices for new employees is that if Auerbach knows your name within three months, you're doing a helluva job, and that extends to anyone appearing below him on the masthead, senior executive VPs included. To a certain extent, in fact, everyone in the world is a potential "What's His Name" to Auerbach, with the exception of those legends who played for him—Russell, Cousy, Heinsohn, the Jones boys, Havlicek. That is part of his eternal power and mystique. There is no other organization in professional basketball with somebody like Red Auerbach, somebody who can what's-his-name" the whole damn league. You can't go out and hire the kind of history that Red Auerbach provides just by showing up in the office. Isiah Thomas once made the point that the Detroit Pistons did not become a winner until he convinced club owner William Davidson to take a more active role in the club's affairs, to make the players feel wanted and a part of some tradition. But Celtics players feel that tradition exists, ipso facto, and Auerbach is the reason, the link between past and present, the continuum, the living proof that being a Celtic is not ephemeral but something you can reach out and touch. Since 1956, the year that Auerbach won his first championship with the Celtics, he has been involved as either a coach or a club executive in sixteen of the thirty-five NBA champions. "I might be wrong," says Kevin McHale wryly, "but it would seem kind of hard for Red not to feel good about himself." And he does.

Still, where would the buck now stop? With Gavitt or Auerbach?

"I will have the last word," pronounced Red. "But there won't be any problems because Dave and I are old friends. We believe in the same things. Dave is the hands-on guy, the basketball guy, the day-to-day guy. We'll be in constant contact, at least five times a week. It's just that I won't be up in Boston as much. [Though Auerbach might be the most famous Bostonian since Paul Revere, he has steadfastly maintained his place of residence in the nation's capital. He keeps a small utilitarian apartment in Boston, but if he lived there full-time, he says, he would've had virtually no private life for forty years.] I don't want to be chasing agents or working the phones. I'll do some scouting and stuff like that so I know what I'm talking about when I have to, but I don't have the patience for the day-to-day. It calls for a younger guy." He popped another piece of candy in his mouth. His passions, besides winning, are Hoyo de Monterrey cigars, Chinese food, candy, and reruns of "Hawaii Five-O," perhaps in that order. "Hey, I'm not a kid anymore."

That is typical Auerbach stubbornness—*there won't be any problems because I say there won't be any problems.*

Auerbach had already made it clear that he wouldn't be a memory. A few weeks earlier, he sat courtside while a group of Celtics free agents worked out at Babson College in Wellesley, a suburb of Boston. Wearing a baseball cap and Bermuda shorts, Auerbach looked something like George Burns in *Oh, God!* Gavitt, Cohen, Gaston, and Volk sat beside him, forming an odd folding-chair tribunal that gave a hard edge to the auditions. "Outside of Red's foul-smelling cigars," said Chris Ford, "I think everyone enjoys having Red sit there." Well, maybe. At one point Auerbach and Gavitt were approached by a fellow named Mirko Novosel, coach of the Cibona Club team of Yugoslavia that was practicing with the Celtics' free agents. Gavitt, who through his work with the United States Olympic Committee knows virtually every basketball executive in the world, immediately rose from his chair and greeted Novosel in the traditional Eastern European style, the coach touching first his right cheek to Gavitt's left, then his left to

Gavitt's right. Auerbach barely glanced at them, but Novosel could hardly contain his joy when Gavitt tapped Auerbach to make introductions. None were necessary, at least from Novosel's standpoint. It turned out that he had met Auerbach in 1964 when the already-famous Celtics coach brought a group of touring NBA all-stars through Europe, and Novosel had been a member of a Yugoslavian team. Through the haze of Auerbach's cigar smoke, Novosel and Gavitt listened enraptured as Auerbach reminisced about that trip. Red Auerbach may not know international protocol, or give two hoots about it, but he knows history.

His mind, when focused, is still sharp, but it can wander during long conversations and interviews, making him sound like one of Billy Crystal's old Jewish gentlemen, rambling on in a singsong rhythm while scattering cigar ashes hither and yon. Of the dozens of signed photographs on the wall, he says his favorite is the one of Jimmy Durante, "a great, great entertainer." If Red Auerbach were a talk show, he'd be Joe Franklin. But though it's easy to lampoon him for being caught up in the past, how many men of his age are not? Besides, the past is precisely what *is* relevant about Auerbach, it's what people want to talk about *to* him, as much as he wants to use it as his frame of reference. What is the value of asking Red Auerbach about, say, the NBA's complicated salary cap? He doesn't understand it and leaves it to Volk. Why ask Auerbach about the administration of the Milwaukee Bucks or the Houston Rockets? They're all What's His Names as far he's concerned. Donnie Walsh, general manager of the Indiana Pacers and a man with a fairly high profile among NBA people, says he's never even had a conversation with Auerbach.

Auerbach is amazed that Volk can actually call up on a computer the name and salary of every player in the NBA. "Can you imagine that?" he said. "Just push a button and all that stuff is right there?" He waved his hand. "I don't get involved with it." And that is the essence of Red Auerbach—if he doesn't need to know it, he doesn't get involved with it. He is the ultimate big-picture guy. "I'm still a little in awe of Red," says owner Alan Cohen. "He never ceases to be someone who has incredible perception and sensitivity. Red could literally be president of the United States with his ability to understand what makes things happen." That's the kind of overstatement one is likely to hear around Celtic Land, of course, but Cohen's underlying point is accurate—that Auerbach, like Ronald Reagan, doesn't get bogged down by the little things. He keeps his eye only on long-range goals, and the crocodile-infested moat that lies just ahead is somebody else's problem. His great strength as an administrator down through the years has been his ability to divide the world into "us versus them," the Celtics versus the infidels. Whenever a decision or ruling of any kind went against the franchise, NBA Commissioner David Stern says that he knew a phone call would be forthcoming. "And the message from Red usually was: 'You have no balls,'" said Stern.

The conversation drifted here and there. Auerbach does not have the patience to deal with one subject for too long. His visitor wanted to know if he still thought, as he once did, that the Celtics, the NFL Cowboys, and the baseball Yankees were America's only true "national" teams.

"I think the Cowboys have fallen out," answered Auerbach. "I think that movie [*North Dallas Forty*] hurt them. Plus the fact that they stopped winning. The Yankees are still there but in a different way. You go around and people still talk about the Yankees but not so much for being a dynasty. But I think it's still the same with the Celtics. I really do. The Boston Celtics were, and still are, the number one recognizable team in the world."

Does he feel that the impact of the foreign invasion, which the Celtics were feeling with Shaw at the time, will be a lasting one?

"Hell, I saw that foreign thing coming years ago because I gave clinics for the State Department over there," said Auerbach. "Wherever there's money, you'll see international. They're playing golf in Russia. Golf in Russia for crissakes! I predict a common draft someday. Not with all the European teams but with the best in Italy, Spain, wherever they're paying the big money. It's going to present tons of problems, no doubt about it, but eventually something will come to pass where they'll respect our players and we'll respect theirs.

"This thing with Shaw—right now the owners over there are on an ego trip. That's the only way to describe some of the stuff that's going on. It seems that the teams over there go after success. They come after us because we're successful. The Lakers are going through the same thing. But some of these other teams—Utah, the teams in Texas—the Europeans don't bother those teams. Know what I mean?"

Does he feel as close to the current Celtics as the old-timers?

"Some of them, maybe, like Bird," said Auerbach. "I used to play Bird in tennis maybe five, six years ago before he got good and I got a little older. I used to beat him, too, and afterwards I'd take my racket and point it at him and say, 'How can you let a sixty-eight-year-old man beat you?' I used to shoot with my guys all the time, Havlicek primarily, until my hands went bad." He looked at his hands. "Handball wrecked them for shooting. The doctors want to fix them, but I say, what for? I can still hold the racket for tennis and racquetball.

[For the record, Bird claims that Auerbach often beat him in tennis because of his creative scorekeeping.]

"Anyway, the players today, by and large, are a little different. The good majority of them come to work with an attaché case when years ago they came with a gym bag. But I'll say this—fortunately for the sport of basketball, and maybe most sports, the more you pay the great athletes, the more they earn it, the more they want to show they deserve it. The Magic Johnsons, the Michael Jordans, the Larry Birds—it's hard to overpay those kind of guys." [That was fortunate for the Celtics, who would be paying Bird about $7 million for the 1991–92 season.]

"I talk to my older players all the time. Bones McKinney. Freddie Scolari. [Frank] Ramsey calls once a month. I see [Celtics broadcasters] Cousy and Heinsohn all the time. The list goes on."

So do the questions from his visitor, who was fascinated by the treasure trove on Auerbach's walls.

"Christ, I thought you knew your history," Auerbach said after being asked another question. "You don't know shit." It was as if he suddenly remembered he was supposed to be irascible. "Look, I gotta get outta here. I'm supposed to pick up my car at noon. Here, you want some candy?"

And so Arnold Auerbach rose from his chair and carefully peeled the foil off another piece of candy. He is the last of a dying breed, men whose personality and spirit and guts held sway over an entire franchise. The old Philadelphia Athletics were Connie Mack. The Chicago Bears were George Halas. And the Boston Celtics were Red Auerbach, a guy with a cigar and his own agenda. He was arrogant, self-centered, conservative, old-fashioned, brilliant, and successful, and so, not coincidentally, were the Boston Celtics.

But this was 1990 and times were changing. Arrogance is fine when you're on top of the world, not so fine when the world has caught and passed you. And, clearly, with the 1990–91 season three months away, Red Auerbach's Celtics had been caught and passed.

Five-year-old Michael Ford was ready to go to the mall and that was that.

"Later, Michael," said his father, Chris. "Leave us alone now."

"I wanna go now," said Michael. "I don't want to leave."

"Michael, I'm warning you," said Ford.

"No," said Michael, "I'm warning *you*."

Ford half-rose from the chair, and Michael scurried away. He was back a few moments later, peeking around the corner. Ford shook his head.

"Chris, if you can't handle a kid," said Ford's visitor, "how the hell can you . . ."

"Handle a team like the Celtics?" finished Ford with a smile. "Listen, I'm not worried about that."

It was a rainy morning at the summer home of the eleventh head coach of the Boston Celtics. Ford was born in nearby Atlantic City in 1948 B.C. (Before Casinos), and he still returns to the Jersey Shore with his family (wife, Kathy, and four children) every summer to renew a love affair with the beach and the boardwalk and the salt air and the blacktop playgrounds where he learned the game. Well, not the play-grounds so much—his knees are bad and he plays his once-a-week summer games with his old high school buddies in gymnasiums. "I grew up poor," Ford said of his boyhood, "but how poor are you when you're walking distance from the ocean?" The Fords own a pleasant, stately home two blocks from the beach. Kathy's family lives just a couple miles away, she being a Jersey girl who started dating Chris when they were in high school.

The summer had been anything but typical. Rookie camp, free-agent tryouts, a week with his team in the L.A. Summer League, and other assorted responsibilities associated with his first head-coaching job had left little time for vacation and cruising on his boat, *The Beautiful Kate*, named after his daughter. And all that was after Ford had spent most of May and the first week of June swinging in the breeze while the Celtics brass played footsie with Mike Krzyzewski. Jimmy Rodgers had been fired on May 7—Ford heard about it the next morning when he was "recuperating," as he puts it, from the traditional breakup dinner—and the Celtics hadn't officially promoted him until June 12. That's a long time in employment limbo when the story is being played out daily in newspapers and on televi-sion. Even an hour after Gavitt called Ford at home to tell him that he had the job, in fact, the eleven o'clock news breathlessly reported that Pat Riley was flying in to Boston to be interviewed. The overwhelming support Ford had received from the Celtics players and others around the NBA in the interregnum was gratifying. The Boston media, too, had been squarely in Ford's corner, which was nice, but somewhat disturbing, given the media's propensity for siding with losing candi-dates.

Ford had been a Celtic since 1978, the year that Pistons coach Dick Vitale traded him and a draft pick to Auerbach for Earl Tatum, a flashy, spectacular player with a big potential but not a scintilla of Ford's smarts and instincts for the game. Pitting Auerbach against Vitale in a basketball deal was a mismatch of epic proportions, and Vitale, to his credit, later admitted the trade was a big mistake, one of several he made before the Pistons booted him out. Every time Ford runs into the broadcaster these days he tells him: "My wife and kids say prayers of thanks to you, Dick." Ford had a good year with a terrible team—only the expansion New Orleans Jazz (26–56) lost more games than the 1978–79 Celtics (29–53)—but Ford hung around for three more seasons, one of them the championship year of 1980–81, as a young player named Larry Bird arrived and turned around the franchise once again. Ford was a typical Celtic, a team player who relentlessly sought victory, loyal to the organization, not particularly popular with the opposition.

Then-coach Bill Fitch cut Ford before the 1982–83 season, and to this day Ford doesn't pretend to be happy about it; he felt he had at least one more good season in him. Nevertheless, he told Auerbach that he'd be interested in staying with the club in some capacity. As luck would have it, veteran broadcaster Johnny Most was taken ill a few months later and Ford stepped in to do radio commentary on WRKO. He was also a volunteer assistant coach at Boston College and was named a full-time assistant for the 1983–84 season. Soon after that, however, Fitch left as head coach of the Celtics, assistant K. C. Jones was elevated to the head job, Rodgers became the first assistant, and, after getting a release from Boston College, Ford came aboard as the second assistant.

Under both Jones and Rodgers (who took over the head job in 1988 when K. C. was kicked upstairs to player-personnel director, a move that did not pan out), Ford was the classic "loyal assistant," which meant he did his job and did not back stab the boss, a frequent practice in the NBA where many assistants would offer their firstborn for a head coaching job. The media considered Ford fair but not particularly forthcoming, a guy to go to for the x's and o's but not the real skinny. Reporters don't necessarily love a guy like that but they usually respect him, and Ford was widely respected.

The relationship between Ford and Rodgers, his immediate boss, had been a close one—their wives saw each other off the court too—but a rift, not overtly noticeable except to those close to the team, gradually developed between them as the strain of the difficult 1989–90 season started getting to Rodgers. Ford felt that the Celtics should be a running team and was frustrated that Rodgers, while pledging outward acceptance to the idea, still went with the cautious, down-tempo style that had won a championship in 1986. The problem came to a head during a February road trip. Dennis Johnson, Boston's respected but aging point guard, had seen only limited action in the first two games of the trip because he was recovering from a torn right thigh muscle. With John Bagley, a running, fast-break player at point guard, the Celtics had won both of those games in sometimes spectacular fashion. But D. J., as was his wont from time to time, sulked and told the media that he didn't go west just to sit on the bench. Rodgers then announced, prior to the third game of the trip in Portland, that D. J. would be back in the starting lineup, a slap in the face of logic, even to those Celtics who admired Johnson. Several players immediately glanced at Ford when Rodgers said "D. J.," and Ford's anger and surprise were evident. He never confronted Rodgers, but things were never the same between the coaches from that point on. When it came time to make a change, both Auerbach and Cohen perceived, accurately, that it was Rodgers and second assistant Lanny van Eeman on one side, Ford on the other. (Van Eeman, who was not considered the most electric of assistant coaches to begin with, was fired along with Rodgers.) Rodgers went into self-imposed isolation on the day he was fired and didn't talk to Ford for over a year. They finally chatted in August of 1991, after Rodgers had been named head coach of the Minnesota Timberwolves.

On this August morning, there were at least four questions that the average Celtics fan had for Ford:

- Did he want Shaw (who at that point was still not in the fold) running his team? Or would he stick with the tried and true, as Rodgers did, and invite back D. J.?
- Would he be able to coexist with Bird better than Rodgers, whose offense had sometimes been subtly criticized by the superstar?
- Would it be hard for him to command respect as the head man? Owing to his status as both an ex-teammate and assistant coach, Ford was much closer to the players than Rodgers was.
- And, finally, how badly was his ego damaged by the six-week waiting game imposed on him by Gavitt and Auerbach?

The answer to the first question was that Ford wanted Shaw very, very badly, and it was his biggest fear that the other members of the brain trust would want to bring D. J. back. As much as he respected D. J., Ford felt he was finished. Ford had kept in touch with Shaw throughout the summer, even as the words flew hot and nasty between the Celtics' brass and Shaw's agent, and Ford went out of his way to show Shaw that he would be more than welcome in the new regime. Ford was not particularly enamored of the Shaw-Stanley maneuvering—with a salary that topped out at $200,000 late in his playing career, Ford says wryly that "I never made enough money to have a contract problem"— but, still, he was a former player, and somewhat of a union man at that. He could understand a player trying to maximize his financial position. So, Ford was able to look at Shaw and see speed, quickness, and youth, rather than greed, disloyalty, and avarice. Had the new head coach not been so adamant that the Celtics needed Shaw, Auerbach and Gavitt just might've traded him.

As for the last question, Ford confronted the Krzyzewski issue head-on. "There will always be the perception that Krzyzewski was first choice and I was second. But it doesn't matter to me. I don't have the big ego. I was comfortable throughout the whole thing with the way Dave and I were getting along." Ford said he understood that Gavitt couldn't come in and immediately rubber-stamp Auerbach's choice of a coach. "He had to pursue his own man," said Ford. Perhaps, but the oddest aspect of the pursuit of Krzyzewski was Gavitt's close contact with Ford, the rival. Ford even started calling his almost daily talks with Gavitt "debriefings," and he sensed that Gavitt, who was strongly aware of his own status as an NBA novice, was listening to him. "Well, if he's going to keep picking your brain," Kathy Ford would tell her husband, "get him to tell you who's getting the job." Once Ford got it, it was not in his nature to kill himself with introspection about exactly *how* he got it.

As for questions two and three, well, Ford was not the only ex-player coaching an NBA team but he was breaking some new ground, for none of the others would be coaching former teammates. Ford's position was comparable to that of ex-Lakers coach Pat Riley, who had been an L.A. player for five and a half seasons and, like Ford, an assistant coach and team broadcaster before getting the head job. But Riley had only one ex-teammate to coach when he was hired in 1981, Kareem Abdul-Jabbar; Ford had at least three strong-willed, ex-teammate veterans—Bird, McHale, and Parish. Ford was particularly close to McHale; in fact, shortly after he was named coach, he and McHale were part of a small weekend fishing party at a lakeside cabin in Maine owned by Ordway. Like frisky teenagers, they had set off fireworks in the evening, and McHale referred to it as "Chris's coronation."

Ford sipped a cup of hot tea and pooh-poohed any possible problems. "I'm confident in my own abilities," said Ford, as his wife and four children darted in and out, bound, variously, for the mall, tennis lessons, and in-laws. "I never questioned Mike Krzyzewski's ability as a coach, but I did question his ability to make the jump from college to the pros. But I'm here now. I never thought about not taking the job, because I have ambition and I wanted to keep moving along.

This seems logical to me. I feel this is where I belong. I know I belong."

He paused and smiled. "But you know what else I know? I know we won fifty-two games last year and the coach was still fired. My eyes are open."

CHAPTER 2

A Question of Color

SEPTEMBER

On the twenty-first day of the month, Celtics rookie Dee Brown walked across Route 16, the main drag that runs through the tony Boston suburb of Wellesley, and climbed into his rental car. Next to him on the passenger's side was his fiancée, Jill Edmondson. Jill and Dee had fallen in love with a house in Wellesley (they planned to move in in October) and Dee was receiving his mail from general delivery in the town until they were settled. They were going through the letters when they were suddenly surrounded by seven policemen, weapons drawn.

"Get out of the car! Get on your knees!" the officers shouted. Brown later said that he and Edmondson were forced to lie face down, while the police claim that they were told only to kneel. Brown's first thought was that it was some kind of joke. "It's not like I was used to having a gun on me or anything," he said.

But it was no joke. A secretary from the nearby South Shore National Bank had called the Wellesley police and told them that a man who fit the description of the suspect in a robbery at the bank three days earlier was sitting in the car. The description was of a tall, slender, light-skinned black man, between twenty-five and thirty years old. Brown is tall and slender, but he was only twenty-one at the time and looked, if anything, even younger. And he is darker skinned, by his own conjecture, than 95 percent of the African-American population. In other words, he does not look anything like the robbery suspect except that they are both black. Brown told the policemen who he was and they said, "Make sure you're right." After a few minutes, they let him reach for an ID. When the matter was cleared up to the officers' satisfaction, Brown and Edmondson, who was extremely angry and upset, protested. The officers were not apologetic. "You got a problem," they said, "take it to the chief." Later, one of the officers accused Edmondson, who is white, of saying, "I hate fuckin' cops." Edmondson admitted she said, "I hate cops," but said she did not swear. Edmondson had been involved in another incident in Orlando years before when guns were needlessly drawn and her tolerance level for such incidents was much lower than Brown's. The Wellesley police chief did not officially apologize until two days later. At that time he denied that it was a racist incident and said that "the procedure for responding to a bank robber was utilized."

Which is what he had to say, of course. But it is patently ridiculous to reach any other conclusion except that Dee Brown was victimized by his skin color. The white bank clerk would probably not have over-reacted and misidentified a white man, and the seven white Wellesley policemen would probably not have handled a white suspect so aggressively. It could've happened anywhere in the United States to any black man, and probably does on an almost daily basis. On two occasions during the 1990–91 NBA season, David Dupree, the respected NBA writer from *USA Today*, was stopped by police in Atlanta and Philadelphia, asked for identification, and frisked. The officers in Philadelphia admitted to him that he "fit the profile" of a drug courier—black, fortyish, casual dress. But the Dee Brown incident was special, obviously, because it happened in the Boston area, and it happened to a member of the Celtics.

The fact that Brown had been a model Celtic in the three months since he had been drafted somehow made it, at least in the microcosm of the Celtics' world, that much more of a travesty of justice too. Indeed, if there was a book on how NBA rookies should act in order to please their employers, then Brown must've spent the summer reading it. In an era when many young players show a remarkable ignorance of history, history being anything that happened more than five years before their birth, Brown dazzled reporters on the night he was drafted with his knowledge of Celtics lore and legend. He didn't just know Bill Russell and Bob Cousy—he knew Frank Ramsey and Jim Loscutoff. Hell, he knew an obscure Celtic named Togo Palazzi. He related the excitement he had felt just walking through Boston Garden during his predraft visit. Brown said he was an avid reader of stat books and sometimes he perused old NBA guides, staring at the black and white photos of championship teams (comprised, in the NBA's first decade, mostly of white players). He said he had followed the NBA "forever" and pronounced himself "in awe" of Celtics tradition. "I always followed the favorite of the moment, whoever was playing good," said

Brown, "and, chances are, that was the Celtics." This knowledge isn't absolutely necessary for a Celtics rookie, of course—Larry Bird didn't know Tommy Heinsohn from Tommy Tune when he came into the NBA in 1979—but don't think the Celtics' hierarchy didn't like to hear it. They couldn't buy the kind of positive public relations Brown gave them, particularly since the negative vibes from the Bias selection four years earlier were never far from anyone's mind.

Then, too, it was difficult not to contrast Brown's behavior with that of Brian Shaw, though no one did it publicly. The Celtics had spent much of the summer in enervating court battles to keep Shaw from reneging on a signed contract and bolting back to Italy, and the issue was still cloudy even in September. It looked like Shaw was returning but only because he had exhausted all of his legal options and would've faced a contempt-of-court charge if he once again said *arrivederci*. Public opinion was squarely in the Celtics' corner on this matter—*Globe* columnist Dan Shaughnessy called Shaw a "contemptuous little creep"—but that hardly compensated for the time, energy, and resources involved in the court battles. Ironically, the one thing that was not suggested, either by the Celtics or in the press, was letting Shaw go and simply handing the point guard position to Dee Brown. Had Brown been a higher draft pick and a big-time college player, that would've been everyone's logical solution. But though everyone liked Dee Brown, no one was exactly sure how good he was going to be.

Brown further distinguished himself by diligently working out alone and showing up at rookie and free-agent camps in July and August even though he had not signed a contract. He did not participate officially, but there he was, hour after hour, wearing a Celtics cap, dribbling a basketball, talking to the coaches, joking with the guys, listening to Auerbach expound on basketball in general and point guard play specifically. "No, 'How ya doin'? How's your life?' " said Brown. "Just basketball." Brown confirmed a report that he had been approached by Il Messaggero, the Italian team that had stolen Shaw, and offered $800,000, plus a BMW, a maid, and a cook, but had turned them down flat. "I don't need all that," Brown said. "I want to play in the NBA. That is my dream and my goal, not money. It's good to know there's interest out there, but it wouldn't have mattered how much they offered. A million. A million and a half. I was not going to take it." It was as if the kid were reading from a script written by Dave Gavitt. That's exactly what Jerome Stanley, Shaw's agent, was thinking—Stanley harbored a quiet resentment toward Brown all season, particularly after Brown showed no interest in switching from his agent, Steve Zucker, to Stanley.

Yet, at the same time, Brown never came across as anything less than genuine. He showed, in fact, an exuberant confidence that bordered on cocky. Before the draft, his size (six one) and quickness had drawn loose comparisons to two of the league's waterbugs, Atlanta's Spud Webb, who is five feet six, and Charlotte's Muggsy Bogues, who is just five three, and Brown didn't particularly care for those comparisons. "I'm a player—period," Brown said. "I can come in and contribute to a team, not just as a utility-type player. I can do a lot of things Muggsy and Spud can't do. All they do is get in the game and be a pest because they're so small." No one held such comments against Brown because, first, they were so honestly held and expressed, and, second, because he backed them up with an intelligence and quick wit that removed them from common jive, or "trash-talking" as it's known in the NBA. (Not to mention the fact that he was probably correct in his assessment of Bogues.)

Brown's easy conviviality with young and old, black and white, came about naturally. Christened DeCovan Kadell Brown, Dee was raised in a stable, middle-class, two-parent family in Jacksonville, Florida. He attended private schools with a predominantly white student body most of his life because his parents thought the educational opportunities were better. Brown's particular interest was computers. During his days at Jacksonville University, he put his opponents' tendencies on disc and consulted them from time to time. He was an inveterate watcher of games on cable too, and when it came time for his big moment—the Orlando All-Star Classic, which is where the Celtics became convinced that he was their man—Brown had a step up on the competition. "I knew that [Loyola Marymount star] Bo Kimble liked to drive real hard, then cross over," said Brown. "I knew that [Texas star] Travis Mays, once he got in the lane, was not going to pass the ball. He always shot it. That kind of stuff gave me an edge." It was probably not coincidence that Brown singled out those two players—both are guards who were picked ahead of Brown in the draft (Kimble at No. 8 by the Clippers, Mays at No. 14 by the Kings) but who subsequently fared less successfully than he in their rookie season.

Brown admitted that the transition from college hotshot to rookie nobody was a difficult one. That, too, contrasted with the attitude of most rookies, who say there's no problem and then get their personal lives off to a disastrous start. "I thought you got drafted, go to that city, move right in," said Brown. "But it's not that simple. You're a businessman now, and none of the Celtics are going to take you by the hand and help you find a place or open a bank account. You're away from home and you've got to take care of your assets." Brown did his homework, researched his options, made his decisions carefully. And he had one major advantage in the person of his fiancée, who had lived in the Boston area as a young girl and returned to study at Northeastern University from where she had graduated a year earlier. Edmondson loved New England and prayed that Brown would be drafted by the Celtics, and Brown described her as "ecstatic" when it happened. In some respects, then, the incident was harder on Edmondson. It was she who had extolled Boston's virtues to Brown, and, being white, she undoubtedly felt some measure of subconscious guilt. "I loved living here before," Edmondson said soon after the incident. "Now I feel like a jerk. The way they came at Dee and the way they just treated us, I have to think at least part of it was because Dee is black. I'd heard things like this about the area, but I didn't want to believe they happened."

"After I was drafted, I heard, 'Well, you're going *up South* to Boston,' " Brown said. "They told me Boston was a prejudiced city. They said, 'You're not going to be happy there.' I'm sure the people who told me this are patting themselves on the back." Brown said he took such stories with a grain of salt. He had heard his share of racial slurs during his formative years, but he also had many white friends from his schooldays and a white fiancée. Race was never much of a conflict in his life. Now he wasn't so sure. "It affects you all kinds of ways," he said. "I'm feeling paranoid already. I was used to having people look at me in this town, but that was okay because, when they'd find out who I was, they were very nice and wanted to talk basketball. Now I'm going to wonder, 'What are they staring at me for?'

"I was very comfortable here. I was having a great time. The house was perfect. We were looking forward to living in it. But one incident can change your whole attitude. I am having a hard time getting over the fact that not one, not two, but several guns were waved in my face."

In the aftermath of September 21, other incidents came to light, other abuses committed by the Wellesley police, other black men unjustly hassled by other police departments around Beantown. In the broad sociological context, the most telling comment was made by Brown when he said that he was used to people staring at him, but when they found out who he was they wanted to talk basketball. The problem is that the converse is just as true: if he were a nobody, instead of a member of the Boston Celtics, they would *not* have been very nice. That was the experience of the average black man around Boston. And in days gone by, it was the experience of some of the black Celtics too. Indeed, racial prejudice was the shadow that hung over the organization, the dark doppelganger that hitched a ride with all of the success.

Celtics legend Bill Russell claimed that he could not buy the house he wanted because a white real estate agent didn't want to sell it to him. Later, bigots broke into his home in the suburb of Reading, broke his trophies, and scrawled racial epithets on the walls. In what was the most memorable passage of his 1979 autobiography, *Second Wind*, Russell wrote: "To me, Boston itself was a flea market of racism. . . . If Paul Revere were riding today, it would be for racism. 'The niggers are coming! The niggers are coming!' he'd yell as he galloped through town to warn neighborhoods of busing and black homeowners."

Even some contemporary black Celtics, though never as outspoken as Russell, would joke about the little difficulties of being black in Boston, the subtle differences between themselves and the white players. Eddie Pinckney, who had been traded to the Celtics midway through the 1988–89 season, liked Boston and felt comfortable in the city, even when he was in public with his wife, Rose, who is white. But Pinckney had been pulled over in his car on one occasion by white policemen for no good reason, and released only after they realized he was a Celtic. Dennis Johnson always claimed that, if the Celtics lost, the local papers would invariably carry a photo of him or Robert Parish, but if they won the newspapers would run a photo of Bird, McHale, Ainge, or one of the other white players. He said it laughingly but he truly believed it. At the same time, black players like him and Robert Parish were sensitive enough not to complain too loudly because the "average, black, nonprofessional unknown," as D. J. put it, had it a lot worse. And one black ex-Celtic, M. L. Carr, had turned himself into one of the most popular of all Celtics alumni simply through dint of his outgoing personality and enthusiasm for the organization.

The one thing that every black player noticed right away, of course, was the dearth of black fans at Boston Garden. It is simply the tradition in Boston that the Gah-den is not a place for blacks. Later in the year, *Herald* columnist Joe Fitzgerald reported a scene that almost defies credulity in America in the nineties. During a National Hockey League game at Boston Garden between the hometown Bruins and the Calgary Flames, a white fan stood up and yelled, at the top of his lungs, "Hey, Buckwheat! Come on, Buckwheat, let's get goin'!" every time the Bruins' lone black player, Graeme Townshend, touched the puck. Just as incredibly, no one said anything to him until a black fan, one of the few in attendance, finally turned around and confronted him. Then and only then did the Boston Garden ushers move in to throw out the abusive lout. That probably would not have happened during a Celtics game, where the appearance of black players is not exactly unprecedented, but it says a lot about the atmosphere at Boston Garden.

The fact that the racial climate in Boston is tense and uneven does not make the Boston Celtics' organization a racist entity. But it has been criticized for that; or, put less forcefully, it has been purported from time to time that the Celtics make personnel decisions based on race. Auerbach has been hearing that for two decades, and it still drives him crazy, for he believes the record is clear. In 1950, three years after Jackie Robinson broke the color line in major league baseball, Celtics owner Walter Brown drafted the NBA's first black player, Chuck Cooper. (Cooper did not earn the distinction of being the first black to play in an NBA game, however—Earl Lloyd of the Washington Capitals, who was drafted after Cooper, actually saw action before Cooper did.) Under Auerbach, a number of black players—Russell, Sam Jones, K. C. Jones, Satch Sanders—achieved success even before the league became predominantly black. And if a restaurant or hotel refused to serve his black players, as sometimes happened in the fifties or early sixties, then Auerbach wouldn't let any of his Celtics eat or stay there. In 1966 Auerbach made Russell the first black coach of any major sport in the United States, and later he would elevate Sanders (in 1978) and K. C. Jones (in 1983) to the head job. The overwhelming majority of pro sports franchises haven't had one black head coach; the Celtics have had three.

Still, down through the years critics have cited the predominantly white makeup of the team. For every black player like Russell or the Jones boys, there were four or five white players who did more to forge the Celtics' identity—Cousy, Bill Sharman, Heinsohn, Ramsey, Havlicek, Larry Siegfried, Bailey Howell, Dave Cowens, Paul Westphal, Don Nelson. And the Celtics' reputation as the last bastion for the white player continued well into the eighties with the coming of Bird, who, to much of America, became a symbol of a tradition lost. Only after Bird joined the team, remember, did Boston Garden consistently sell out. A quick glance at a photo of the 1985–86 championship Celtics team is almost startling: there are eight white players (Bird, McHale, Ainge, Bill Walton, Jerry Sichting, Scott Wedman, Rick Carlisle, and Greg Kite) and only four blacks (Parish, Johnson, Sam Vincent, and David Thirdkill), just about the opposite racial percentage that one might expect in the NBA at that time. (Ten blacks and two whites comprised the top twelve players for the Los Angeles Lakers during that season, for example.) But what does that prove? Seventeen years earlier, the Celtics' championship team consisted of eight blacks and four whites. Now, most assuredly the Celtics have been charged over the years with keeping a white player or two at the bottom of their roster at the expense of a more talented black. Though everyone denies it, that is a common accusation in the NBA even today. But at the same time, the Celtics, Auerbach in particular, have simply done an outstanding job of recognizing good white players. There was not an NBA team in 1986 that wouldn't have wanted Bird, McHale, Ainge, or Walton, and both Wedman and Sichting were outstanding role players.

They did win the championship, after all, even if the contributions of Carlisle and Kite could have been matched by black players.

There is no doubt, though, that the Celtics quietly reveled in being somewhat the antiteam, the minority outpost of the NBA, where racial politics were turned upside down. They were different and they got away with it. And if the predominantly white audience in Boston Garden was inclined to overpraise Bird, as it sometimes did, or favor Walton (the reserve) over Parish (the starter), as it sometimes did, then that was hardly the fault of the organization. At worst, one could say that the Celtics' brass knew its constituency and did an outstanding job of keeping it happy. And, certainly, no one could accuse the Celtics of trying to perpetuate a white tradition in recent years: Their top draft picks since the 1986 championship season have been four blacks (Bias, Lewis, Shaw, and Brown) and one white (Michael Smith).

At any rate, race was indeed the subtext of the Reggie Lewis–Jerome Stanley subplot that had boiled over a month before the Dee Brown incident. And it was still sitting on the stove, simmering away, in September.

With Bird and McHale getting older, Lewis seemed to be the obvious player to lead the Celtics into the nineties. He was not the extroverted, vocal, Magic Johnson–type of leader, but rather the quiet Gary Cooper type, who, like Bird, would lead by example. It would be "Reggie's Team," an honor that in Celtics tradition had customarily rested on the shoulders of a white man. The exception was probably the sixties when Russell was easily the dominant Celtic, but even then Cousy and Hondo (Havlicek) were around to bear much of the leadership role. It was "Cooz's Team" in the fifties, "Hondo's and Cowens's Team" in the seventies, and "Larry's Team" in the eighties.

Early in August, even as the Celtics were still at odds with Stanley over Shaw's contract, the club was informed that Stanley was now representing Lewis, who had left ProServ, the top sports agency doing business with the NBA. Stanley, who was then thirty-two, called the surprise move a "gigantic knuckleball" to the Celtics organization, and that it was. It also seemed fraught with symbolic sociology: The black player leaves the establishment agency to join the angry young black man with whom he will fight the powerful white organization.

In reality, though, it was not that pat. First, Shaw was able to sell his close friend, Lewis, on Stanley, and it is only logical that a young black man would like to do business with another young black man. Second, Lewis was not altogether happy at ProServ, believing that the agency lavished most of its attention on its All-Star clients, like Michael Jordan and Patrick Ewing, at the expense of less-known players like himself. And finally, Lewis, though he felt a quiet black pride deep within him, did not consider the Celtics a racist organization. Lewis's major reason for changing agents was the standard one—with his contract due to run out at the end of the 1990–91 season, he thought that his new agent would do a better negotiating job than his old agent. Stanley's pitch to Lewis was right on the money. "ProServ does a good job," Stanley told him, "but the difference between them and me is that, for me, you're a superstar. I think you should have your own TV commercial, your own poster, and be paid as a top player. Can they honestly say that to you? They have Jordan, Ewing, Mitch Richmond, Dominique Wilkins. They probably have twenty guys they consider better than you. They like you, but can they honestly go to the Celtics and say, 'Reggie should have more money'?" It was a good sell for Stanley, exactly the one he should've used.

And best of all for Lewis, he backed it up. Within three weeks after they became a team, Stanley had gotten his player a five-year contract extension worth about $16.5 million. Much of the package is in deferred monies, so Stanley could not be accused of looking for the quick kill and not having his client's best long-term interests at heart. Granted, it was a sometimes sloppy negotiation game that Stanley played. He first said that he had no intention of negotiating with the Celtics, which was way too strong, and then, just hours before he reached an agreement with the team, he sent an uneasy Lewis out to face a throng of reporters and give the impression that things weren't working out. But ultimately, even the most severe critic of Jerome Stanley had to admit that the new kid in town had scored a coup.

The backlash was immediate in other quarters. Bob Wolff, the agent for Bird and Parish, called the deal "disgusting," and said it "made me sick to my stomach." Privately, Wolff complained that Auerbach, for whom he had enormous respect (their many and varied contract battles over the years notwithstanding), had broken an unwritten but long-standing Celtics rule that loyal, longtime veterans (read Bird and Parish) be the best paid; Lewis's new contract, on a per-year average, made him the highest-paid Celtic. Such gripes did not represent a high point in Wolff's distinguished career—Stanley did his job for his client, and did it well, and that's what Wolff should've said. And in dredging up tradition and *Red's way of doing things*, Wolff missed another point: These were modern times and Auerbach was no longer calling all the shots.

Stanley believes that it is the private fear of Wolff and every white agent who deals with the NBA that more black agents will get into the business and steal most of the black players. He never hesitated to express that opinion or the related view that the white world in general hopes that he is a failure. Such comments led *Herald* columnist Fitzgerald to brand him, variously, as "a jerk," "a lucky jerk," "a bozo," "a coward," and "a well-dressed bag of wind." Stanley was careful, though, to stay away from racial characterizations when the subject was the Celtics. "Although some may view the Celtics as a racist organization, I am not comfortable with that label," said Stanley. "From a basketball standpoint, what person in his right mind would not like to have Larry Bird, Kevin McHale, Danny Ainge, and Bill Walton? I'm not so sure about other teams in the NBA. The Cleveland Cavaliers, for example, ship out an all-star guard [Ron Harper] and a couple other black players, and come back with Danny Ferry, Craig Ehlo, Mark Price [all white players]. Utah, Denver, some of those teams I'm not sure about. But if I was running the Celtics, I don't know how much different I would've done. They've got a packed house, they've got Larry Bird. You can't fault success."

Still, Stanley felt racial antagonism, he says, in other parts of Boston. "I went on a radio show and about one-third of the calls had some racial comment," said Stanley. "I was called 'an antagonist.' Or they said I was trying to 'stir something up.' See, in the nineties, the new racism is not talking about lynching or calling someone a nigger. I never heard the word 'nigger' at any time in the Brian or Reggie negotiations. But it's more subtle than that, more of a stay-in-your-place type of thing." Shaw said he sensed a change, too, once Stanley actually showed up in Boston and began to get his picture in the paper. "People didn't know he was black," said Shaw. " 'Jerome Stanley' was just a name, and all the stuff that went on with me in June and July had no racial basis at all. But when people saw he was black, then all of a sudden I started hearing, 'Oh, you're being represented by some *slickster* from L.A.' or, 'Oh, these poor kids are getting bad advice from an *outside* guy.' "

Stanley said that a walk through Roxbury, Boston's predominantly black area, was illuminating. "I stopped in this barbershop, the kind of place where the old black guys sit around playing checkers and dominoes, drinking brandy, and telling lies. And these guys were all saying, 'Yeah, man, you took it to 'em. Red Auerbach thinks all he has to do is buy a brother some Chinese food and he wants to play for the Boston Celtics. Well, the black player wants money, too.' " Stanley said he neither agreed nor disagreed with that perception of Auerbach; in fact, throughout the long and sometimes intense sessions concerning both Shaw and Lewis, Stanley had never even met Auerbach. That can be attributed to both Auerbach's distaste for such negotiations, as well as the degree to which he was entrusting daily matters to Gavitt.

Taken as companion pieces, the Dee Brown incident in Wellesley and the Jerome Stanley–Reggie Lewis negotiations offer a fascinating, if murky, look at the state of race relations in the Boston area. On the one hand, a black man and his fiancée are terrorized by gun-toting white policemen in broad daylight in a town that still is not accustomed to seeing blacks in public. And on the other, a black sports agent with almost no negotiating experience stares down one of the most experienced franchises in all of sports and comes away with a lucrative contract for his young black client. One of the remarkable things is that both stories, as big as they were when they broke, quickly faded from newspapers, television, and, seemingly, the public consciousness in general. But another juicy story that began on the sports pages and quickly found its way to page one, in Boston and beyond, went on and on, for months and months, and really hasn't died yet.

On September 17, the Monday morning four days before Brown and Edmondson were sorting their mail in Wellesley, a twenty-six-year-old sportswriter from the *Boston Herald* named Lisa Olson arrived at Foxboro Stadium for a scheduled interview with Maurice Hurst, a cornerback for the New England Patriots. Olson, who was in her first year of covering the team, had asked to interview Hurst in the Pats' media room, but Hurst said he'd rather meet in the locker room. Olson didn't feel particularly comfortable in that male enclave—indeed, even some male reporters who share a history of locker-room hijinks with pro athletes, not to mention a sexual organ, don't always feel comfortable there—but a job is a job, so Olson showed up at the appointed hour. So did several other Patriots players, who were evidently waiting to ambush her. The day before, after a Patriots victory, Olson was forced to linger long after the game in the locker room to wait for an interview with a couple of players who were getting treatment; after the fact, she learned that several Patriots had interpreted this as her hanging around to get a glimpse of them naked.

Anyway, about two minutes into her interview with Hurst, several players lingered near her, apparently on their way to or from the showers. Suddenly, a couple of them removed the towels and made suggestive and outright lewd comments. "Is this what you want to see?" was one of them. Olson turned away quickly but thought she identified Zeke Mowatt, a Patriot tight end, as one of the men. "One of them was Zeke, right?" Olson said a few minutes later to Patriots' public relations director Jimmy Oldham, who was in the vicinity when the incident occurred. Oldham confirmed it. "Who else?" Olson asked Oldham, and he singled out a player named Michael Timpson. Later, Oldham told another reporter that there were five Patriots involved.

Shaken, Olson left the stadium, and reported the story to her sports editor at the *Herald*, Bob Sales. Word spread quickly, and a number of reporters from other newspapers heard about it too. It was a tough call for Olson's paper. Journalistically, was it a legitimate story? Or was it more a private matter between Olson and the players, and, by extension, the *Herald* and the Patriots? Sales decided to let Olson make the decision, and she elected not to go public, but, rather, to meet with the Patriots to discuss not only that situation but also future relations between herself and the team. Sales and Olson talked several times to Oldham, but got nowhere, largely because the owner of the club, Victor Kiam, who is better known for peddling his Remington razors on television than being a team executive, refused to take Olson's complaints seriously.

Meanwhile, the editors of the rival *Boston Globe*, who had heard about the story from their Patriots beat writer, Michael Freeman, decided that it was a legitimate news story, and it ran in the September 21 morning edition of the *Globe*. Many people were reading about it when the Wellesley police were surrounding Brown and Edmondson in their car. But unlike the Brown story, this one did not go away. It had sex appeal. It had the kind of wink-wink, elbow-in-the-ribs, tabloid element that could be rehashed endlessly in locker rooms, on golf courses, and over hands of poker. Then the rival newspapers got into it in a big way, the *Globe* attacking the *Herald* for trying to cover up the story, the *Herald* attacking the *Globe* for printing the story for no other reason than sensationalism. Did it get personal? Well, the *Herald*'s Fitzgerald managed to mention *Globe* columnist Mike Madden's receding hairline, and *Globe* columnist Will McDonough called Sales "a spineless wimp," just to mention two highlights. McDonough, the most powerful voice in town, came down strongly, and rather pathetically as it turned out, on the side of the Patriots. At times he made it sound like Mowatt, who (along with Timpson and another Patriot named Robert Perryman) was ultimately fined by NFL Commissioner Paul Tagliabue, was one of the original American patriots, engaged in a courageous battle against injustice. McDonough became a mouthpiece for Mowatt's lawyer, an old friend of his named Robert Fraley, and whenever he mentioned Olson, whom he had never personally met, it was in a patronizing tone that must've escaped him and his editors. ("People I like and respect tell me she is a very nice young woman," he wrote at one point.) Meanwhile, two other *Globe* columnists, Ryan and Madden, were strictly in Olson's corner.

To further fan the flames, McDonough is also a commentator on NBC's NFL telecasts, and the Olson-Patriot story became a network staple for weeks on end, thereby turning it into a truly national, and even international, story. That, in turn, meant that the *Herald*'s TV writer, Jim Baker, could comment negatively on McDonough's television reporting on the Olson matter. On and on and on it went. The Boston media can try to justify it all they want, but, in retrospect, the Dee Brown story got far too little coverage, and the Lisa Olson story got far too much.

But perhaps that was inevitable. Dee could get out there on the court and make everybody forget what happened to him on a Friday morning in Wellesley. The first time he got together with his teammates after the incident, McHale suggested a new addition to the Celtics' exercise regimen, "the Dee Brown stretch," hands behind the back, cuffed together. It became a staple of team humor, and perhaps that's a good thing. But Olson was just one of those sideline cynics with a tablet and a tape recorder. She had no defense, no one with whom to share her anguish, and her professional and personal life was all but ruined by the incident. The anonymous phone calls to her home were of either a blatantly sexual nature or downright life threatening; one of them mentioned battery acid. Her name appeared in graffiti on bathroom walls and on mailboxes. The hate mail she received at home and at the office was described by one of her lawyers as "the worst stuff I've ever read." When she covered a Patriots game at Foxboro Stadium on September 30, fans spit on her, threw beer, tossed one of those inflatable rubber dolls around the stands while chanting her name, and jeered in unison, "Classic bitch," the latter a reference to a comment directed at her by Kiam. Incredibly, the clownish owner later reinforced his sensitivity by telling an Olson-Patriot joke at a banquet in Stamford, Connecticut, several months later. "What do the Iraquis have in common with Lisa Olson?" asked Kiam. "They've both seen Patriot missiles up close." A few days later, after a torrent of negative publicity, he publicly apologized, calling it "bad judgment."

Who could explain the hatred? What was Olson's crime? There is, no doubt, some portion of the Boston populace that secretly cheered the actions of the Wellesley police, and believed that Brown deserved to have seven guns drawn on him simply because he is black or because he was in the company of a white woman. But it is no longer fashionable to hold that opinion publicly unless one is wearing a hood. Sexism, however, is just fine in many circles, even recommended behavior. What also became clear in the Olson incident was that America, years after the subject of women reporters in the locker room should've become passé, has little or no understanding of what is essentially a civil-rights issue. One of the things that drove Olson to distraction during the whole mess was how many times she heard that "other women reporters don't have to go into locker rooms to do their job." Of course they do. There might be as many as ten females in the crowded Boston Garden locker room after a Celtics game, a happenstance that forces many Celtics to don a remarkable invention called the bathrobe. The short, white terrycloth number doesn't do much for, say, Kevin McHale, but it seems to make the issue of privacy nearly irrelevant.

Was Olson's treatment worse in Boston than it would've been in other large American cities? Perhaps. Boston is difficult to fit into a neat little sociopolitical package. Home to the nation's largest concentration of colleges and universities, it is in some respects a haven for liberals and intellectuals, and the tradition of Hawthorne, Emerson, Longfellow, Thoreau et al. who found the Boston area an ideal place to contemplate this vale of tears continues today. However, there is about the place a certain rough edge, too, a blue-collar, working-class immigrant ethos. And the degree to which Boston has maintained its blue-blood tradition, that air of Beacon Hill snobbery that gave rise to the famous expression that defined the city's two first families, "The Lowells talk only to the Cabots, and the Cabots talk only to God," must be thrown into the mix too. It is hard to say exactly which of the warring sociologies predominates, which probably means that none of them do. But what one feels in Boston is a sense that the order of things is to be preserved, not shaken, that traditions are to be upheld, not torn down. Does that make Boston backward or stupid? Of course not. But backward and stupid incidents happen there, and, to be sure, two of them occurred within four days of each other last September. And both resonated, to one degree or another, throughout the 1990–91 Celtics season.

CHAPTER 3

Ford Sets No Speed Limit

OCTOBER

Brian Shaw walked onto the court at Hellenic College, smiling, confident, and joking with his close friend, Reggie Lewis. He slapped palms with Kevin McHale. Chris Ford said something to him and he laughed. A fan timidly asked for an autograph and he complied. Shaw seemed to be just another Celtic on this, the traditional opening day of training camp—an informal schmooze-autograph-interview session that draws team executives, fans, media, and general hangers-on—and that had to be considered a plus. Less than a month ago, after all, Shaw had been the most reviled athlete in Boston since Bucky Dent, the Yankee shortstop whose unexpected playoff home run had kept the beloved Red Sox out of the World Series in 1978.

If Shaw was worried about the reception he was going to get, he didn't show it. But, then, not showing it is Shaw's style. His demeanor on and off the court suggests a man who has adopted a philosophy of deeply rooted placidity. Either that, or someone long ago had taught him that you're a step ahead of the game if you look like you are. His press conference three weeks earlier to once and for all settle the tortured summer-long legal battles among the Celtics, Il Messaggero, and himself had been a triumph of composure, if not clarity. Not only had he lost the battle to return to Italy, but he also owed $50,000 in contempt fees for failing to heed the rulings of a district court. And the Celtics quietly confirmed that they had no intention of reworking his five-year, $6.2 million contract. Yet Shaw hadn't sounded like a loser. His explanations for trying to run out on the Celtics were contradictory but somehow never sounded so. He was never thrown off guard by a question, as his buddy, Lewis, had been during his embarrassing press conference back in August. He never lost his cool, never stumbled over his words, words that were mildly conciliatory but never repentant. Everyone agreed that it was a masterpiece resting somewhere between diplomacy and bullshit. "I'm with the team I want to be with," said Shaw. "I'm with the team that wants me to be with them. That's why I'm here today." Red Auerbach was not there, however, perhaps because he would've been unable to celebrate the occasion so joyously. The Celtics' representatives were Ford, who needed Shaw to run his fast break, and Gavitt, who needed the whole damned mess to go away as quickly as possible. Indeed, it was this kind of situation for which Gavitt was hired, the "modern" way of dealing with modern athletes being impossible for Auerbach. When a television reporter wanted to know how anyone could ever again trust Brian Shaw's promise to honor a contract, Gavitt grabbed the microphone and said: "We're the party that has Brian's signature on a piece of paper, and we're very comfortable that this obligation will be fulfilled." Auerbach might've demanded a pound of flesh in some form; Gavitt preferred to *press* the flesh and get things moving.

As Shaw met reporters on that first day, he was pleasant and accommodating, "a lounge act," as the *Herald*'s Steve Bulpett described him the next day. "I wasn't really worried about how the team would react," Shaw said. "I was in pretty close contact with the other players and management all through the summer. They weren't really my main concern, because I knew things were all right with them.

"I just want the Boston fans to know I'm going to give them one hundred percent. My goal is the same as theirs—to win games and make everyone happy. I'm sure people will still be bitter about what's happened, but I'm just going to try to use that as a positive motivation to do better and let them know I'm on their side."

That Shaw had handled himself so coolly was not a surprise, for he was always well spoken and composed. Though he described his background as "lower middle class," his upbringing in northern California was somewhat similar to Brown's in that his parents, an auto mechanic and a director of a day-care center, provided a stable environment that put a premium on education. He was still extremely close to both of them; in fact, during his rookie season in 1988, he had taken his mother, Barbara, as his guest when the Celtics traveled to Madrid for the McDonald's Open in October. (The organization loved that.) And he had gotten away for a week during the turbulent summer by taking a fishing trip to Alaska with his father. Shaw attended a Catholic high school in east Oakland that had a predominantly white student population and a strict set of rules. "The girls had uniforms, and the boys couldn't wear jeans, shirts without collars, or tennis shoes," said Shaw. "Tell you the truth, I liked it. It gave me an excuse to dress nice."

Indeed, Shaw shared the honor (with Parish) of being the best-dressed Celtic. His season with Il Messaggero hadn't hurt his fashion sense, either, and these days his suits tended to be of Italian cut. He always looked good, always sounded confident. Shaw excelled in those classes in which participation was valued; his teachers liked him because he was that rare athlete who spoke up. "Confidence was something my parents instilled in me very early, on the court and in school," said Shaw. "They always told me I could do just as well, if not better than anyone else. And I believed it. I caught on to the piano, the trumpet, ice skating, whatever it was, quicker than anybody else. I only went to first grade for a couple of weeks before they bumped me to second. Same for basketball. I always felt inside like I had a special gift for the game, a knack. I never doubted for a moment I could play in the NBA, even when I was little."

His dream was to play for the Lakers, who had thought that he was their own little secret until the Celtics chose him with the twenty-fourth pick of the draft, one before the Lakers. "I had had absolutely no contact with the Celtics," said Shaw, "and the first time I ever thought about them was when the commissioner called my name. I was stunned." Shaw was one of the Celtics' most pleasurable draft picks—not only had they managed to keep their choice fairly secret, but they had been able to steal him from the Lakers, who subsequently chose a point guard who never panned out, Notre Dame's David Rivers. Shaw adjusted quickly to the idea of playing for Boston, particularly when he contemplated the prospect of sitting behind Magic Johnson on the Lakers bench, and from the outset there was a special chemistry between Shaw and then-coach Jimmy Rodgers. Shaw got a lot of early playing time—exhibition games were never Dennis Johnson's favorite form of exercise—and he seemed capable of enforcing his will upon the veterans. And "seemed" is the right word. "I guess I was never as confident as it looked," said Shaw. "The hardest thing for me was trying to carry out Jimmy's orders when guys would start to free-lance. And, obviously, we had guys that could do that, Larry, Kevin, and Robert. They had been here all these years and had won championships, so how could I say to them, 'Hey, Jimmy instructed me to run this play.'? But on the other hand, Jimmy would be telling me, 'Look, you've GOT to tell them if they're out of position.'

"It was always tough. There would be Kevin standing out there wanting the ball, demanding the ball, and I was supposed to be running something else. Sometimes I'd give it to him, sometimes I wouldn't. It was almost like I tried to figure out who I wanted to be mad at me at the time, Jimmy or my teammates. I probably went half-and-half with it and pleased no one because I was always second-guessing myself. It was the worst thing about my rookie year. I know I looked confident on the outside because that's the impression I like to leave. But I didn't feel that way all the time."

Shaw said he felt none of that hesitation now. He had grown up in his year abroad, he said. He had fired one agent (Leonard Armato), hired another (Stanley), taken a stance against one of the most power-ful organizations in pro sports (although he lost), returned to face the music, and was now ready to lead the Celtics to the Promised Land. And his teammates seemed to be behind him 100 percent. Maybe in the old days someone would've mumbled about Shaw's lack of loyalty, but these were the new days, and everyone understood that an athlete did what he could to maximize his earning power. Ten years earlier, after all, a rookie named Kevin McHale had threatened to play in Italy because he didn't like the Celtics' contract offer. And Bird had boycot-ted media day two years earlier because he was unhappy with his contract.

"Why should I be mad at Brian?" McHale said when asked why there was no animosity directed at Shaw. "Look, if he made it personal, if he came out and said, 'I'm not playing because I hate Kevin McHale,' then it would be different."

"Actually, Kevin," a reporter told him, "that's exactly what he did say."

"Where is that cocksucker?" said McHale, bolting out of his seat.

The gymnasium at Hellenic College, a Greek Orthodox institution located in the Boston suburb of Brookline, was a perfect fit for what Auerbach considers the true ethos of the Celtics. It is an old, out-of-the-way place that the most experienced Hub cab driver has trouble finding, even if he somehow knows the way to Hellenic, possibly the Boston area's most obscure institution of higher learning. The gym and its facilities were, at best, utilitarian, at worst, an embarrassment. But that is an outsider's perspective. To Auerbach, it doesn't matter where a team practices as long as the baskets are close to ten feet above the floor and the balls are reasonably round. Peeling paint and cold showers? What the hell did they have to do with winning basketball games? That was the Celtics way: Take what's dealt and kick every-body's ass. Thus, the organization had done little to refurbish Hellenic over the last few years, even though the place had become increasingly rundown and gloomy, evocative of the NBA of the fifties, Auerbach's NBA, rather than the NBA of the nineties.

But the 1990–91 edition of the Celtics found a different Hellenic when they showed up on October 5. The ceiling and walls had been given a fresh coat of white paint—the smell on opening day, in fact, gained a standoff in an olfactory war with Auerbach's cigar—the floor had been refinished, the lighting improved, the training facilities (weights, stationary bikes) significantly upgraded. Away from prying eyes, there were nameplates on the lockers and new carpeting and paint in the locker room. All together, the Celtics probably spent no more than $40,000, a drop in the bucket for a multi-million-dollar franchise, but the changes had symbolic significance. Some of the Celtics' players had begun quietly grumbling about the amateurish aspects of Hellenic, and that led to a general feeling of: "Why should we care? The organization doesn't care about us." Who knows if it cost the Celtics a game or two somewhere along the line? Auerbach would pooh-pooh that notion, of course, but free agency was turning the NBA, more and more, into a buyers' market. Veteran free agents had to *want* to come to a particular team, and things like practice facilities were part of an organization's selling point. Obviously, the Celtics were still one of the more attractive franchises in the league, simply because they were the Celtics, but that was beginning to change. The Detroit Pistons, L.A. Lakers, and Portland Trail Blazers were considered just as desirable (if not more so), while franchises like the Chicago Bulls, San Antonio Spurs, and Phoenix Suns were coming on. With the alterations at Hellenic, the Celtics were saying: "We're ready to do things first class."

"It's amazing," said McHale with some irony, "what one can of paint can do."

The changes were the first indication that things would be different in the Gavitt Era. He had spent most of his professional life in a big-time college environment, where things *had* to look right. If you brought in a hotshot college recruit, you could lose him if he was turned off by, say, holes in the locker room walls. Whereas Auerbach's idea of stroking an athlete was offering him a piece of candy while he showed old Celtics team photos, Gavitt knew all the little seductions of the flesh trade. Furthermore, as commissioner of the Big East, one of the most powerful amateur forces in the United States, Gavitt was accustomed to going first class. He discovered the curious dichotomy that pro franchises (particularly those wedded to the past, like the Celtics) sometimes operate more amateurishly than colleges (particularly those influential ones with which Gavitt was used to dealing). "Tell you the truth," said Gavitt, "I was kind of appalled at how Hellenic looked." Even the press was aware of the difference the first day when it entered Hellenic to find complimentary coffee and donuts. It was classic Gavitt—practices were closed to the media for the first hour, but there *was* coffee and donuts when you finally got in the door.

Just as important as seeing the need for change, of course, was the fact that Gavitt had the clout to make such changes, cosmetic as they might have seemed. One of the major weaknesses of the organization had been the absence of anyone under Auerbach to get the little things done. That "anyone" was supposed to be Jan Volk, but he was wrong for the job. He literally grew up at Auerbach's side, his late father having owned the camp (Milbrook) where Auerbach ran his summer basketball camp. Volk remembers walking into his father's office as a wide-eyed teenager and seeing Celtics legends Bill Russell and Tommy Heinsohn sprawled on the couch. "The thing I remember about Red is that he was always very, very nice to me," said Volk. "Sure, he had a gruff style but you always knew he had a twinkle in his eye." (Many people notice the gruffness, miss the twinkle.) Shortly after he passed the bar exam in 1971, Volk began doing season ticket work in the Celtics' office. His longtime relationship with Auerbach no doubt aided his climb up the executive ladder, but so did his piercing legal mind, his eye for detail, and his indefatigable work ethic. His value to Auerbach and the various Celtics owners under whom he worked only increased as the NBA's rules and regulations, particularly those relating to the salary cap, became more and more complicated. Besides Gary Bettman, the NBA's chief attorney, Volk is the acknowledged master of the cap.

But that doesn't change the fact that, to a certain extent, Volk was and always will be the wide-eyed teenager trailing along at Red's side. Even when he differed with Auerbach on a philosophical point, as happened from time to time, Volk did not have the clout to argue it with him or go over Auerbach's head to the owners. The players sensed that Volk was somewhat of a pawn, too, and never gave him their full respect. That put Volk in a difficult position and he was understandably insecure in his job. Whenever there was a screwup that became public, Volk was usually blamed, when, in point of fact, Volk saved many an administrative screwup over the years. Under the surface, Volk was a much warmer man than he seemed too. When Joe Kleine was traded from Sacramento to Boston, for example, Kleine's wife, Dana, somehow got the idea that Volk was the Celtics' director of public relations instead of the general manager. She called him several times with menial requests—like sending her the Celtics press guide and various bumper stickers and pennants—and Volk cheerfully carried them out, never indicating that such tasks were not exactly in his job description.

Gavitt, on the other hand, was a polished executive, wary, to be sure, of stepping on Auerbach's toes, but outwardly comfortable with the burden of leadership. On many mornings he showed up at Hellenic in a sweatsuit for what several of the players began to call "The Gavitt Workout"—a donut or two, a couple cups of coffee, a couple cigarettes, and 20 minutes on the stationary bicycle. But that somehow fit the executive package, the idea of the once skilled athlete (as Gavitt was) gone comfortably to seed. Gavitt played golf. Volk, insecure, a little edgy, kept himself lean and rhapsodized about his weekend flag-football team.

More to the point, not only could Gavitt approach the owners with an original idea that involved opening the checkbook, but he could somehow convince the ol' president that he, Auerbach, had thought of the idea. "What Dave has accomplished, first of all, is that he has the instant respect of the players," says owner Cohen. "And, second, well, Red still has his certain old ways. And in some respects they're good and in other respects they have to be changed. That's where Dave came in." That is about the closest that the Celtics' hierarchy will come to admitting that things had grown stale and that Dave Gavitt was needed to freshen them up again.

To a certain extent, the sense of mystery and suspense that surrounds the preseasons of major league baseball and the National Football League is just not present in the NBA. Through the decade of the eighties, it had been entirely possible for the astute observer to predict in October, with something like a 90 percent accuracy rate, the teams that would qualify for the playoffs at the end of April. It was even easier to pick the champion; in most seasons, there were only two or at most three legitimate contenders. Consider: Between 1980 and 1990, fifteen different major league teams had played in the World Series and eleven different teams, the maximum, were crowned champion. In the same span the NFL produced twelve Super Bowl teams and eight different champions, with only the 49ers repeating. The NBA between 1980 and 1990? Only six different teams made the Finals (the Lakers, Celtics, 76ers, Pistons, Rockets, and Trail Blazers), and only the first four won championships. Both the Lakers (in 1987 and 1988) and the Pistons (1989 and 1990) repeated. And the Rockets, who lost in the Finals in both 1981 and 1986 to the Celtics, were the only true surprise among those finalists.

Actually, the 1990–91 season promised to have more realistic championship contenders than most years, primarily because of a Western
Conference that was considered strong and balanced. Portland and
Phoenix seemed to be the Western favorites, followed by the Lakers,
the Spurs, and perhaps even the Utah Jazz. But in the East there were
only two contenders, and the Celtics were not one of them. The two-
time-defending-champion Pistons and the Bulls appeared to be the
only Eastern teams with the right stuff. The Celtics were lacking any
number of championship features, not the least of which was the plain
and simple fact that they had come nowhere near the title in the
previous season; history showed that that fact was significant in the
somewhat cut-and-dried NBA. Had the Celtics made a major personnel move, such as they did in 1985 when they landed Bill Walton,
they might've attracted more notice as a contender. But Shaw and
Brown were the only significant additions, and neither of them was
expected to make a Waltonesque contribution. Celticologists had un-
earthed the fact that since 1956–57, Bill Russell's rookie year, the
franchise had never gone longer than four seasons without winning
the NBA title. This would have to be a championship season for that
trend to continue, but only the most ardent diehards believed that was
possible.

The Celtics team that began preseason drills on the sixth day of
October, in fact, was something like the gymnasium at Hellenic—
there was a lot of wear and tear under the fresh paint. But the hierarchy had shown it was serious in its pledge to get younger and quicker
by turning loose Dennis Johnson, a mainstay since 1983 and Bird's
idea of what being a Celtic was all about. Throughout their seven years
together, D. J. was the only player for whom Bird consistently went out
of his way to praise. Johnson noticed it himself. "I think Larry did it
because he sensed that the town rose up for him or rose up for Kevin,"
said D. J., reflecting on it one day. "Larry just wanted to let everybody
know that it was more than him and Kevin on the team. He did it for
Robert [Parish], too. Yes, I was grateful for it." Bird and D. J. had a kind
of built-in telepathy that at least once a game for seven years produced
a backdoor play that was both simple and magical. Bird would be
cutting across the lane near the basket, apparently to either set a pick
or receive one from a teammate crossing from the other direction. He
seemed to be oblivious to the prospect of receiving the ball when
suddenly a pass from D. J. would come whizzing by Bird's defender
and into Bird's soft hands for a lay-up. It was uncanny the way Johnson
always picked the right time to make the pass and Bird always picked
the right time to look for it. "We'd never talk about, never make a signal

for it," said Johnson. "We just knew. I'd be coming down the court and
I'd hear the other team's coach saying, 'Watch it, watch Bird off the
pick, watch . . . ,' and it'd be too late. You know, I only ever hit three of
Larry's defenders with that pass, Dennis Rodman, Bernard King, and
somebody else I don't remember. I could always get it right past their
ear. And only one guy guarding me reached up and stole it. Magic
Johnson. Took it right out of the air. Shocked the hell out of me."

Johnson was not terribly surprised when the news came. He had
been called into the Celtics offices a few days before camp to meet with
Gavitt, Ford, and Volk. "Well, Dennis . . ." began Gavitt, and Johnson's
mind flashed back to 1983 when he was traded from Phoenix to
Boston. D. J. felt the brass handled it about as diplomatically as possible, considering that they were giving him a kind of death sentence.
On his way out the door, Volk said: "You know, Dennis, this wasn't an
easy decision." To which D. J. added: "Well, I hope it wasn't. I'm glad I
weighed on your thoughts." And then he was gone. A few days later he
flew to Los Angeles to tidy up some business affairs and ran into a
friend of Volk's at the airport. "We talked to Jan," the fellow told D. J.,
"and he said you really took this like a man." The comment upset
Johnson and left him feeling mildly betrayed. "Did anyone really expect anything different from me?" he wondered. Athletes are often
emotionally unpredictable—Volk undoubtedly felt the comment was
the highest form of flattery; D. J. took it as an insult.

Ford felt bad about releasing D. J. and was mildly concerned that
they were losing a truly clutch performer; McHale used to say that
Johnson deliberately missed shots during the season so no one would
think to guard him in the playoffs, when he would invariably shine. In
point of fact, though, the release was not a terribly hard decision
considering that Ford wanted speed and quickness, and D. J.'s forays
up and down the court during the 1989–90 season were, as the joke
around Boston went, more accurately calibrated with a calendar than a
stopwatch.

The Celtics also cut loose another relatively slow-moving piece, Jim
Paxson, early in training camp, which was a sign that Kevin Gamble,
who played both shooting guard and small forward, as Paxson did, was
being counted on heavily. How much Paxson's troubles with Bird the
previous season had to do with his being let go was hard to calculate,
but it figured in the equation somehow, and Paxson didn't like it. He
knew his enduring Celtics legacy, if he had one, was to be The Teammate Who Blasted Larry Bird, and he claimed to have gotten a bad
deal.

The trouble had started early in the 1989–90 season when Rodgers
tried to implement a spread-the-wealth offense that de-emphasized a

dependence on Bird. And it wasn't long before Bird began to sulk ever so slightly and make disparaging comments about his reduced role. Several of his teammates, and certainly Paxson was one of them, believed that Bird tried to do too much when he did get the ball, and that he became, for the first time in his career, a selfish player. It was not that Bird was looking to compile gaudy statistics—he had enough of those to last a lifetime. But some of his teammates felt that, first, he had a subconscious desire to show that he had recovered completely from the heel surgery that had kept him out of action for the 1988–89 season, and, second, that he consciously believed the Celtics' best chance of winning was for one L. Bird to take 25 shots a game. In mid-December, press reports surfaced that one or a couple of Bird's team-mates claimed that his play was "tearing the team apart." Bird ignored it at first, then unleashed a few volleys at his unnamed teammate or teammates. "The one thing that bothered me . . . is that they don't have enough guts to stand up and put their name next to it, as having said it. And to me, that's a yellow streak down their back. That's the way I've always perceived it, and I know who said it, so I just look at it and say, 'Hey, they've always been quitters, they've always had no heart, and it's the same now.' "

Bird was somewhat vague on his pronouns, and it was never clear whether he was talking about one player or two. Since then, he never cared to set the record straight, and when Bird says he is through with a subject, he is through with it. But various teammates confirmed unquestionably that he was targeting Paxson. Whether Bird was also implicating McHale was anyone's guess. At times it seemed that he was, and at other times he specifically excluded players with whom he had won a championship, of which McHale was one. Paxson swears that he never made the comments and told Bird the same thing. "He seemed to accept it at the time," said Paxson, "but I don't know what happened after that. What bothered me is that I was never vindicated. I felt more let down by the coaching staff than anything else. No one wanted to talk about it. No one wanted to do anything to clear my name. I was benched and didn't play much after that because, I guess, the coaching staff didn't want the situation to get to Larry. The funny thing is, I never felt the situation with Larry and me was that bad, certainly not when we were on the floor together."

Paxson doesn't deny, though, that he and Bird were never partic-ularly close, even by Bird's distant standards of friendship. Perhaps Paxson just wasn't his type and that was that, but Paxson does have two other theories, both of them plausible. "There are friendship cliques on every team, and the Celtics definitely have them," said Paxson. "Larry and Kevin have a mutual respect for each other—they really do—but they're so very, very different. And usually guys who were close friends with Kevin, like I was, weren't also close with Larry. I think I got pulled into that." Paxson also believes that Bird, who doles out respect warily and rarely to begin with, could never truly respect someone with whom he had not won a championship, the I-never-went-to-war-with-you syndrome. And Paxson had been a Celtic for only two and a half seasons, the worst two and a half seasons of Larry Bird's career. Whatever Bird's true feelings were about Paxson or any other unnamed teammates, the public unpleasantness contributed to what Celtics' trainer Ed Lacerte termed the "aura of malaise" that engulfed the 1989–90 season.

Bird paused on a number of occasions during the early days of camp to comment on the absence of D. J. "I hate to lose him." "He did a lot for us." "It's going to hurt." "It's going to be sad." And so on. But his comments on the departure of Jim Paxson went unrecorded.

During a scrimmage on the fourth day of camp, McHale drove to the basket and was mugged by Bird. The ball squirted loose and neither Don Casey nor Jon Jennings, the assistant coaches who were acting as referees, blew the whistle. (Generally, a player has to be dismembered before a whistle will be blown in a scrimmage.) McHale complained about the call and did not run back upcourt on defense.

"McHale!" Ford screamed at him. "It's a turnover! Get your ass downcourt!" And McHale dutifully got his ass downcourt.

Shortly thereafter, Joe Kleine and Eddie Pinckney bumped into each other while one tried to set a pick for the other—if there were two Celtics voted most likely to bump into each other it would be Kleine and Pinckney—and Ford blew the whistle, and shouted: "What's that? A dance?"

As the scrimmage dragged to a ragged close, the players were near exhaustion, but that didn't stop the rookie coach. Ford blew his whistle and took a step onto the court. "Stop!" he shouted. "One, two, three, four, five, six guys on this side of halfcourt! Next time it happens, it's suicides. Get your asses downcourt! All of you!"

Chris Ford did not gradually ease into the captain's chair at Hellenic College. Rather, he dragged it to midcourt, plunked himself down, and announced, "I'm here! I'm in charge! Get to work!" Ford believed that the only way the Celtics would become a running team, which they had not been since Nate "Tiny" Archibald departed the premises in 1983, was to start running on the first minute of practice and never let up. One day of complacency, one day of Bird hanging back and shooting three-pointers, was a week's worth of retreat, of surrender, of returning to the mistakes of recent seasons. Ford wanted to make this point clearly and early: If you fail to run, I will jump on your butt, even if your name is LarryKevinorRobert. Particularly, in fact, if it is Kevin. What a strange relationship they had. They were ex-teammates, friends, and total equals off the court. Yet Ford was McHale's boss. Yet McHale was ten times more famous than Ford and made about six times more money. Yet Ford had to not only motivate and sometimes criticize his friend, but also do it publicly and demonstrably. *"McHale! Get your ass downcourt!"* At the same time, neither saw anything strange in it. They didn't discuss their changing relationship before the season, not even over beers and fireworks at their holiday get-together at Ordway's. Ford knew that he would have to holler at McHale, both because McHale was sometimes lazy and also because he had to demonstrate that no one was above the law. And McHale knew it was coming.

Ford had one advantage that no other Celtics head coach could possibly have—he didn't have to sell himself to the veterans. They knew and trusted him, and that trust was his to lose; a new coach, on the other hand, would've had to spend precious time gaining it. Ford's other big advantage, obviously, was being an ex-player. It was somehow more acceptable for the veterans to get abuse from someone who had crawled through the same briar patch. The drill-sergeant tactics of Bill Fitch, who had guided the Celtics to a championship in 1981 but was disliked by many of the players, would've been much more tolerated had they been the product of an ex-player instead of just an ex-marine. As intense as Camp Ford promised to be, no one was ready to compare it to Camp Fitch. "I remember my first practice under Bill vividly," said McHale. "We were running some kind of drill and M. L. Carr just couldn't get it right, so he kicked the ball in frustration, just missing Fitch. Fitch didn't see who did it but he whirled around and screamed, 'MARAVICH, GODDAMMIT!' Just like that. And I'm thinking to myself, 'Holy shit, he talks to Pete Maravich like that, what's he going to say to me?'"

Ford would never admit it, but interpersonal dynamics were somewhat touchier with Bird. They, too, were friends off the court, but Bird, by nature, is moodier and more distant than McHale, harder to read. One can push Bird only so far, and then he won't be pushed. He'll tune you out, and Ford could not afford that. But at the same time he had to get Bird in step with his offensive philosophy of fast-breaking. And so he went after Bird, too, probing, testing, all the time weighing how far he could go. During one scrimmage, Bird was slow getting back on defense and Ford made everyone stop and run two rounds of suicides, making it clear who had fouled up. Bird ran them but trudged behind the pack. During another scrimmage Bird took a bad shot from the corner, then ran upcourt, tapping his left hand to his right bicep, indicating he was fouled. "Bad shot, Bird," said Ford. Bird kept tapping his arm, and Ford kept ignoring him. "Bad shot. It's basketball. Move the damn ball."

McHale emerged, not surprisingly, as the Celtic most willing to talk about Ford, being the only veteran with both a sense of security and an overdeveloped sense of humor. "See, Doc Ford is like Francis, that character in *Stripes*, the guy who's always saying, 'Touch my stuff, I'll kill ya.' With Doc, it's, 'You don't run, I'll kill ya. You don't get back on defense, I'll kill ya.'" Many of the Celtics, particularly the veterans, called Ford "Doc," an ironic nickname hung on him years ago by ex-Celtic Cedric Maxwell after Ford surprised everyone by windmilling a dunk shot right in the face of Julius (Dr. J) Erving.

Getting hollered at by Ford was really nothing new, said McHale. "He used to yell at me all the time when we were playing. I used to live close by, in fact, and Chris would come over to my house between practices, sit on the floor, and yell at me. The thing is, when Chris yells at me, he's not yelling at me as a person. He's yelling at me as a basketball player, and I probably need it. When Chris calls me a shit, I know he doesn't mean it. At least I hope he doesn't mean it."

McHale looked over at John Bagley who had reported to camp with tendinitis in his right knee and a few extra pounds on his chunky six-foot frame. Even at that early stage, Bagley, who was alternately brilliant and ineffective as a floor leader, could see he was going to have trouble making the team, and so could everyone else. "Look, Doc told him to report at two hundred and four pounds and Bags didn't do it," said McHale. "That's the thing about Doc—he doesn't screw around. He said two-oh-four, that's what he means. We need that around here. We really do." McHale seemed almost to be convincing himself of it.

The new player who got the most attention in camp, besides Dee Brown, was Eric McArthur, a former teammate of Shaw's at the University of California, Santa Barbara. McArthur had not been drafted after his senior season and thus was eligible to sign with any NBA team that wanted him. So desirous were the Celtics of getting "more athletic"—a phrase that, in effect, meant younger, blacker, and a little wilder and crazier—that they seemed to be placing an inordinate amount of hope on him. McArthur, nicknamed "Freeze" by Shaw and other college teammates because he was always dropping things, was being quietly compared to the Pistons' Dennis Rodman, who had become one of the league's best defenders and rebounders. In point of fact, though, they had little in common. At six feet eight, Rodman was bigger than the six six McArthur, more athletic, and more confident. And though McArthur had shaved his head before camp—"It gets me all psyched up," he said—it turned out that he really wasn't all that wild and crazy, either. He was a nice, polite, young man, who wasn't even sure he belonged. When a reporter asked for an interview, McArthur said: "Whoa! Wait a minute. I'm not even on the team yet. Don't do anything to jinx me." His biggest liability, however, was the complete lack of a shooting touch. McHale watched him bricking jumpers for a few minutes one day and shook his head.

"I think he's a keeper, sure, but the thing about these kids is that they never shoot," said McHale. "You can tell it by their mechanics. We used to just go out and shoot for hours. Hey, Eric, come here!" McArthur dutifully tucked the ball under his arm and trotted over. "Eric, no matter what, keep shooting the same way," lectured McHale. "If you miss fifteen in a row, shoot it the same way. That's important." McArthur just nodded at him, somewhat tongue-tied, feeling, no doubt, even more pressure because McHale had singled him out. "Got it? The same way. Every time?" McArthur just kept nodding. "Okay," said McHale, wrapping up class, "keep shooting."

On the morning of October 16, Jon Jennings gathered himself, took a deep breath, and strode to the center of the court at Hellenic College to present the Celtics with the game plan for that evening's opening preseason game against the Pistons. It was the first real moment in the spotlight for perhaps the most unlikely assistant coach in the NBA. Jennings was only twenty-eight years old, had never played basketball at any level beyond informal competition at the YMCA, and had never spent a moment as a coach on the bench of any NBA team. And now he was going to tell LarryKevinandRobert what they should do to beat the NBA champions that evening. "I was nervous," said Jennings. "I'm a meticulous planner, so I knew I'd be ready. But on the other hand, there were three Hall of Fame players out there, and it was a little disconcerting."

Jennings had been with the Celtics since 1986 as a video coordinator and scout. Ford saw in him a gifted basketball mind, one that could break down both teams' offense and defense almost instantly, and made it clear that he wanted to elevate Jennings, though Auerbach was somewhat resistant to the move. "Christ, the kid's only twenty-eight!" he'd say. (Of course, Arnold Auerbach was only twenty-nine when he became the head coach of the Washington Capitals in 1945.) But, as was the trend, Auerbach let Ford have his man after Gavitt backed the recommendation. There was much quiet resentment about Jennings around the league, most of it from a roving band of would-be coaches now working as scouts, video coordinators, or team broadcasters, who had formerly been NBA bench coaches and were looking to get back. "Who the hell is Jon Jennings to be working for the Celtics?" they wondered. Improbably, Jennings not only had the Celtics job, but would've also been able to work for K. C. Jones in Seattle had the situation in Boston not worked out. It was Jones, then the Celtics' head coach, who had pushed for Jennings's hiring five years earlier. Jennings's strength was working efficiently, relentlessly, and without obvious designs on the head job. He seemed older than his years, less emotional, and even at twenty-eight one could picture him behind a general manager's desk, making personnel decisions. Certainly, Jennings could picture himself doing that. When he was asked by Gavitt during a prehire interview what his professional goals were, Jennings said: "Well, Dave, the job I really want is yours." As the second assistant, though, advance scouting was primarily his responsibility. He told the Celtics what the opposition was going to do; Casey told the Celtics what they were going to do to counter the opposition. And Ford worked the middle.

Jennings's presentation was brief, dealing mainly with Detroit's personnel and breaking down five different defensive stratagems it was likely to use. It lasted about ten minutes, though it had probably taken Jennings, who sifted through old videotapes to see how Detroit defensed Bird, McHale, and Parish, about four hours to prepare. It had only been within the last decade that NBA teams had bothered much with advance scouting, and some still didn't take it very seriously. Jennings would soon find that the Celtics were pretty good about it, though far from perfect. McHale generally acted bored and hung near the back of the pack, but Bird and Parish at least pretended to listen most of the time, and that set the tone for the other players, particularly Reggie Lewis and Kevin Gamble, who were avid listeners.

McHale was stretched out on the press table at the Hartford Civic Center an hour before tip-off against the Pistons when someone asked him about the significance of opening preseason games.

"I'll tell you how significant they are," said McHale, "I don't remember anything at all about my first one when I was a rookie. Nothing.

What I do know is that I'm happy to get the hell away from Hellenic College and Chris yelling."

The *Herald* had dispatched Lisa Olson to write a sidebar about the game. By this time she had been taken off the Patriots' beat—the antagonism of Kiam and some of the Patriots and the abuse heaped on her at Foxboro Stadium had made it impossible for her to do her job. Women reporters considered the NBA, along with the NHL, the best of the professional leagues to cover. They heard a sexist comment from time to time, but it was rarely nasty or personal, as such comments tended to be from baseball or football players. Perhaps it was because, in the case of the NBA anyway, most of the players were black and thus more sensitive to intolerance. Or maybe it was just because the fewer number of players simply reduced the number of potential incidents. But as she sat courtside before the opening whistle, both Isiah Thomas and John Salley of the Pistons came over and wished her good luck. Ford had mentioned it to the Celtics too (not that anyone needed reminding, as the saga of Lisa, the Patriots, Victor, and Will continued unabated in newspapers and on television), and most of them went out of their way, she felt, to make her feel welcome.

Dee Brown was out of action due to an infected toe, and thus missed the traditional opening-day embarrassment foisted upon all rookies and free agents. The team walked out of the locker room together and told the newcomers to lead the way onto the court. So out ran Eric McArthur, Stojko Vrankovic, Carrick DeHart, and Aleksandar Sasha Dordevic . . . with no one behind them. McArthur, DeHart, and Dordevic all managed weak smiles when they realized they had played the fool, but Vrankovic, the big Yugoslavian center, looked confused. It would not be the last time. As the Celtics lined up for "The Star-Spangled Banner," Ford hissed at his two Yugoslavian players: "Sasha! Stojko! Get in line." He looked at Casey, shook his head, and smiled. Trainer Ed Lacerte snapped his fingers backward, trying to clip Jennings in the zipper area, as Jennings cracked up. And then the Celtics stood at attention (sort of) for the first of some one hundred national anthems they would hear through May 17, 1991.

The starting lineup announcements held more suspense than usual because the Celtics were eager to hear the response that would be given Shaw. The real test would be the opener at Boston Garden a month hence, of course, but the Hartford crowd, though traditionally laid back and appreciative to just about everything the Celtics do, would give somewhat of an indication. If Shaw were booed lustily in Hartford, certainly he would be destroyed in the Garden. But when he was announced and trotted onto the court wearing his usual half-smile, there were only scattered boos. Everyone, Shaw included, later agreed that they were expecting much worse. And when he scored the Celtics' first basket of the season a few seconds into the game, there were cheers.

Ford's coaching style emerged in the early seconds, and it surprised no one. "Run! Push! Go!" he screamed whenever the Celtics got a defensive rebound and, on occasion, even after the Pistons scored. Run-push-go became his offensive mantra. When the Celtics were on defense, Ford had a strange one. "Boxes and elbows!" he'd yell constantly. "Boxes and elbows!" That was the warning to the Celtics' defenders not to allow their man to beat them to the boxes (the areas of the court near the basket marked by little rectangles) and the elbows (the foul line extended on both sides), as had been the custom with the previous year's team, which Ford felt had played far too unaggressively, or "softly," as NBA terminology went. Ford was determined that his team would be much more assertive on defense and surrender far fewer easy baskets than Rodgers's teams had done. "Larry! Close to him!" Ford screamed when Bill Laimbeer, the most hated member of the opposition, hit a jumper over Bird. Later, an obscure young Piston named Mark Hughes made a jump shot over McHale and Ford shouted, "Kevin! Get up on him!" McHale glanced at the bench with a questioning look on his face as if to say, "Get up on *him*?" To which Ford replied, "Hey, he's on the court, isn't he?"

Midway through the first period, Bird was falling out of bounds when he fired a bullet pass to Reggie Lewis, who was cutting down the middle, for an easy basket, and the arena erupted. It was a typical Bird play, the kind that Ford expected to see a half-dozen times a game during the regular season, when Bird was in shape. He still had a few pounds to lose and looked generally sluggish, particularly when the Pistons' roundish Mark Aguirre, who *always* has a few pounds to lose, beat him to a loose ball. "I took off in the beginning of the summer, then got into good shape, then took off again," said Bird. "I really haven't done that much in the last couple weeks. So it's not like I came to camp in shape. I'm going to use camp to get in shape. I used to do that, back in '83 and '84. Sometimes when you go into camp in real good shape, you feel like you don't get nothing out of it. You sorta get bored. I think that this year I decided to come in out of shape so I can take it more serious." If it was a rationalization, it was a doozy, but Bird was absolutely straight-faced when he delivered it. He did acknowledge one gnawing problem, however—his back was a little sore.

Bird made only 2 of 8 shots for 4 points in thirty minutes. But Parish made all 6 of his shots from the field, Shaw and Lewis played an

Ford Sets No Speed Limit 67

energetic backcourt, and Gamble came off the bench in place of starter Michael Smith to score 21 points as the Celtics won 116–98. Nothing to get overly excited about, but from Ford's perspective, it beat the hell out of Jimmy Rodgers's debut, a 121–80 loss to the Cavaliers in 1988.

A loud cheer erupted late in the game when Ford installed the mysterious seven-foot-two Vrankovic. He was big, muscular, quiet, laconic, evocative of a film noir star, someone who would be at home perched on a motorcycle, smoking cigarettes, and making ambivalent eye contact with blondes in leather skirts. Part of that was plain wrong—Vrankovic was a confirmed family man with a wife and young daughter—but some of the Celtics were certain that Stojko, like many European athletes, smoked cigarettes away from the team. They found that the only logical explanation for the endurance problems that surfaced during scrimmages when Stojko would suddenly puff his cheeks out like Dizzy Gillespie in midnote and stop running, unable to keep up with the pace. Otherwise, he was a pure physical specimen, raw and tentative, but a specimen nevertheless. Stojko picked up a quick foul, blocked a shot, then committed another quick foul, his every action, positive or negative, drawing applause. "Now there is a guy," said Mike Fine of the *Patriot-Ledger,* one of the Celtics' beat reporters, "destined to be a folk hero."

Lisa Olson, meanwhile, had had a pretty good evening as she gathered up her notes after the game. Her flaming red hair made her an easy target at Foxboro Stadium and on the streets of Boston, but she seemed to go unnoticed in Hartford. As she headed into the locker room for interviews, however, some leather lung spotted her and yelled: "HEY! LEAVE OUR PATRIOTS ALONE!" She paid him no mind and continued on her way. Six nights later, after the Celtics lost an exhibition game to Atlanta at the Centrum in Worcester, Massachusetts, a fan dumped beer on Olson's head as she left the arena.

Bill Walton was a visitor to the October 17 practice at Hellenic. Dressed in conservative tan and sporting a short haircut, Walton looked like an exceptionally tall family dentist ready for a golf outing. He was trim and fit a few weeks before his thirty-eighth birthday, and there was no doubt that he could've gone out that day and dominated most of the centers in the league ... except for the unmistakable limp he displayed when he got up and walked on the court to shake hands with Bird and McHale. Walton's legendary foot problems had from the outset plagued what would've surely been a Hall of Fame career. Walton had won a championship with the Trail Blazers in 1977, but though he played in Boston for only two seasons, he considered himself more of a Celtic than anything else. He was a member of the Celts' last championship team, in 1985–86, and anyone who played on that team—Bird, McHale, Parish, D. J.—considered it special. (Fitch, among others, considered it the best team in history.) Walton was an integral part of it. Almost by magic, he stayed healthy that season, appearing in eighty of eighty-two games and playing the role of the best backup center (to Parish) in NBA history.

Moreover, Walton added an off-the-court energy just by being Walton. He was such a flat-out contradiction—the selfish, spoiled, ego-driven, modern-day athlete waged a daily competition (of which Walton seemed blissfully unaware) with the politically liberal, sixties-era, flower child—that he could hardly help but be larger than life, even on a team with the larger-than-life Bird. But on the Celtics he was just "Bill," and became, along with Ainge, the lightning rod for abuse. His teammates kidded him about being friends with Patty Hearst ("Where did you hide her?" they'd ask him all the time), criticized his politics, laughed off his history of injuries, lampooned his occasional stuttering. One day McHale and a couple teammates hung Walton's jersey on the wall at Hellenic and told him, "You'll never make it at Boston Garden, Bill, so we're honoring you here." Walton, for his part, loved every minute of it. He often said that his entire career had led to this season with the Celtics, a team that played basketball the way he liked to play it, unselfishly, cerebrally, *cleanly*. His respect for Bird, Parish, McHale, and Johnson was so out of balance from a player who was capable of showing utter disdain to those he considered inferior that it sometimes seemed bogus. But it wasn't. When a reporter would ask him how he was faring with his new team, Walton would put his hands on his hips, get very serious, and answer in his basic Californiaese: "Without a d-doubt, Larry, Kevin, and R-Robert are, like, the best. D. J.'s like the b-best guard I've like ever p-played with." McHale did a deadly imitation of Walton, and whenever he felt depressed, McHale might harken back to the moment in 1986 when, after a rare loss, Walton announced to an otherwise quiet locker room: "Th-that was like the worst e-exhibition of b-basketball in like the en-entire history of the g-game. We like set b-back the sp-sport like twen-twenty years." Everybody cracked up. Or, once, when Walton was telling McHale about his family, he explained: "The only bl-black sheep in my family is my brother Bruce. He's a Re-Republican."

Walton's relationship with Bird was particularly fascinating. Bird was the kind of athlete Walton would've probably criticized a decade

ago—politically unaware, disinterested in academics, overly concerned with basketball. And certainly Walton's intellect, by any other
measure than what happened on a basketball court, was superior to
Bird's. Yet Walton seemed almost obsequious in Bird's presence, the
eternal backup, the role player ready to service the superstar. That did
not, however, change the genuine affection they shared. They kibitzed
under the basket as Walton tried to hobble through a few moves.
McHale came over—it was rare to see McHale and Bird joking around
together; they always seemed to be most comfortable with a third party
present—and then Parish ambled over. Pretty soon, ex-Celtic Dave
Cowens, who had been hired to work with Vrankovic, joined the group
too. The scene was too much for Don Casey.

"Look at this," he said to no one in particular. "Would you look at
this? Dave Cowens, Bill Walton, Robert Parish, and Kevin McHale.
Four of the greatest ever at the center position under one basket at one
practice session." He shook his head. "I tell you, I love it here. You
think I saw this kind of thing when I was with the Clippers?"

Like many superstars, Bird is not a diplomat. If you want someone to
say all the right things, Bird is generally not your man. In the month of
October, as the Celtics worked toward putting a team on the floor that
was utterly different from Celtics teams of the recent past, the diplo-
matic and right things to say were: "We believe fully in Chris's offense."
Or: "We're all behind the running game a hundred percent." Or:
"We're going to begin running on opening night and keep running to
the championship." Everybody was saying those kinds of things.
Everybody but Larry Bird, that is. When asked about the up-tempo
offense, Bird would invariably be somewhat unenthusiastic and non-
committal. It wasn't that he didn't want to run, he would say, it was just
that he doubted that the running trend would continue. "We always
start out this way," Bird would say, "but pretty soon we're walking it up
again." Reading between the lines, some interpreted his message as:
"When the going gets tough, everybody knows we'll just slow down
and get it to me. That's our best chance of success, not running the
ball." That was the superstar in Bird talking, of course, and it was
understandable. Bird had scored many, many points off the fast break
over the years, and his passing and ball-handling skills were such that
he could never be an outright bad transition player, as Dennis Johnson
was. But there was no doubt that he was at his best in a halfcourt game,
where he could post up and overpower smaller defenders, or take
larger defenders out on the floor and shoot over them.

But it was also true that with each passing year Bird's ability to carry the Celtics with his halfcourt skills diminished. Ford read Bird's lukewarm comments—to his credit, Ford wasn't one of those coaches who claimed never to read the newspapers; he read them carefully and wasn't afraid to challenge a report with which he disagreed—and decided, in the immortal words of Mayberry's Deputy Barney Fife, to do "some bud-nipping." Those close to Ford claimed that he had been angling for a confrontation with Bird about the offense, if only to assure himself that the type of Larry-vs.-the-team situation that had occurred last season was not repeated. Ford's most dominant personality trait, according to his wife, Kathy, was a compulsion to attack problems head-on without letting any time elapse. And this situation, felt Ford, could become a problem.

Shortly after the first preseason game with Detroit, Ford gathered the team together and read a newspaper account that noted Bird's lukewarm comments about the offense. When he was finished he added a short but very specific speech about how the Celtics will run and run and run, and anyone who doesn't want to run can leave the premises immediately.

"Do we understand each other, LARRY?" Ford said, shooting a glance at Bird.

"Fuck you, Doc," Bird said.

And Ford came back with a few expletives of his own. So did Bird. So did Ford. But when it ended, the coach had had the last word. The incident occurred when the media was not present, during "the quiet hour," as someone dubbed the behind-closed-doors segment of the Celts' practice, and thus was open to only secondhand interpretation. Ford would never discuss the incident and Bird claimed it was overblown after *USA Today* columnist Peter Vecsey chronicled it weeks after it happened. Indeed, a player saying "fuck you" to the coach might've been news on other teams, but not on the Celtics. Yet others on the scene said it made an impression, and that impression was: Chris Ford was clearly in charge. Bird may have differed with others on the significance of the confrontation, but he *did* read Ford's lips, and his ambivalent public comments about the offense stopped.

The Denver Nuggets came to Boston on October 24 as the most talked-about team in the NBA. Also the most laughed-at team in the NBA. Like Boston, Denver was a team with a rookie head coach (Paul Westhead), and an up-tempo offense. The difference was, Denver played no defense and had no LarryKevinandRobert, or, for that matter, no BrianReggieandDee. Their forty-eight minutes of nonstop movement executed by a squad of extremely young and in some cases marginal NBA players was a prescription for disaster, and, indeed, the Celtics had already put 173 points on the board in a win at Denver four nights earlier. "The worst thing I've seen in forty-five years," proclaimed Celtics broadcaster Bob Cousy after Boston's 173–155 victory. And Cooz had seen some bad ones.

At any rate, the presence of the Nuggets brought new meaning to the word "exhibition." The only suspense was whether or not the Celtics would break 200 points—it had already been theorized that that would happen for the first time in NBA history with the Nuggets on the floor—and whether or not Shaw would be booed off the parquet in his Garden debut. Already the Celtics were joking that they didn't want to stand by him during the national anthem in the event that the fans started throwing things. Shaw did draw a lot of boos when his name was announced and he was jeered lustily after he lost a ball out of bounds in the first period. During an early time-out, a pair of young boys leaned over the first row of the lower balcony and yelled: "Hey, Shaw, you suck!" Shaw held their gaze with a big smile, and they didn't repeat the comment. When play resumed, Shaw went into the stands chasing a loose ball and the crowd nearly gave him a standing ovation.

"Ah," said the *Globe*'s Jackie MacMullen, "Boston at its consistent finest."

Bird, who had a triple-double by halftime, was beginning to play himself into shape. In the first period he went up for a long rebound, grabbed it, turned himself half-around in the air, and rifled a long pass to Michael Smith for a lay-up. It was the type of play for which Bird has no peer in the history of the game. No one has ever thrown more good passes off defensive and offensive rebounds than Bird, passes to get a fast-break started or passes to get the Celtics a second shot. It speaks to the essence of Bird as a player, the move requiring him to be mentally one step ahead, to be thinking about the next play while everyone else is concentrating on where the rebound is going to go. Later, in the second period, Bird found himself alone on the wing, too far from the basket to shoot, even in an exhibition game against the Nuggets. He faked a pass inside, faked a pass to the corner, and, when no Celtic worked himself free, he shrugged and faked a pass to referee Jake O'Donnell. O'Donnell smiled slightly but didn't flinch. Finally, McHale came out to the three-point line, took the pass, and sank a three-pointer, just about the last option Ford would want. It was that kind of night. "Real defensive struggle here at the Garden, sports fans," said reserve center Joe Kleine as he walked by the press table en route to the locker room at halftime with the Celtics leading 90–61. The final was

158–135. Eric McArthur, whose shooting continued to be erratic at best made a rim-rattling tomahawk dunk in the third period, missed another a few minutes later, and had another rejected as time ran out. McArthur hit the floor hard after the last one. "Eric had an ego-ectomy," said McHale, and no one any longer expected McArthur to be around on opening night.

CHAPTER 4

A Quick Start

NOVEMBER

Chris Ford walked into the locker room at about five o'clock on the Friday evening of November 2, the time he usually arrived when he was an assistant, to officially begin his Boston Celtics head coaching career. Tip-off was seven-thirty against the Cleveland Cavaliers. He wore a double-breasted gray suit—no sportcoats now that he was head coach, he had decided—a white shirt and a red paisley tie. He looked a lot different than he did back in the early seventies when, while a Detroit Piston, he went for the "Superfly" look in a big way—black velvet jumpsuits, big hats, long leather coats. Kathy Ford had picked out the suit and tie. The dry cleaners had done the shirt, but Ford had reironed it. "He doesn't like to shop, but the funny thing is that he's very, very fussy about his clothes," said Kathy. "I don't mess with them once they're bought. He doesn't even like the way I hang up his pants. He rehangs up pants and reirons shirts. Can you imagine that?" Jan Volk could—later in the season he bought his coach a travel iron as a present. Ford also carried, as has been his custom for the last decade, a small Italian leather pouch, which, coming as it did from The Sharper Image, no doubt cost more than the three or four checkered sportcoats that constituted Red Auerbach's entire coaching wardrobe. At one time or another, Auerbach probably referred to such purses as "fag bags," but now the eleventh head coach of the Boston Celtics carried one. Times had indeed changed.

Typically, the Celtics had planned no special ceremony for Ford's debut and it seemed like any other season opener. Up in the press room, the *Globe*'s Jackie MacMullen walked in, sniffed the air, and remarked, "Boy, smells like throw-up in here, doesn't it?" It did. Meanwhile, organist Ron Harry, who has been playing for the Celtics almost continuously since 1946, banged out such modern-day standards as "The Mexican Hat Dance" and "Three Blind Mice." During the pregame introductions, the fans booed Shaw rather lustily, screamed "Chief" when Parish trotted out, brought the roof off the place when Bird was announced, and applauded strongly but not hysterically when Ford's name was called. Standing implacably with his arms folded, the new coach appeared not to notice. He stood up for the opening tap and remained standing the rest of the game. Ford hadn't realized, he said, that he would be "a stander," but he did know that he wouldn't be a "kneeler," as some head coaches were; he was a baseball catcher for a couple of seasons and never enjoyed crouching. His counterpart on the Cleveland bench, veteran coach Lenny Wilkens, meanwhile, rarely stood or raised his voice. It was entirely too pat, of course, but the coaches seemed to symbolize their teams, the Celtics a running, gunning, newly rejuvenated bunch, the Cavs a down-tempo, defeated band even on day one of the season.

Ford professed not to be nervous and didn't look it. Reporters who approached and asked him for the cosmic significance of his debut were disappointed. "I'm here, I'm ready, it doesn't feel much different than it ever did," Ford said with a shrug. Kathy Ford had already been surprised by how smoothly her husband had made the jump from assistant to CEO. "It's like he was born for this," she said. (McHale felt that Kathy, too, had made the jump well and had begun calling her "The First Lady.") Ford drank coffee and from time to time glanced at a cassette of the Celtics-Cavs exhibition game, which the Celtics had lost by 121–115 a few days earlier. Many NBA coaches isolate themselves from the locker room before games, but assistant Ford had tended to hang around, enjoying the pregame witches' brew of banter and tension, and apparently he would do the same as head coach. Dave Gavitt came over about an hour before tip-off, shook Ford's hand, smiled, and said, "Chief [the team nickname for Robert Parish] wanted me to report that he's here." The Chief was usually the last Celtic to arrive.

All seemed calm. Lewis and Shaw talked quietly together. Dee Brown stretched. McHale expounded on the Boston Bruins, his favorite subject whenever the NHL is in season. Bird laughed and joked with Joe Kleine and Michael Smith and wondered if Ford would call a Sunday practice if they lost. One reporter mentioned how vividly the atmosphere contrasted with the last, jittery days of the Rodgers regime. But that wasn't quite fair. It was only November 2, after all, and every team in the league, including the Miami Heat and the Minnesota Timberwolves, was undefeated. There was plenty of time for the train to derail.

Still, the 6–2 preseason had been an unqualified success. The coaching staff had wanted to get the Celtics running, and they had run; even Bird was with the program. Most of the time the fast break had taken on the desired controlled and structured aspect too. Ideally, Parish, Bird, or McHale would get the defensive rebound, outlet to Shaw, while Lewis and the other small forward, Smith, Eddie Pinckney or Gamble, would go to the middle and then fan out to create lanes. If the break wasn't there, Shaw could pull back and wait for the rest of the Celtics to set up. "We wanted it to be like Iwo Jima," explained Casey, who, despite being a political pacifist, read military history and often used war metaphors in his strategic explanations. "See, we hit them with the first wave that comes in quick—bang!—the young guys and all that speed and quickness. Then, here comes the second wave, the heavy equipment, Bird, Parish, McHale." The Celtics' defense was tougher and improving every day too. The roster moves had been relatively simple: Bagley was placed on injured reserve, Dave Popson was kept on to battle it out with Vrankovic for the eleventh-man role (the loser would be twelfth), and DeHart, Dordevic, and McArthur had been cut, the latter's offensive weaknesses having canceled out the benefits of his athleticism.

Ford's main problem—and it was not a small one—was finding a fifth starter at the forward position to go with Bird, Parish, and guards Shaw and Lewis. For the opener, he tapped Pinckney. Ford had made an early decision that, if at all possible, he wanted to bring McHale off the bench. Rare was the successful NBA team that didn't have one reliable scorer who could enter a game and put points on the board right away, and McHale was ideal. He came out shooting, he needed absolutely no time to warm up, and he enjoyed the role. Indeed, it had been all but understood since the first day of training camp that McHale would be a super sub, and Ford had not even felt it necessary to consult with him.

The Celtics led by only 6 points midway through the third period when Ford called for a time-out and gave one of his "Francis" speeches. "Get over here!" he yelled at his players on the floor, who included LarryKevinandRobert. He read them the riot act, told them to get their asses up and down the floor, practically pushed them back onto the court, then roamed the sidelines, arms folded, and watched the Celtics start to pull away. Later in the quarter, McHale came over to the bench huffing and puffing after Cleveland called a time-out, raised his hand before Ford could say anything, and wheezed, "Doc, let me shoot my free throws first, then yell at me." The Celtics won 125–101 and the Chris Ford Era had begun smashingly.

There were many positive signs. Lewis, whom the Celtics wanted to become a big-time player, had a big-time game with 32 points. Parish had 23 points and 14 rebounds, and looked, at times, like the youngest player in the league instead of the oldest. Bird took fewer shots (15) than Lewis and McHale (both 18) and didn't appear to have a frown on his face; he had 15 assists and 9 rebounds to go with 18 points. Shaw continued to play erratically but enthusiastically, bent on showing his teammates and the Garden faithful that he was a player and not just a money grubber, and, for right now at least, Ford was satisfied with that. McHale had predicted that as long as Shaw played well the fans would forget all about Italy, and, true to form, the booing was pretty much contained to the opening introductions. But the big problem remained. Pinckney had gotten only twelve minutes, compared to McHale's thirty-three, and, at that rate, Ford might as well give up the charade and just start McHale. Perhaps, wondered Casey and Jennings after the game, Gamble, though he was as much a guard as a forward, could become that fifth man; in seventeen minutes against Cleveland, he had made 7 of his 8 shots.

November 8 was officially celebrated as " 'Cheers' Day" in Boston. The cast of the long-running sitcom, which is set in a Boston bar, had been honored with a ceremony at City Hall Plaza, and most of them were coming to the Friday night game against the Bulls at Boston Garden. On the morning of the game, Bebe Neuwirth, who plays Lilith, and a dozen or so other assorted producers, writers, technicians, family members, and friends gathered at the Garden for the NBA ritual known as the morning "shootaround." If the "Cheers" group had come to experience the Garden's spartan ambience, they weren't disappointed. The place was freezing and it smelled like sour beer. Out on the court, Gamble blew on his hands as he shot free throws and Pinckney wore a gray sweatshirt zippered up past his neck. The night before, Gavitt had encountered George Wendt, the roundish character actor who plays the beer-drinking Norm, at a health club, but didn't realize it.

"This guy was real nice to me, talking and everything as we rode the stationary bike," said Gavitt, "but I had no idea who he was until I went home that evening, switched on the news, and watched him getting the key to the city. All I knew was that the guy made me feel pretty good." (Physically, Gavitt is somewhat of a smaller version of Wendt.)

"Wait a minute, you never watched 'Cheers,' Dave?" someone asked him. "Christ, the show's been on for nine years."

"Think I've seen it twice," said Gavitt. "I basically have the TV for news and sports." This Auerbach hire was no lollygagger, that much was certain.

As they walked onto the court, most of the players paused for a few seconds and nodded at Lilith, looking no doubt for Rebecca and Sam Malone, but the "Cheers" people were waiting for Bird. One could hear whispers of "Larry" and "Bird" and "When's he coming?" Finally, Bird walked out, cast a look neither right nor left, grabbed a ball from the rack, twirled it behind his back, and dribbled onto the court, altogether underwhelmed by the Hollywood invasion. McHale came out a few minutes later, though, and the response was entirely different. He engaged Neuwirth in animated conversation, waved at various others, signed autographs for the kids. McHale had appeared as himself on one of the show's more memorable episodes a couple months earlier, demonstrating an on-camera ease that can't be taught. He even contributed an original line (caustic, of course) about the Pistons' Laimbeer and suggested that Woody Harrelson, who portrays a hick bartender from the Indiana farm country, refer to Bird as "a dufus." McHale pooh-poohed a future acting career—"About all I could play is monsters, Lon Chaney types with long arms," he said—but he was obviously smitten with his taste of Hollywood.

The Celtics convened briefly to discuss the Bulls' offense (though the idea of hypothetically defensing Michael Jordan is somewhat laughable), then broke into an end-of-practice shooting game. White players versus black players with Parish on the sidelines, cheering on the blacks, and Kleine doing the same for the whites. Kleine's "brothers" eventually triumphed, helped by an improbable jumper by Vrankovic. "Hey, whites are *supposed* to be better shooters, right?" said Jennings. The Celtics deserved no special commendation for race relations at this stage of the season, but the game was just a little sign that the players were comfortable with each other.

Immediately after practice, Parish began his slow, loping walk to the locker room only to be headed off by Ford.

"Where you going, Chief?" said Ford.

"Treatment," said Parish.

"Uh uh," said Ford. "Foul shots."

And Chief turned back around.

When McHale was finished, he walked back to the "Cheers" group, stepped into the first row of seats where they were congregated, and held court for an hour, like the executive producer at a story conference.

Chicago coach Phil Jackson had many memorable moments in Boston Garden as a player for the hated New York Knicks in a twelve-year career that began in 1967. "I remember in '73 Red had us switch locker rooms four different times," said Jackson, sitting on the Chicago bench an hour before game time that night at Boston Garden. "We finally landed up changing in some unbelievably small room, like a broom closet, right off the hallway." He could laugh about it now.

"I guess that kind of stuff doesn't happen these days, right?" someone said.

"Well, maybe not that bad," answered Jackson. "But even today we wanted to shoot around at the Garden in the morning and we were told the ice was down and we couldn't practice. So we went to some health club." Jackson smiled meaningfully. "Of course, the Celtics shot here. Must've been some kind of mix-up."

The Celtics were living in a perfect world on the night Jordan came to town. They stood at 3–0, the last of those victories having come at Chicago three nights earlier in a most improbable, but promising fashion. Bird and Lewis sat on the bench during crucial stages of the game in favor of Dee Brown and Gamble. But Bird, when he did return, had a stretch of 9 field goals in a row, most of them on jumpers far out on the floor. The score was 108–108 when Shaw rebounded Parish's airball and put it back in at the buzzer for a 110–108 victory. The fast break was clicking, the spread-the-wealth offense was working, and the enthusiasm of the young players, Shaw and Brown in particular, seemed to be contagious. "You made a play that you made a zillion times before," said McHale, "and there, all of a sudden, is Dee coming up to you with that look in his eye, slapping palms."

But then Jordan brought that perfect world crashing down. He scored 41 points in a 120–100 Bulls victory, the Celtics' worst home defeat since March 27, 1981, and a reminder that Boston was a long way from being of championship timber. At times, the Celtics looked very old and very tired against the Bulls' young athletic trio of Jordan, Scottie Pippen, and Horace Grant, and even Ford's repeated ministrations to "Run!" and "Hustle!" did no good. After the game, he complained about the Celtics' lack of effort, while McHale said they showed "a lack of discipline." Perhaps. No one wanted to consider the alternative—that the Celtics had not played that bad but just weren't nearly as talented or as athletic as the Bulls. In any case, the game demonstrated that for all the promise showed by Reggie Lewis, Brian Shaw, and Dee Brown, none was anywhere near as good as Michael Jordan.

New Jersey Nets' coach Bill Fitch leaned back in his office chair and reminisced about Chris Ford, the player, whom he had coached in Boston for three seasons (1979–80, 1980–81, and 1981–82). Ford had never been a great fan of the driving tactics and incessant film-watching of "Captain Video" (the nickname hung on Fitch by McHale), but no one could deny that Fitch knew his x's and o's. In his four seasons, Boston had won sixty-one, sixty-two, sixty-three, and fifty-six games, as well as a championship in 1980–81. From Fitch's standpoint, the bitterness that led to his departure after the 1982–83 season was a thing of the past. Hell, it looked like a honeymoon compared to what he had been through in Houston, what with drug problems and the unpredictable seven-foot-four Ralph Sampson to deal with. And now he had landed at New Jersey, one of the league's least stable franchises.

"I knew Chris would be a coach someday," Fitch said. "He was never afraid to take a player to the side and chew him out. There was only one problem I had with Chris—he never wanted to come out of the damn game. Frankly, I left him out there sometimes so I wouldn't have to sit next to him. Sure, coaching ex-teammates could be a problem for him. He came up with those guys. But on the other hand, they won't misread him, and that's a big advantage. I know one thing, he won't accept loafing from anybody. And he's probably one of the smartest players ever. Bird, too. And I'll tell you something else—there's two guys who never beat anyone in a footrace, Bird and Ford."

Fitch was rarely able to talk about basketball without bringing Bird into it somehow—it was almost as if he had never coached any other player. Indeed, the words "Bird" and "Magic" had a way of creeping into many conversations around the league, and it had been that way since they broke in together in 1979. Both had made so much out of what were seemingly modest innate athletic skills that they became the standard of comparison whenever coaches wanted to talk about the *intangibles*. "Well, he's good, but he just doesn't have Magic's intelligence on the floor," a coach might say of a point guard. Or: "Well, he's got talent, if only he'd work as hard as Bird." Such comparisons were patently unfair—Bird and Magic, whose innate skills were never as modest as some would believe anyway, are simply two of the greatest players ever to pick up a basketball. But it happened time and time again. All-stars who had come along later in the decade—Jordan,

Philadelphia's Charles Barkley, and Utah's Karl Malone foremost among them—were never used as the standard of comparison because their God-given athleticism seemed too extraordinary. But who knows how many times Bill Fitch sat over on the Houston Rocket bench, watching Sampson consistently fail to live up to his potential, and wished he were back in Boston watching Bird dive for loose balls and make impossible no-look passes. Or how many times he would do the same thing this season while watching his own talented but enigmatic rookie, Derrick Coleman, the No. 1 pick in the draft.

Over in the visitors' locker room, meanwhile, Bird looked over the roster of a rotisserie league team on which he had been chosen. (Bird thought carefully about what skills he thought were important for a player, and, indeed, one such rotisserie league was named "The Larry Bird League" because it had adopted Bird's method of evaluating players.) He pointed to the name "Benoit Benjamin" and gave a look of disgust. Benjamin was a Los Angeles Clipper center (since traded to Seattle) for whom the words "inconsistent," "unpredictable," and "overweight" were hopelessly insufficient.

"Remember that team chemistry doesn't count in this league," his visitor told him. "Only numbers."

Bird shrugged. His visitor told him that one of his teammates was his close friend, Brad Lohaus of the Milwaukee Bucks.

"If you were gone for numbers," said Bird, laughing, "why'd you pick Brad?"

To that point, Bird had not attempted a three-point shot in four games and his visitor suggested, jokingly, that the rotisserie team desperately needed some help in that area.

"Don't know about that," said Bird. "I'm trying to git my field goal percentage up, and shootin' threes don't help it. What I gotta do somethin' about is turnovers."

"Turnovers don't count in this league," his visitor said. "Only positive stats."

"Guess ya don't mind if I try to do somethin' about 'em anyway, do you?" Bird said.

Early in the first period, Bird sank a jumper from about twenty feet, and Stojko Vrankovic rose off the bench and shouted, in his deep, accented bass: "WAY TO GO, LAZLO!" Everyone around him cracked up. The game was no crackup, though. Lazlo continued to have turnover trouble—he would finish with 5—and Brown experienced a bout of rookie uncertainty when called upon to run the offense. "Dee," Ford said to him during a time-out, "you're dribbling the shit out of the ball and not going anyplace. Give me some confidence!" Bird, sitting on the bench for a breather in the second period, suddenly and uncharacteristically rose out of his seat at one point and shouted defensive encouragement at McHale: "Play 'em, Kevin!" That's because McHale was guarding the rookie hotshot, Coleman, who had recently signed a five-year $15 million contract that made him, on a per-year basis, one of the highest-paid players in the league. Bird has always been known for treating rookies on his own team extremely well but would prefer the oppositions' to earn their respect. Even on an otherwise boring Saturday night at Brendan Byrne Arena in East Rutherford, New Jersey, he didn't want any high-paid rookie stealing his thunder, or McHale's. The Celtics finally salted the game away late in the final period when Bird sneaked around Nets' center Sam Bowie, slapped the ball out of his hand from the blind side, and made a great no-look pass to McHale for a 101–91 lead. The final was 105–91 and the Celtics stood at 4–1.

Through the first six games of the season, Ford tinkered with his fifth starter, using Pinckney in the opener, Smith in the second game, Pinckney again in Games 3, 4 and 5, Smith in Game 6. The problem, Ford knew, was that neither player was a true small forward, or "3-man" in NBA parlance. "Eddie is more of a '4' [power forward] in that he doesn't really have the offense to be a small forward," Ford would say. "And Michael, who's a pretty good passer and a pretty good shooter, can't guard the real '3's' because, defensively, he's more of a '2' [shooting guard]." When the Charlotte Hornets came to Boston on November 14, Ford decided to go with Gamble, who wasn't the classic 3-man, either.

The Celtics had picked up Gamble from the CBA in December of 1988, but though he was at times spectacular, he could never quite earn Rodgers's full respect. In the 1989–90 season he had averaged just fourteen minutes per game and had collected 11 DNPs (Did Not Play). Late in the season, his agent, Ron Grinker, proclaimed: "I can absolutely guarantee you that Kevin won't be back. They have humiliated him." After Ford got the job, Grinker altered his stance (agents do that from time to time, sometimes hourly) and wanted Gamble to stay. He encouraged his soft-spoken client to accompany Ford and Volk on the Celtics' late-summer cruise to clarify his status. But every time he encountered either one, all they talked about was the weather.

Truth be told, Ford wasn't sure at that time how much he needed Gamble. On the one hand, he didn't feel that Rodgers had used the player wisely, but on the other, he, like Rodgers, distrusted Gamble's sometimes "matador" style of defense. The big problem was that Gamble is a "tweener," the NBA tag hung on players who aren't quite big enough to be dominant forwards and not quite quick enough to be successful guards. Still, that didn't seem to bother Gamble on offense. He moved with a kind of heavy-legged gait—the initial rap on him after he was drafted by Portland in 1987 was that he was overweight—yet his forte was slashing to the basket and scoring in the open floor, either from the "2" or "3" position. Once Gamble made a move with the ball he was not easily deterred, and it didn't matter how slow he *appeared* to be moving. Gamble felt that he was ready. It had been three years since then-Portland coach Mike Schuler knocked on his hotel door and said, "Kevin, you're a good player, and I think you can make it in the NBA, but there's just no room for you here. We're letting you go." The Trail Blazers were in Philadelphia at the time, and Gamble, a wide-eyed rookie, was excited about playing against his boyhood idol, the Sixers' Julius Erving, that evening. After Schuler gave him the news, he just packed his bags and left, bound, as it turned out, for the CBA and even a short stint with a pro team in the Philippines.

When Ford said, "Okay, we're going with Oscar tonight," Gamble was determined to play well and never give the job back to either Pinckney or Smith. (Ainge had given Gamble the name of "Oscar," after a former major league baseball player named Oscar Gamble, and one had to struggle to remember that his given first name was actually "Kevin.") With the $300,000 contract he signed the previous season, Gamble had fulfilled his dream of making enough money to move his mother out of the ghetto on the northeast side of Springfield, Illinois, and he was extremely proud of it. "We live on the west side of town now," said Gamble, who returned to Springfield to stay with his mother each summer. "It's not real unusual for a black family to live there, but it is very unusual for a black family to come over to the west side from the east side."

The story of the Charlotte game, though, was Bird. The night before in Milwaukee he had passed up several obvious shots and finished with only 5 points on 7 field goal attempts in a terrible 119–91 loss to the Bucks. Some observers felt that Bird, despite public proclamations to the contrary, was still not enamored with Ford's offense and would stage such protests of ennui from time to time just to make that point. But he came out shooting against Charlotte and scored 45 points to go with 8 assists, 8 rebounds, 2 steals, and 5 blocks, a performance so close to the vintage Bird of four or five seasons ago that it was almost scary. Bird has always feasted on those defenders who hang back and dare him to shoot his variety of fallaways and fadeaways from seemingly impossible distances—can they still not believe a six-foot-nine player can make those shots?—and he abused two of those types in this game, Johnny Newman and Armon Gilliam, the latter one of the league's true loafing dogs. After sinking one long rainbow shot over Gilliam, Bird backpedaled with a contemptuous look on his face, shaking his head at Gilliam's refusal to come out and play him. "Too much Bird," said Charlotte coach Gene Littles after the game, a 135–126 Celtics victory. "And it's not like it was one of those nights. He can do this every night. There was a time when he *did* do this every night."

In the Celtics' big picture, though, the contributions of the new starter were more significant. Gamble scored 26 points, missing only 4 shots, and was clearly the most effective of Casey's "first wave" strike force, more potent in the open floor than even Lewis. Ford still didn't know whether to call him a small forward or a big guard because, on occasion, he still needed the six-foot-seven Lewis's size to guard bigger people near the basket, and he liked to define his players' position by what they did on defense. But he did know that having both Gamble and Lewis on the floor gave him offensive flexibility, forced the opposition to adjust to the Celtics, not vice versa. Semantics aside, Ford knew that he had found his elusive fifth starter.

"Ladies and gentlemen," said Boston Garden public address announcer Eddie Jick, "it's time for the Northwest Airlines halftime shootout!" From his post high above the parquet floor in Boston Garden, Celtics' radio announcer Glenn Ordway was taken aback. "Whoa!" he told his listeners. "Here's something new."

On November 16, with the Utah Jazz in town, the Celtics ran their first-ever halftime promotion. There was a palpable buzz when the announcement was made, for there was a consistency to the halftimes at Boston Garden, i.e., nothing happened. Oh, every once in a while, some group would present an award to a deserving Celtic for one thing or another, but there was none of the carnival aspect that went on in most other NBA arenas. Tradition. "Our fans don't like to watch things at halftime," said Tod Rosensweig, vice president of marketing and communications. "Our fans like to smoke and drink beer." That was true. The hallways in the Garden during halftimes were the American Cancer Society's biggest nightmare. It was the same thing before games. The Celtics never saw the need for celebrity crooners, not with local legends Guy Rotondo and Freddie Tagg ready, willing, and able to sing the national anthem. But Gavitt had given approval to start a few modest promotions, and some team officials were a little, well, sheepish about it.

"There will be no cheerleaders, no dot races on the scoreboard, and I don't think you'll ever see a 'wave' in the Garden," said Rosensweig. "In terms of glitz we're at the bottom, and we like it there." The Celtics felt that some franchises, Chicago and Atlanta to name two, were far too tacky with their constant promotional drum-beating. Like most Celtics employees, Rosensweig felt that some changes were desperately needed, but he still felt Auerbach's touch on his shoulder. (To Rosensweig, it probably felt more like a strong tug; his father, Stanley, is an old friend of Auerbach's who shares an office with him in Washington, D.C.) Rosensweig promised that there would never be a Celtics mascot either.

"Not many people remember this, but we actually tried out a mascot one time," said Rosensweig. "It was during one of our bad stretches in the late seventies. [Boston went 32–50 and 29–53 in the two seasons before Bird arrived.] This woman mime showed up at our offices one day dressed as a leprechaun, and the funny thing is that she was pretty damned good. Red even liked her, so we tried her out at a preseason game." He shook his head. "Poor woman. Didn't make it until the beginning of the game. The fans hated her and hooted at her so much. Always wondered what happened to her."

After the Northwest Airlines Shootout, the Celtics broke away from a desultory 47–47 halftime tie with a shootout of their own en route to a 114–89 rout. Lewis had 24 points and Bird had 23, but best of all was the performance of Parish, who had his first good game since the season opener with 20 points. At one point in the third period, Bird drove, spotted Parish, and threw a high pass near the basket but well to the side of it. Parish got control of the ball and in one motion laid it off the backboard for a basket. Chief probably dunks less than any scoring seven-footer in the history of the game.

"That pass," remarked the *Globe*'s Ryan at courtside, "was an alley-ooo. No 'p' at the end, just like there was no dunk. An alley-ooo."

On a blustery cold Tuesday evening two days before Thanksgiving, Reggie Lewis and Brian Shaw, along with their agent, Jerome Stanley, stood behind a table in a large room at Roxbury Community College tossing around turkeys. They wore gloves to handle the three hundred frozen birds that were to be handed out to needy Boston families. "I don't think Chris Ford would like it if Reggie and Brian showed up tomorrow night [for the Celtics' home game against Houston] with 'turkey elbow,' " joked Willie Maye, sports director at WILD, the Boston area's best-known black radio station. "You guys better take it easy." Lewis had wanted to do something for the black community but didn't want to make a big deal about it, so he and Stanley put together the turkey idea, announcing it only on Maye's program and downplaying the fact that any Celtics were involved. Helping out, besides Maye, were Lewis's fiancée, Donna Harris, and a few other friends. Donna actually had the toughest job—checking public assistance cards and turning away anyone who didn't have one. And some didn't go very quietly. When Stanley and the players arrived at about six-thirty, a half hour before the designated pickup time, the line wound all the way around the building and into the street. A policeman told Shaw that families had begun gathering about four o'clock.

"Mister, listen to me, Mister," a young mother with several children in tow said to Lewis. "I got five kids. Can I have two turkeys?"

Before Reggie could answer, Stanley came over. What are agents for if not to handle the delicate politics of turkey distribution?

"I'm sorry, ma'am, but we have to limit it to one per family," said Stanley.

"But how can I feed five children and myself with one turkey?"

"I don't know, ma'am, but there's a lot of people out there and we can only give you one turkey."

She threw the turkey into a bag and left in a huff.

"Sir, sir, you're doing this all wrong," said another woman to Stanley.

"Now, how is that, ma'am?" said Stanley.

"Outside you've got people cutting in line," she said. "I barely made it in here. Gotta be more organized."

"I'm sorry, ma'am, but we're doing the best we can," said Stanley, smiling, nodding his head, patient but firm, just like when he told Dave Gavitt that, yes, Reggie Lewis needed more money.

It was a portrait of frustration all the way around. Some families never made it into the room and went home empty-handed. Others found one turkey insufficient. And there was Lewis, who only wanted to help, being told that he was "doing this all wrong." It was the flip side of what most athletes experience in their carefully orchestrated public appearances at autograph signings, award ceremonies, and banquets. Incredibly, most of the Roxbury pilgrims didn't even recognize Lewis or Shaw, or, at least, paid them no mind if they did. They had come for the turkeys, not for the gravy of meeting a Celtic or cadging an autograph. That was fine with Lewis, for if there was one Celtic who was used to the shadows, it was Reggie Lewis.

He grew up in the hardscrabble, predominantly black section of East Baltimore, one of four children of Irvin and Inez Lewis. His parents separated when Reggie was young and he saw his father sporadically. He was saved, he said, by the neighborhood recreation sports programs. He was a decent switch-hitting first baseman and a speedy wide receiver motivated by fear. "I remember catching a ball in the middle of the field and going all the way just because I was so scared of being tackled," said Lewis. At the same time, he would fight if he had to. "Kids tried to take your money, so what could you do?" he said. "I remember I had one fight that seemed to go on forever, me and this guy rolling under parked cars, because nobody would ever break up a fight. We finally just gave it up ourselves."

At Dunbar High School, Lewis was a member of the nation's best scholastic basketball team—and arguably one of the best of all time— but never got the headlines. Even in his senior year, he came off the bench as the sixth man, while other players like Muggsy Bogues, Reggie Williams, David Wingate, and Gary Graham got more attention. His coach, Bob Wade, who later moved on to the University of Maryland where he got in trouble with the NCAA for recruiting violations, used to tell him he had "the ugliest jump shot in the history of basketball." Lewis took such joshing quietly, but it hurt inside and he never cared much for Wade's coaching. Reggie vastly preferred the summer-league games at Madison Square Park, which they called "The Dome" (it had a roof), Lewis and Wingate playing for the Cecil Kirk Rec Center, Muggsy and Williams in the uniform of Lafayette Red. To this day, the men he most respects are Calvin Dodson, Anthony Lewis, and Vernon Francis, the unknown rec-league coaches to whom he looked up to as father figures. When it came time to choose colleges, Muggsy, the team leader, went to Wake Forest and the high-profile Atlantic Coast Conference, Williams and Wingate went to the high-profile Big East program at Georgetown, Graham went to the high-profile program at UNLV. Reggie Lewis went to the low-profile program at Northeastern University.

Much to everyone's surprise, including his own, Lewis was an instant star at Northeastern. He took to the city of Boston, and Boston took to him, at least to the limited degree that it noticed Northeastern's basketball program. "I made a great adjustment to college right away," said Lewis. "Maybe it had to do with being away and, at last, being the main guy. I mean, in one year I went from not starting for my high school team to people talking about me going hardship in the NBA draft." When Lewis ended his four-year career as the NCAA's ninth all-time leading scorer, the university retired his number (35). Still, Lewis was surprised when the Celtics made him the twenty-third pick of the 1987 draft. He would bump into Dennis Johnson at a neighborhood pizzeria (Johnson was that rare Celtic who lived inside the city limits), and Celtics scout Rick Weitzman would talk to him after Northeastern games from time to time, but Lewis had no idea that Auerbach even knew he existed. At the press conference after he had been selected, Lewis was again overshadowed . . . by the ghost of Lenny Bias, who had stood where Lewis was standing just one year earlier. "How do *you* plan to celebrate?" someone asked him.

Lewis considered himself pretty much a Bostonian now that he had spent most of his time there since 1983. He said he never sensed any racial animosity and had certainly never experienced anything like what Brown went through in Wellesley. That's why some Celtics officials were worried when Stanley suddenly materialized in Lewis's universe. They feared that Stanley would feed Lewis with negative ideas and turn him against the Celtics and the city. Lewis said that was nonsense. "Anything I felt about being black, I felt inside me, and Jerome had nothing to do with it," said Lewis. He remembered being chased by a group of white youths when he walked through a white section of Baltimore on his way home from the rec center; thereafter, he changed his route. The only college course he remembered with fondness was one called "The Sociology of Prejudice," in which he and a white coed wrote a script for a skit that paralleled *Guess Who's Coming to Dinner?* "Her family wanted to serve me greens and fried chicken and a bunch of other stuff that I really didn't like that much," said Lewis. "Writing it and acting it out taught me a lot."

When Lewis decided to give out free turkeys in Roxbury he was not making a grand statement about prejudice in Boston. But he was remembering the times that he had gone hungry, when his mother couldn't quite feed four children with the salary she earned at a paper-cup factory, and he definitely *was* making a statement about integrating the Celtics and the black community. But it was difficult for him because he sincerely does not like the limelight.

And so, he stood behind a table in a pair of gloves giving away turkeys until the supply ran out. The Celtics' organization didn't know he was there, most of the media outlets didn't know he was there.

"I don't know what else I could've done," he said. "Buy more turkeys next year, I guess."

The first event ever held at Boston Garden, on November 17, 1928, was the Crosscup-Pishon Post's American Legion boxing show to benefit the wounded soldiers' welfare fund. To kick off the festivities, Harry Lyon, an Army captain who made the first solo flight across the Pacific, re-enacted a World War I bombing mission outside the Garden. The First Corps Cadets gave a demonstration of dismantling and reassembling machine guns at high speed. One Doris Erskine sang "1492." Local hero Dick "Honey Boy" Finnegan won a ten-round decision in a nontitle bout against world featherweight champion Andre Routis of France.

And all of it, no doubt, went off more smoothly than the Boston Celtics–Atlanta Hawks game did some sixty-two years later, on the evening of November 28, 1990.

The Hawks carried an eight-game losing streak into Boston that evening, but that did not explain why Hawks players began losing their balance, slipping, and in some cases falling at the east end of the court, where they were shooting. It wasn't as evident at the Celtics' end (although Shaw appeared to slip when he went in for a lay-up early in the game), and Boston quickly built a substantial lead. McHale, ready to check into the game late in the first period, ambled over to the Hawks' bench, pointed to the dry side of the court, and said to Atlanta assistant coach Kevin Loughery: "Watch, next half the wet spots will mysteriously be over there." Loughery sniffed. "I think what'll happen, they'll turn the goddamned court around." Play was finally stopped with 10:45 left in the second period while chief referee Dick Bavetta went in to call NBA officials. Record-high temperatures in Boston that day (the mercury had reached 74 degrees and it was still 67 at game time) had partially melted the ice underneath the parquet, producing the dangerous condensation on the floor. The Celtics could not be faulted for the weather, of course, but the problem would never have developed if the ancient Garden had air conditioning or a temperature-control system of any kind, or, for that matter, if the floor were not wooden and so susceptible to condensation.

During the half-hour delay, the Garden took on the aspect of an informal cocktail party with spectators. Bird slapped a towel across the floor, just killing time. "Hey, why don't we go finish this thing at Hellenic," he suggested finally. Vrankovic was mildly amazed that everyone hung around. "In Europe," he said, "everybody go home now." When the action resumed, it took Atlanta's Tim McCormick only fifteen seconds to take a bad fall near the sideline, at which point the Hawks rose off their bench en masse, heading for the locker room. "Let's get the hell outta here," said Loughery. Bavetta reached the same conclusion, postponing the game with 10:30 left in the second period and the Celtics leading by 37–22. The spectators didn't even boo; they were simply stunned by Dick's announcement: "Due to unsafe playing conditions, tonight's game has been postponed." It was to be continued from the point at which it was stopped, on December 23.

Auerbach made his way across the court en route to the locker room, as he always does, stopping at the spot where McCormick had taken the final tumble. He scuffed his feet along the floor a few times, then shrugged his shoulders. "Hey, Don, come here," he said to owner Don Gaston. Together, they scuffed the floor like a couple of ol' soft-shoe hoofers and looked at each other. Auerbach shrugged his shoulders again. As far as he was concerned, there was not a damn thing wrong with the parquet and the Hawks had simply wormed their way out of what was destined to be defeat. Hell, he'd seen such treachery before. "I'm really impressed with Red Auerbach," McCormick said later. "I thought I had heard about all his tricks, but climate control, that's one I never expected."

Out in the hallway leading to the locker room, local broadcaster Bob Lobel prepared to interview Celtics assistant Jennings. Inexplicably, he introduced Jennings as "Dave Checketts," an NBA executive at the time, now the general manager of the Knicks. There was an ongoing Rodney Dangerfield contest between Casey and Jennings to see whose name would be more tortured during the season—Casey was constantly being called "Don Chaney," who was in fact the coach of the Houston Rockets, while Jennings's problem was more one of outright anonymity—but this was unquestionably the highlight to date.

"Dave, what happened out there?" Lobel asked Jennings.

"Well, Bob," said Jennings, "my name's Jon, but the floor was wet."

Twenty minutes later, the Celtics, one of the NBA's notoriously slow teams in opening its locker room doors to the media, were still dressing behind closed doors. It was only eight forty-five P.M., they figured, and no one was missing a deadline.

"You know, the Celtics have to be the only team that won't open their locker room after a game that *wasn't* played," said Jackie MacMullen.

All in all, the evening was rather amusing, but it didn't hide the fact that Boston Garden, one year older than the NBA's next-oldest arena, Chicago Stadium, had proven to be, once again, a national embarrassment for the Delaware North Corporation, which owned the Garden (as well as the NHL Bruins), and, by extension, the Celtics. Game 4 of the 1988 Stanley Cup Finals between the Bruins and Edmonton had to be postponed when a generator in North Station blew, putting Boston Garden in near-darkness. At other times when outside temperatures were high, the Garden ice had fogged up so badly that the players seemed to be skating around in Jack the Ripper's London, or, perhaps, at the climactic moment of some surrealistic ice show. And any number of NBA teams have complained about the heat, the smell, the overall circus-just-left-here *feel* to the place. Only the most avid Gardenite—and granted, there are thousands—could see anything quaint about a game having to be postponed in a league where nightmare travel schedules already test the athletes' endurance limits. Even most of the Celtics' staff, Auerbach included, had by this time quietly reached the opinion that the Garden had outlived its usefulness. But

no one said it too loudly, for that would be like the monks suggesting
that the monastery wasn't up to snuff. It didn't matter what anyone
thought, though. All the influence of Auerbach and all the persuasive
power of Gavitt would not make one iota of difference in this battle.
Plans for a new Garden were hopelessly hung up by financial problems, and it would be several years at minimum before the Celtics
would be playing anywhere else. Gavitt, a man who wants to go first
class in everything, could only hold his breath that nothing else of
major consequence would go wrong in the building to embarrass the
franchise. And when walking through most parts of Boston Garden,
holding one's breath is not a bad idea.

With an 11–2 record (not including what would probably become a
win over Atlanta), the Celtics had started to feel pretty good about
themselves and each other. Ford felt it was a positive sign that a lot of
players were hanging around after practice, either working on individual moves or challenging each other in informal competition. On this
November 29 afternoon, a day before the final game of the month (at
home against Washington), Bird and Dee Brown were at one end of the
gym engaged in a game that juxtaposed experience and youth. Bird
stood in the middle of the lane, about five feet from the basket, tossing
up short shots, while Brown, standing under the basket, leaped out
and tried to goaltend them. Even in the earliest days of his career, Bird
would've never been the one to goaltend. More than half the time
Brown's incredible leaping ability enabled him to jump far over the rim
and either catch the ball or bat it away.
   "Okay, twenty dollars," said Bird.
   "Okay," said Brown.
   "Ready?" said Bird.
   "Ready," said Brown.
   Bird made just the slightest adjustment, shooting the shot lower but
also quicker, disturbing Brown's timing. Despite a heroic leap, the
rookie just missed and the ball settled into the basket.
   Bird turned away and laughed.
   "Oh, he's just a rookie," he warbled in a singsong voice.
   A group comprised of McHale, Kleine, Pinckney, Smith, Popson, and
Vrankovic had begun to engage in an informal but eagerly awaited
three-on-three competition after most practices. The games were
played on what Kleine called "McHale Standard Time," i.e., they began whenever McHale finished dillydallying and deigned to amble
over. McHale's incredible talent of maneuvering around, between, and
over the opposition to make shots was even more evident in these

contests than in regular-season games—he totally dominated even as he expended half of his energy "broadcasting" the action.

"He's going to the hoop," McHale said, and promptly drove on Kleine for a basket.

"He's taking him inside again . . . No! It's the old step-back move," said McHale as he stopped dead in his tracks, stepped back, and hit a jumper over Pinckney.

The McHale team needed one more basket to win, when McHale took two dribbles and released an awkward-looking half-hook from around the foul line. "Oh, yes, it's the . . . the . . . Big Daddy Lipscomb shot!" he shouted just before the ball settled into the hoop for the victory. (McHale and his brothers used to fight over who would be the celebrated defensive lineman during their football games on the front lawn of their home in Hibbing, Minnesota.) The losing team of Kleine, Pinckney, and Smith was miffed but was also having trouble not collapsing into hysterics. Popson was laughing hard, too, as he high-fived his teammate. Bird dribbled by to watch, a half-smile on his face, looking perhaps even a little wistful. His postpractice competitions— and no one had engaged in more—tended to lack the surreal element that McHale provided. Only Stojko looked a little confused.

"Whatta you figure Stojko's thinking when Kevin mentions Big Daddy Lipscomb?" Popson asked Kleine.

Kleine considered it. "Unfiltered cigarettes?" he suggested.

For reasons known only to himself, McHale had decided that Kleine reminded him of the tightly wound Jimmy Piersall character portrayed by Tony Perkins in *Fear Strikes Out*. Or, rather, having just seen the movie on a late show a few nights earlier, it might've been that McHale just needed *someone* to be Piersall, and Kleine was the logical choice. Indeed, Kleine had become more or less the team's lightning rod of abuse, now that Ainge and Walton were gone, and he was a natural for the role. He was incredibly intense and competitive on the court, but easygoing, affable, and quick-witted off it. He was one of the few exceptions to Paxson's rule of being either a "Larry guy" or a "Kevin guy." Kleine was both. He was a Parish guy, too, and a Pinckney guy. Joe liked everybody, and everybody liked Joe.

At any rate, Kleine was practicing jump shots when McHale's piercing yell cut through the gym.

"DAD! DAD! HOW WAS THAT, DAD? DID MY JUMP SHOT LOOK OKAY, DAD?"

McHale continued in this vein for a couple minutes until Kleine dropped the ball, looked quizzically at McHale and said, "What the hell are you talking about?"

"*Fear Strikes Out*," said McHale. "Classic. Tony Perkins finally flips out because his father, Karl Malden, is on him all the time, and he starts climbing the screen at a baseball game. 'HOW WAS THAT, DAD? HOW WAS THAT BUNT, DAD?' "

"So, I'm Jimmy Piersall?" said Kleine.

"Well, just seemed to fit," said McHale.

From there, they segued into a discussion of the Disney movie, *The Rescuers Down Under,* to which they had just taken their young sons. From there it was onto a conversation about their own youth. One of McHale's fondest memories as a teenager, he said, was the day he and a few buddies walked into a theater in Minnesota, parka pockets loaded with beer, and sat down for a Clint Eastwood triple feature. "All you heard was the sound of cans popping," said McHale. "It was beautiful."

From there, it was classic television shows. Both McHale and Kleine are family men who complain that the job takes them away from their wives and children, yet here they were, a full hour and a half after practice had ended, still lounging around the bleachers at Hellenic College, keeping company with men they saw all the time. They settled on "Gunsmoke," "The Fugitive," and "The Honeymooners" as all-time classics.

"And 'The Andy Griffith Show,' " said Kleine. "Remember the one when Barney thought everybody was jinxed? They were in Floyd's barbershop, and Barney told them they had to reach around and touch their ear with their opposite hand while saying this rhyme. I still remember it. 'Rigamus, rigamus, rigamus, rex. Save us from the man with the hex. Rub your nose, give two winks. Save us from the man with the jinx.' "

"It is definitely," said McHale, "time to go."

Minutes before the Celtics and Bullets took the court on November 30 at Boston Garden, a blind man was led to his front-row courtside seat by a German shepherd seeing-eye dog. The man sat down and the dog waited obediently at his feet, just a foot or so from the out-of-bounds line.

Leigh Montville, a *Sports Illustrated* writer who formerly worked as a columnist for *The Boston Globe,* eyed the dog dubiously.

"Let's not forget this is Boston Garden," said Montville, "and I say the dog comes into play at some point."

Actually, the game was destined to be somewhat of a dog, with the struggling Bullets unable to offer much of a challenge to one of the NBA's hottest teams. But the night was of enduring interest because Bird was just 12 points shy of becoming only the fifteenth NBA player to score 20,000 points. Only two others in the club were still active,

Atlanta's Moses Malone and the Spurs' Alex English, and neither of them was contributing to his team in a full-time capacity, as Bird was. More significantly, Bird's 20,000th point would make him one of only five players to reach 20,000 and also register 5,000 assists, proof positive of an all-around, unselfish game. The others were Oscar Robertson, Jerry West, John Havlicek, and Kareem Abdul-Jabbar. As starting fives go, that one wasn't bad. Bird finally passed the milestone with 8:19 left in the third period, hitting a jumper over the immortal Haywood Workman to put him at 2,001. The crowd started the obligatory "LA-REE! LA-REE!" cheer that has filled Boston Garden for the last decade, and Bird looked slightly embarrassed as he took the ball from referee Jake O'Donnell. He waved ever so slightly to the crowd, shook hands with a few teammates, and then pretended he was going to throw the ball into the seats. He looked eager to get the game going again, and when it did, he immediately hit another jump shot. Early in the fourth period, Bird swatted away an entry pass intended for Bernard King, chased the ball down before it went out-of-bounds, and sent a behind-the-back outlet pass to Gamble that led to a basket. It was the kind of hustling play that typified the Celtics' first month of the season.

Boston won the game 123–95, leading McHale to quip that, "We've got an eight-and-a-quarter game winning streak going." Bird didn't have much to say about his 20,000th. "It isn't really that big a deal. You want to git it out of the way and go on with it. Hey, if they paid us by the point, I'd have 50,000 by now." He smiled, slipped on his coat, and left.

McHale, who was closing in much more quietly on 15,000 points, was asked if he would be around to score 20,000.

"That's a good question," he said. "I've got a ways to go."

"You think you'll get 5,000 assists like Bird?" he was asked, somewhat facetiously, for McHale is not known as a passer.

"I sincerely hope not," he said.

CHAPTER 5

McHale and His Missed Milestone

DECEMBER

If the Celtics were truly to be something special, they would have to win on the road against teams like Philadelphia, Eastern Conference rivals with less talent. On the first day of December, they did not, losing 116–110 at the Spectrum. Ford had reason to be concerned. Once again, the Celtics showed that they could be exploited by the superstar, and that they really didn't have that special defensive quality championship teams must demonstrate. Just as Jordan had torched them for 41 points at the Garden three weeks earlier, so did Philadelphia's Charles Barkley dominate them in this game, scoring 37 points, grabbing 13 rebounds, and showing a general contempt for the Celts' meager attempts at stopping him. Barkley exposed the heart of Boston's defensive weakness. Bird had the size to check Barkley but was sadly overmatched in the quickness department, as he was against most of the better forwards in the league. (And quite a few of the not-so-better ones, too.) Gamble was completely overmatched in size. Putting Lewis on Barkley was like asking a toothpick to stop a tank. The one player with the size and ability to deal with Barkley was McHale, whom Barkley had often singled out as his toughest defender over the years. But though McHale did a decent job of stopping Barkley when he was matched up on him, the Sixers star simply rumbled through everyone else, which left McHale grumbling about the decision to use Gamble on Barkley so much. But what could Ford have done? Sooner or later, he had to get a fifth starter, if the McHale-as-sixth-man rotation were going to continue. As it was, Gamble played only twenty-eight minutes, McHale thirty-seven. And many of Barkley's points were in transition and weren't really Gamble's fault.

Actually, the Celtics could've won had Bird not missed 11 of his 17 shots. "I don't care what else you say," said Philadelphia guard Hersey Hawkins after the game, "*that* is why we won." He pointed to Bird's below-average line on the stat sheet. "No matter how much they've changed, if you hold that man down, you'll probably beat them."

Cutting the most forlorn figure after the game was Eddie Pinckney. He had played his college ball in Philadelphia, and his coach at Villanova, Rollie Massimino, had come to see the game and take him out afterward. Three weeks earlier Pinckney had been a starter, and now, in a game where the Celtics needed a defensive stopper, he didn't play a single second. Ford, too, was a Villanova man, but that didn't mean anything; Pinckney had been given the chance, as far as Ford was concerned, and had failed to deliver. As they left the building, Massimino drew Pinckney closer so he could say something to him, and Pinckney, more than a foot taller, bent down to hear him. It was a touching sight. Five years earlier, in the 1985 NCAA title game, they had been part of one of the most memorable games in college basketball history, Villanova's upset victory over Georgetown. But on this night Eddie Pinckney hadn't even gotten off the bench.

On the evening of December 3, with K. C. Jones and his Seattle SuperSonics in town, the Celtics officially said good-bye to radio broadcaster Johnny Most in an emotional halftime ceremony. His "retirement" had been announced in the preseason, though he would continue to do a pregame show from his home when his health permitted. Most received a gold lapel pin with thirty-seven diamonds, representing the number of years he was with the Celtics. He got a ring from Auerbach that symbolized the franchise's sixteen championships, every one of which Most was a part. He got a three-minute standing ovation, one that he can endlessly replay in his mind. The Boston papers were full of tributes. The *Herald*'s Fitzgerald called him a "poet" and admitted to being a "Johnny Most junkie." The *Globe*'s Ryan called him an "intelligent announcer, a bit biased, perhaps, but intelligent. And witty." In a somewhat more restrained tribute, *Globe* TV critic Jack Craig said of Most that "you sensed there was more there."

Really? Some people missed that. Some missed Most's poetry too, others his intelligence, others his wit. But almost all of those naysayers lived outside of New England. Most represented, by any objective standards, the clearest example of Celtics arrogance gone berserk, a man absolutely unable to separate fact from fiction whenever his beloved Green was involved. Yet he was—make no mistake about it—a living legend. Game after game, year after year, decade after decade, otherwise-intelligent human beings in the Boston area bought into his us-against-them view of the world, a mentality invented, perhaps, by Auerbach but spread like margarine by Most. He was very nearly an untouchable in Boston. Even Auerbach would take heat in the newspapers now and then, but Most remained the crotchety Teflon commentator, the tell-it-like-it-isn't-but-I'll-say-it-is franchise mouthpiece.

And, frankly, he didn't deserve the accolades. Not all of them, anyway. Yes, he was entertaining and even innovative in his early years, and as his sidekick Ordway claims, he was probably the first broadcaster whose distinctive voice, coated with years of nicotine and caffeine abuse, compelled fans to turn down the volume on their television sets and listen to him. But other broadcasters are entertaining and innovative. Most's legend was largely the result of his having a ringside seat to history; like Ringo Starr, he just happened to be there when the revolution broke out. Most's famous call in the 1965 playoffs—"HAVLICEK STOLE THE BALL! HAVLICEK STOLE THE BALL!"—is replayed so endlessly and talked about so frequently that it is worthwhile to remember that Havlicek stole the ball, not Most. His most significant characteristic behind the microphone was absolute blind loyalty, which makes for a great employee but not always a great broadcaster.

The amazing thing about Most, said everyone who knew him, was that, if he was putting people on, he seemed to have absolutely no sense of irony. After he'd finish laying waste to some Celtics opponent, calling him every name in the book and altering whatever events had occurred to fit a Celtics view of the world, he never poked his partner in the ribs and said, "Boy, we really took care of him, didn't we?" The only logical conclusion is that he believed everything he said, or, at least, came to believe it in later years. His paranoia grew worse as the years went on, particularly on the road. Other broadcasters read out-of-town newspapers for information; when Most read them, which was not often, it was for ammunition. He would take a story about, say, Bird being in a shooting slump quite personally, and somehow the criticism would become not the fault of an individual writer, but, rather, of the team, of the whole city. *They hate Bird here. What the hell do they know?* His private and professional lives were impossibly entwined. If the maid service in a Milwaukee hotel was bad, Johnny Most would take it out that night on, say, Bucks' center Jack Sikma. Bad cab ride in Portland? Clyde Drexler is a bum. And whatever passion he felt about a particular player or call, he would transfer to the Celtics. Ordway remembered Most screaming into the microphone, "K. C. JONES IS ABSOLUTELY FURIOUS ABOUT THAT CALL!" when Jones was, in fact, calmly standing in front of the bench.

Most's health had been steadily deteriorating over the last several years—he had been admitted to the hospital with fluid on the lungs just two weeks before the ceremony—as had his perspective, which was, at best, severely damaged even in his energetic years. Still, when the Celtics put him out to pasture as gently as they could, announcing that he had retired because of medical reasons, TV critic Baker blasted them in the pages of the *Herald*. Baker used phrases like "behind-the-scenes manipulation" and "carefully choreographed fadeaway" to put a sinister spin on the whole thing. But, really, what else could the Celtics have done? Announce that Most had been fired? Or that he had grown increasingly irrelevant? Or that he had grown too sick to make it through an NBA season but didn't realize it? Though the Celtics coasted to a 135–102 victory over Seattle that night, the evening had a sad aspect to it, no doubt about that. Most looked weak at the ceremony, a withered shell of a man, and his departure truly marked the end of an era. With the much less biased and much more professional team of Ordway and analyst Doug Brown manning the mike, the 1990–91 Celtics broadcasts took on an aspect that had been missing for years and years and years—reality.

Don Casey made Celtics halftime-speech history on the evening of December 5. The excrementitious Nuggets were in town, and the Celtics promptly sunk to the occasion, allowing Denver to race out to a 78–75 halftime lead. In all probability, none of the Celtics felt they were going to lose, but their apathetic defensive approach—we'll-score-then-you-score-then . . . —was driving Casey, who had seen too many such performances as a Clippers coach, absolutely crazy.

"You know," he said at halftime, "you guys are going to blow this game if you keep standing around whacking your willies."

Even Ford found it difficult to keep a straight face. No one could remember having heard the term "whacking your willie" since sixth grade, if then. The Celtics went out and won 148–140, as Bird scored 43 points.

Jennings could never forget it, and subsequent games against inferior opposition were invariably called "willie whackers." Halftime speeches aside, Don Casey's contributions were most evident at Hellenic College where he immediately added a certain off-the-wall, high school spirit to the Celtics' practice sessions. If any coach anywhere in the continental United States had run a drill since James Naismith tacked up the first peach basket in 1891, Casey knew it. When Ford needed to instill his running mentality back in October, for example, it was Casey who suggested the eight-second drill, a particularly devilish aerobic endeavor in which a team of four offensive players tries to get a lay-up off three passes at one end and a pull-up jump shot off two passes at the other end. When the Celtics first started the drill, the eight-second buzzer went off about 90 percent of the time before they even attempted the jumper; as time went on, they beat it with regularity. Casey brought a unique brand of experience to the Celtics bench that was desperately needed. Ford, for all his strengths, had never been a head coach at any level, except for his son's town team in Lynnfield, Massachusetts, and Jennings hadn't even done that. But Casey had been a head coach at every level of basketball—high school, college, European pro, NBA; hell, he had recruited a hotshot New Jersey player named Chris Ford nearly twenty-five years ago—and he retained that hands-on, down-on-the-floor-with-the-troops approach to the game.

As with Jennings, though, Auerbach had not exactly welcomed Casey into the Celtics fold with open arms. When Ford said he wanted to hire Casey back in June, Auerbach's first words were, "Who the hell is he?" Considering how much he kept up with or cared about the lower teams in the league, it was entirely possible that Auerbach did not realize it was Casey who had brought the Los Angeles Clippers into Boston Garden on January 5, 1990, and scored a 114–105 upset victory. Less than four months later, the Clips had fired Casey, and he drifted in job limbo until Ford could get his hire, as Casey put it, "through Congress." His interview with Auerbach had been direct and to the point.

"Everybody tells us you're good," said Auerbach, "but what I want to know is, if you're so goddamned good, why don't you have a job?"

"Good question," said Casey.

But, eventually, Gavitt backed Ford's strong recommendation— Gavitt had to overcome concerns that, first, Casey was too soft, too much of a players' coach, and second, that he was too far out of the Celtics' mold, being extroverted and actually friendly with the press— and Auerbach fell into line, too. As the season progressed, Casey felt Auerbach warming to him but only slightly. "I was like the new in-law," he said. "Red basically looked at me and thought, 'Well, you're in the family now. Let's see if you can come to the picnic.'" Shortly after Casey was hired, he and his boss loaded up Ford's van for a few days of working vacation at the Jersey Shore. Bereft of mechanical inclination, they required a couple hours to strap the luggage onto the roof of the car with bungee cord, only to watch their work come undone just a few miles into the trip, bags dangling down the side of the car. "You guys appear to be a good match," said Kathy Ford.

Much of the Celtics' basic offensive and defensive arsenal came from Casey. Ford knew his x's and o's, but, as a former player, he tended to coach instinctively. Speaking independently, Casey and Jennings described Ford's coaching style similarly. Jennings: "With Chris, it's kind of a seat-of-your-pants type of thing, a 'feel' that he really can't explain." Casey: "It's like your grandmother makes chicken soup. Chris doesn't exactly measure any of the ingredients, but he knows what he's doing, and it comes out tasting great." But Casey had been a head coach too many years not to measure the ingredients. "Case has a theory on everything," said McHale. "A team will come down with a one-three-one zone trap, say, and everybody else will take a minute just looking at it, but Case will say instantly, 'Okay, here's what you run against a one-three-one zone trap.' Everybody doesn't necessarily agree with him all the time, but he's positive and confident in what he says and that makes a player feel positive and confident."

The one thing Casey had to battle against was overcoaching but, with Ford holding the reins, that was pretty much impossible. The assistants' roles were clear during games. Jennings did little on-the-bench coaching, his scouting work having been done before the game. Casey sat next to Ford and fed him input whenever he felt it necessary; Ford took some, rejected others. Clearly, as he patrolled the sidelines like a Prussian sentry, Ford ran the show. The combination had worked fine in the first month of the season, and in fact, Casey's air of calm on the bench had surprised many Celtics observers. At one point in his life, some twenty-five years earlier, Case had been a crazy man, ripping off his coat, screaming at his players, intimidating officials. Off the court, he popped pills, mostly uppers, and nearly became addicted while trying to live up to the tag of "Boy Wonder," which had been hung on him by the Philadelphia area press when he won consecutive state championships at Bishop Eustace High School in Camden, New Jersey, while still in his early twenties. The tag of "space cadet" followed him around, but he had cleaned up his private life, and these days the only pills he popped were various and sundry vitamin supplements, along with energy bars, high-fiber cookies, and other varieties of what Jennings called "California food."

Still, Casey was perhaps the only NBA coach who read Thoreau during the season—he used a Celtics scouting report as a bookmark—and made sure to visit the GREENPEACE store on road trips to San Francisco.

Since Jennings tended to act a few years older than his twenty-eight years, and Casey quite a few years younger than his fifty-two, Ford's assistants seemed roughly the same age. Casey was the former head coach who carried the onus of having been fired; it shouldn't be an onus in a league that spits out head coaches at the same rate McDonald's spits out french fries, but it was, and Casey couldn't quite shake the feeling. Was he worthy enough, respected enough, to get another chance at a head job? And Jennings was the young coach without a track record, who was trying to live up to the incredible opportunity he had been given. Did he earn this spot, or was it just handed to him? Did the players take him seriously? Ford, from time to time, had some fun with their insecurities. For example, Casey had made a rare scouting trip to Milwaukee the night before the Celtics played the Bucks at Boston Garden on December 12, and that caused Jennings, who generally handled all the scouting, some anxious moments. Since the Bucks had blasted the Celtics 119–91 in Milwaukee on November 13, is that why Casey went this time? Jennings wondered. Ford played along.

"Look, we've got to *know* these guys a little better than we did the first time," Ford told the team in the shootaround prior to the rematch at the Garden.

Sure enough, the Celtics destroyed Milwaukee by 129–111 that evening, the Bucks' near-exhausted state (they had played eleven games in seven cities in seventeen days) having had much more to do with the win than Casey's scouting report. Nevertheless, McHale, never one to miss an opportunity to do some bustin', said, as he passed by Jennings on his way out of the dressing room, "I don't know what it was, but I just felt we *knew* those guys so much better tonight."

The victory over the Bucks gave the Celtics a 17–4 record, best in the East, and the peace and goodwill among men continued. Winning does that for a team.

Bird continued to get a kick out of Dee Brown. In *Drive,* his autobiography authored with Ryan, Bird had talked about the chilly reception he had received from Kent Benson during his brief stay at Indiana University and how it later affected the way he treated rookies when he got to the NBA. "He [Benson] treated us freshmen as if we were idiots," wrote Bird. "That's why to this day I never treat rookies badly. I always try to take them under my wing." And that's what he did with Brown. He ragged Brown about being a rookie from time to time, and like the other veterans, he made sure that Brown carried the bag of balls on the team bus. And when someone would ask Bird about the influence of the young guys, a favorite question during the first two months of the season, Bird would deadpan: "Hey, they haven't done a thing to help my shot." But then he would grow serious and talk about their contributions. He took time to work with Brown after practice and never seemed to be threatened by Brown's skills or the attention he was getting. The fact that their skills were not at all comparable might've had something to do with that, of course. While Michael Smith had come to Boston with the reputation of being "a poor man's Bird" (although, as it evolved, he wasn't even, as someone put it, "a street person's Bird"), that tag would never be attached to Brown, who had quickness and jumping ability that Bird could only dream about. Bird seemed almost fascinated by those gifts and constantly tested them, ultimately trying to prove, of course, that his own manufactured talents were just as formidable.

In a December 13 practice at Hellenic, with the defending-champion Pistons coming to town the following evening, Bird and Brown stayed after practice testing each other with high-arching rainbow jumpers. Bird would toss the ball to Brown, run at him, and try to block the shot. Then they would switch. Brown blocked three of Bird's shots, but, of course, Bird couldn't get any of Brown's. Actually, it was atypical of Bird to be expending such energy, preferring those games, as Reggie Lewis pointed out, "where nobody moves, because that's when he always wins." At times Bird looked almost awkward sailing through the air, lunging, and coming up with only air, and one was again reminded how much he had done with natural gifts that in some respects were rather modest. Finally, Bird stood at a spot about twenty-three feet from the basket just inside the three-point line. He waved to Dee, who was under the basket. Brown waved him off. Bird waved again, and Brown came out after him. Bird waited until the rookie was right on top of him, then shot a ball at least thirty feet in the air, well over Brown's outstretched arms. It settled into the basket, and Bird shook his fist in the air.

"Ever notice how much Bird loves that last word?" said Casey.

Over at another basket, Celtics legend Dave Cowens was tutoring Vrankovic, whom the Celtics had begun to call "Brother," as in "Big Brother," a reference to his Eastern European background. It didn't make complete political sense, but it didn't have to. Opinion was divided on whether or not Vrankovic would ever be a player—and was still divided when the season ended five months later—but, like the awkward but tall freshman at a high school practice, Stojko got a lot of attention. Eventually, Auerbach, who had watched practice that day, wandered over and began giving Vrankovic some pointers. They made an incongruous pair, the short, Jewish senior citizen and the huge Yugoslav, but, then, no more incongruous than Auerbach and Russell had made thirty years earlier. Eventually McHale dribbled over and began talking, and then Kleine joined the group, too.

"You know what that is for Stojko?" said the *Herald*'s Steve Bulpett. "Circuit overload from four decades."

Soon afterward, the McHale sextet continued its three-on-three games with the usual result: McHale's team won despite its concentration problems caused by McHale's play-by-play. On this day, though, Kleine had an answer. He kept calling McHale "Jim Henson," and, when the game was over, he ran behind Popson, held his hands above Popson's head, and said in a high, squeaky voice, "Ooh, Kevin, you're so funny, work my strings, Kevin, I'm just one of the Muppets. I'll laugh at anything you say, Kevin." It was very nearly as good as a McHale routine.

On his way out the door, McHale was asked by a reporter if he thought that the Celtics' preseason game against the Pistons, won by Boston 116–98, would have an effect on the game tomorrow night.

"You're kidding, right?" said McHale. "Preseason games are meaningless. They're like shitting in an outhouse."

After practice, a contingent consisting of McHale, Kleine, Pinckney, Gamble, Smith, Ford, Casey, and Jennings drove to Children's Hospital in Brookline for the Celtics' annual (and unpublicized) Christmas visit to the pediatric cancer ward. One Celtics official (not a coach) was already dreading the most frequently asked question: "Where's Larry?" Bird's reticence at attending such official charity functions rankled some of the Celtics' brass from time to time, although this official held no such animosity toward Parish, another reluctant good-will ambassador. "Robert doesn't do it because he's a private person," said the official. "Larry doesn't do it because he's selfish." Others in the organization believed precisely the opposite, that Parish was the selfish one and Bird the private one. At any rate, McHale was a fixture on such excursions, providing still another version of the "good Celtic, bad Celtic" routine he played, knowingly or not, with Bird. McHale did the charity work, Bird didn't. McHale accepted whatever playing role (sixth man) was given him, Bird sometimes sulked. McHale chatted up the press, Bird sometimes disappeared out the back door. So it went.

Gamble, whom Kleine had started to call B. K. ("because he's the black Kevin," Kleine explained), was a quiet man, unaccustomed to representing himself as a Celtic, and looked nervous. So did Michael Smith, who enjoyed such functions but desperately wanted to make a good impression. (No one enjoyed being a Celtic more than Smith; were he a real player, some of the press corps believed, he would own the town.)

"Anything we're not supposed to ask them?" said Smith to McHale.

"Let your spirit be your guide," said McHale. Then he barged into the first room and immediately turned off the TV.

"Okay, no soap operas," McHale said to the patient, a teenage male. "They'll fry your brain. Didn't your parents tell you that?" He turned to the boys' parents, who were sitting bedside. "Oh, that must be you," he said. "I'm Kevin. This is Mike."

As McHale moved easily from room to room, he received the news that someone in the hall had recognized Smith but not him. "You've got to be kidding," he deadpanned. "This is like the lowest moment of my career." He knocked on the next door. "Okay, you know who I am, right?" Back in the hall he bumped into Ford, who was leading another group through the hospital. "Hey, Chris," said McHale, "the last kid wanted to know why I only played eleven minutes last night. What should I tell him?"

A couple of the younger black patients were plainly uninterested in McHale and Smith.

"Did Dee Brown or Brian Shaw come?" they asked McHale.

"Sorry, they couldn't make it," said McHale. "We'll have to do."

Toward the end of the afternoon, Kleine's group came across a young boy, rendered almost bald by radical chemotherapy, sitting in a treatment room dressed in full Celtics regalia, hat, sweatshirt, green sweatpants. In his hand he held a Celtics pennant.

"How long's he been waiting for us?" a nurse was asked.

"Tell you the truth," she said, "he didn't even know you were coming. He dresses this way all the time. He just loves the Celtics."

Tears worked their way into the corners of Kleine's eyes.

"Can you believe that?" he said. "You know, my dad died of this disease." He shook his head. "But these are kids. I guess this really puts basketball into perspective, doesn't it?"

Whatever perspective that was, it had again changed by the following night. The December 14 game at the Garden was the season's first true checkpoint, a chance for the Celtics to see if they were really a team that could make a run for the title or merely an early bloomer that would fade in the dead of winter. The Pistons brought an uninspiring 14–7 record into the game, clearly showing the strain of defending a championship they had won two seasons in a row, but they were still the Pistons, and the game was something special.

Indeed, Boston and Detroit had been engaged in a fascinating pas de deux over the last four seasons. It was no coincidence that the Celtics' descent as an NBA powerhouse had coincided with the Pistons' rise, and the teams shared an intense, competitive relationship. It began back in the 1986–87 season, one in which the Pistons first started to flex their muscles and call themselves "The Bad Boys." "A physical game by Piston standards," said power forward Rick Mahorn, "is when everyone is bleeding from the mouth." The Celtics were not exactly pacifists, but they considered Detroit's physical style antithetical to pure basketball, particularly Parish, who absolutely despised his Pistons counterpart, Bill Laimbeer. Both Parish and Bird had tangled with Laimbeer, and McHale had mixed it up with Mahorn on occasion too. Detroit had an excellent chance of eliminating the then-defending champions in the conference final when Bird made one of the most famous plays in Celtics history, stepping in front of a lazy inbounds pass thrown by Isiah Thomas, making the steal, and having the presence of mind to search for, and then feed, a cutting Dennis Johnson for a buzzer-beating basket that gave Boston a 108–107 victory in Game 5. The Pistons won Game 6 easily in Detroit, but the Celtics captured the decisive Game 7 with a 117–114 victory in the Garden to win the series 4–3. Clearly, Game 5 had made the difference.

That single errant pass was a nonstop flashbulb of a nightmare for Thomas, one that blinked over and over in his mind, and when the series was over, he let his frustration rise to the surface. Teammate Dennis Rodman, then a rookie, had made the unfortunate comment that Bird was overrated; some reporters thought he had said an "overrated *white* player," though Rodman vehemently denied it. At any rate, the question was put to Thomas in racial terms: Do you agree that Bird is overrated because he is white?

"I think Larry is a very, very good basketball player, an exceptional talent," answered Thomas. "But I'd have to agree with Rodman. If he was black, he'd be just another good guy."

Thomas was mortified when his comment made national headlines and he claimed that he made it in jest. Anyone who heard him knew that that explanation didn't wash. Thomas was frustrated to distraction at that moment after Game 7, and so he made the comment; given time to think about it, he would not have made it and probably didn't subscribe to it. Thomas underwent a torrent of abuse, much of it fanned by a white, pro-Bird press corps that didn't care all that much for Thomas to begin with. It got so bad that the NBA brought Bird and Thomas together for a press conference the following week in Los Angeles where the Celtics were playing the Lakers in the Finals. Thomas pleaded his case, while Bird basically stood by with a bemused look on his face, professing that the story was no big deal. "The only thing that bothered me was that Isiah had agreed with a rookie," said Bird, laughing. Everyone agreed that it was a masterpiece of aw-shucks, Hoosier diplomacy, though, in fact, Bird probably was not upset by the comment, having heard variations of it his entire career. But the affair scarred Thomas and kept some of America from completely respecting him, even though in subsequent years he proved to be a tough, intelligent clutch player. There didn't seem to be any lingering animosity between Bird and Thomas—Isiah played in Larry's all-star game—and McHale and Thomas never failed to chat each other up when they got together at All-Star games and the like. But there was still a definite edge, a tension, to the Detroit-Boston relationship. No Celtic liked Laimbeer and none was crazy about Rodman. (Mahorn was gone.) And Laimbeer, for his part, felt that the Celtics owed his team respect after two straight championships, but had failed to give it, particularly Bird and Parish.

When the teams took the floor, in keeping with custom, Laimbeer strode directly out to the court, eyes focused straight ahead. He didn't shake hands with any Celtic and no Celtic shook with him. Isiah shook with everyone. Bird took his place and shook with anyone who came by to shake (Thomas and Joe Dumars), but didn't seek anyone out. He and Rodman only pointed at each other, half-greeting, half-challenge.

The game was no classic, but it offered several moments of great basketball theatre. At one point, Bird found himself isolated underneath with Dumars, who is some six inches shorter. "LARRY'S GOT A LITTLE ONE!" Ford screamed at the top of his lungs, but the Celtics couldn't get him the ball. Later, Bird again found himself facing Dumars, who is known for his relentless, fundamentally sound defensive play.

"Come on, come on," Bird goaded him, "I'm going to the basket." When Bird begins talking on the court, it's a sign that he's really into the game.

"Come on, Larry, bring it in here," Dumars yelled back at him.

Dumars won that battle, forcing Bird, after a few moves, to pass off.

But Bird won the war. After the Pistons had cut a huge Celtics lead to just 97–94 late in the fourth period, Bird came down on the wing, launched a three-point shot, and put his fist in the air as it went through. And the Celtics went on to a 108–100 victory.

The Pistons were quietly frustrated after the game, not only by the loss but also by the fact that they had to spend the night in a hotel. Boston was one of the few cities where airport noise restrictions prohibit the Pistons from chartering out after the game on *Roundball One,* their much-ballyhooed and ultra-luxurious jet. (They wondered, half-seriously, if Auerbach had pull with the control tower at Logan Airport.) But, this being the age of Pistons diplomacy, most of them had the predictable praise for the "new Celtics," particularly Dee Brown, who had scored 12 meaningful points, dished out 6 assists, and on a few occasions simply blown by Thomas, an outstanding defensive guard. Laimbeer, alone, was unmoved, or pretended to be.

"No, I don't really see a difference in the Celtics," said Laimbeer, staring straight ahead, expressionless, a form of "communication" he adopts from time to time to discourage questions he doesn't want to hear. "What are you referring to?" Then he planted the dagger. "It was an opportunity for them to measure themselves against us," said Laimbeer. "It's probably a big deal for them."

Considering how the status of the teams had flip-flopped over the last few years, he was absolutely correct, even if the Celtics wouldn't acknowledge it. They *had* measured themselves against the Pistons . . . and liked what they saw.

The win over Detroit gave Boston a 19–4 record through the first six weeks of the season, but the search for an elusive "final piece" continued unabated. As optimistic as the fans were about the Celtics' chances in the East, the coaches and players knew that they still weren't tough enough to grind their way through the meat of the schedule, which had been relatively kind to them so far. The Philadelphia game on the first of the month had proven that. "We're not good enough to win a championship right now," Bird said flatly after the Pistons game. Ideally, the "final piece" would be a hard-nosed forward who liked to mix it up, rebound in the trenches, and shut down the opponent's leading frontcourt scorer. In other words, he should be everything that the Celtics wanted Pinckney to be but didn't feel he was. Eventually, the "final piece" took on a name, Derek Smith, a twenty-nine-year-old, six-foot-six free agent who had been cut loose by the 76ers. Proven, hard-nosed NBA forwards, as Smith most definitely was, were not in limbo without a good reason, of course, and in Smith's case that reason was knees. He had already undergone several operations, the last of them only three months earlier, and would need weeks of rehabilitation, making him, in a best-case scenario, playoff insurance, albeit of premium value. Gavitt thought Smith worth the risk. When Gavitt coached the 1980 Olympic team (the one that stayed home because of the boycott), Smith, who was at the University of Louisville, had been one of his favorite players; Gavitt ultimately made him one of the final cuts, but he didn't feel comfortable about it. Ford liked Smith too, but he was hesitant about making any kind of change that might disturb the delicate team chemistry. Eventually, though, he agreed that Smith was worth a look-see.

The Derek Smith tryout was one of the worst-kept secrets in town. Smith's representative, Grinker, is rather the Broadway Danny Rose of NBA agents, and the only way to pry information out of him is to call him up and have nothing to do for the next two hours. Smith, too, is an outstanding talker. Yet the Celtics' brass insisted on making fools out of themselves with a mishandled cloak-and-dagger operation, possibly because Auerbach had been in Boston the last few days and was orchestrating it. Here's what Gavitt should've said to the media and possibly *would have* said had Auerbach not been around:

"As you know, we're bringing in Derek Smith for a tryout. We want to do it behind closed doors because Derek is still rehabbing a knee that was surgically repaired in September. If you stick around, we'll give you a short statement when it's over."

Instead, here's what they did:

They sent equipment manager Wayne Lebeaux around to chase the press out of the Hellenic gym after practice. "School function," said Lebeaux. Lebeaux is dutiful to a fault in carrying out the instructions of higher-ups, but even he looked rather embarrassed. "What is it?" Mike Fine asked Lebeaux, "the Greek Orthodox prom?" When a reporter asked Gavitt when "Derek" was coming in, Gavitt said, "Derek who?" Ford wouldn't answer questions at all. After the press was herded out into the hall, the Celts locked the gym doors and covered the quarter-inch slats with white tape, not before, however, prying eyes had spotted several orange cones being placed at strategic places along the court. McHale, of course, found the whole thing somewhat ridiculous.

"The poor guy comes in to try out for a basketball team and they got him running around cones," said McHale. "He'll probably be on the first plane outta here. Tell you what, if some team brought me in and asked me to run cones, I'd say, 'See you tomorrow at practice . . . when we're playing basketball.' "

A few minutes later, a white, late-model Toyota with out-of-state plates ("So they can't be traced," cracked Peter May) pulled up just a few feet from a side entrance to the gym, and out jumped Derek Smith, Jan Volk, and Ron Grinker, using, as May wrote the next day, "a forsythia bush as a pick." Volk forgot to look furtively in both directions and hold the trench coat over his face. A few reporters found an upstairs peephole through which to watch Smith's hour-long workout, but the session was too boring to hold anyone's attention for long.

"We're looking at all the options we have," said Gavitt, who finally *had* to say something to the reporters who hung around. "There is no timetable. I think today was a good day. We accomplished what we wanted to accomplish. Now we'll sleep on it."

He never mentioned the "final piece" by name. Over the next two days Ford continued to deny that a Smith signing was imminent; "Celtics Lukewarm on Derek" proclaimed a *Herald* headline on December 20. On December 22 Derek Smith signed a one-year contract for about $437,500.

In the waning moments of a routine 115–105 win over the 76ers in the Garden on December 19, Kevin McHale scored the 15,000th point of his NBA career. But the game was not stopped, there was no announcement, and no one gave McHale the ball. No one knew it. Not the Celtics PR staff, not the Celtics beat reporters, not McHale himself. Already that season, two scoring milestones had been recognized in the Garden—Bird's 20,000th and the Nuggets' Orlando Woolridge's 10,000th—yet no one picked up on McHale's until the following morning. McHale found out about it as he sat on the bench during a game in Charlotte that night when he heard Ordway mention it on the air. "If it was Larry, they would have given him the ball, stopped the game, the whole thing," Parish complained later to the *Globe*'s MacMullen. "But because it's Kevin it's okay to do nothing? I'm sorry. That's bull." Gavitt was mortified, having missed the ambassador's forte—ceremony. "It was absolutely an unforgivable mistake," he said. The slight stung McHale more deeply than he admitted but soon it became just another piece of ammunition. "Doc Ford and Tod Rosensweig feel so bad about it," said McHale, "I can bust them forever."

The incident was a perfect microcosm of McHale's first-rate/second-banana career. Yes, he was initially overlooked. But then everyone felt bad for him and stumbled over themselves to comment on how overlooked he is. And, ultimately, what McHale got out of it was a big laugh, more ammunition to "bust someone," another chuckle for the man MacMullen calls "The Fun Master." If, indeed, living well is the best revenge, then Kevin McHale seems way, way ahead of the game.

Anyway, for someone who is overlooked, McHale is pretty obvious. His selection to the 1991 Eastern Conference All-Star team in January would be his seventh. Opposing coaches design a good part of their defensive game plan to stopping him. And the media votes him to the all-interview team on a regular basis. It's just that fate happened to put him on the same sailing vessel as Larry Bird, and their voyage has been a long and complex one, sometimes stormy, sometimes calm, never dull.

In the endless search for differences between McHale and Bird, it's easy to miss the similarities. One of the prime motivations in each of their lives has been the desire to remain "regular people" or "one of the guys," a product of his environment, which in both cases was definitely blue-collar, lower-middle class. Neither has completely succeeded, of course—the excessive celebrityhood extended to successful pro athletes made that impossible years ago. But each has tried in his own way. Both frequently refer to the common-man status of their brothers (Bird has four, McHale one), and sound, at times, like they envy the anonymity and simplicity of the *other* Birds and McHales. Perhaps they do, perhaps they're just fooling themselves, but the struggle is sometimes touching and even a little honorable. At root, though, is one major difference between them. While Bird's past in French Lick, Indiana, at times crossed into the dark, Gothic side of the American working-class ethic—an alcoholic father who committed suicide, periods of true economic deprivation—McHale's boyhood in the mining town of Hibbing, Minnesota, was one of happiness, stability, and good memories. He didn't have it easy, but he didn't have it as rough as Bird, either.

"I think what I got from my father," said McHale, one winter afternoon, relaxing in his sprawling home in suburban Boston, "was that a man got up and went to work every day, whether it was thirty below or thirty above. I think that has a lot to do with my attitude about playing hurt." Paul McHale worked shifts in the mines for thirty-five of the forty-two years he toiled, battling frostbite all the time. Middles were the worst—he'd go to work before his children got home from school and they'd be in bed when he got home. He always told Kevin about the preunion days when company men would come by and just point. "Okay, we'll take you and you and you, but not you." It made an impression.

Not that McHale ever wanted to follow in his father's footsteps. He began talking about his three summers in the mines when his wife, Lynn, a Hibbing native herself, walked in.

"He'll make it sound like he put in grueling summers in the mills," said Lynn. "Tell him what you did."

"I was on the blast crew," said McHale, somewhat defensively.

"Oh, give me a break," said Lynn. "You blasted one day a week."

"Okay," said McHale. "There was a lot of dead time when the drills would break and we'd just ride around the mines in trucks and look like we were busy. My legacy in the mines was my ability at mine stickball. We hit rocks with an axe handle."

Lynn Spearman's family was a step up the economic chain from the McHales—her father owned a business that sold equipment to the mines. She went to parochial school, McHale went to public school.

Lynn did the socially acceptable things, while McHale and his buddies hung out at a place they called "the dump," catching rabbits, smoking cigarettes, and learning how to swear.

"I remember my mom warning me about that 'tall McHale boy,'" said Lynn, laughing. "The rumor about this place where they hung out was that they lured the young girls up there and made them take off their undershirts."

"That's crazy," said McHale. "I can't remember any undershirts coming off. We just had a bad rep. Of course, for Hibbing, we were like the guys from 'the projects.' We wore jean jackets and stole apples."

McHale was interested in Lynn before the feeling was reciprocated, and she dated the point guard on the high school team, Monte Mitchell, before she went out with McHale. "He's bald now," said McHale. "I'm clearly the catch."

Bird has always maintained that, as a kid, no one knew less about the NBA or, for that matter, any basketball world beyond his hometown. McHale claims he was just as ignorant as Bird. "My idea of being incredibly successful in basketball was being the best player on your high school team," he said. "When I was a senior, I couldn't believe it when the University of Minnesota actually offered me a scholarship to play basketball." McHale had no intention of going anywhere else. If you were an Iron Ranger, which is what the strong, beer-drinking people from the mining area were called, you dreamed of being a University of Minnesota Gopher. The Big Ten was Nirvana.

As a freshman, McHale began developing his carefully choreographed low-post moves in practice to neutralize the shot-blocking abilities of his All-American teammate, Mychal Thompson. He enjoyed the perks of being a jock, a BMOC, rambling around campus with his buddies, a party-hardy McHale's Navy, parka pockets stuffed with beer, a little mischief on their minds but goodness in their hearts, talking about Gopher hockey, women, Big Ten basketball, Clint Eastwood movies. Studying was something to do when the beer ran out. McHale was an avid reader of Jack London stories and other books about the outdoors, but he had always been the kind of kid whose report card said: "Kevin could be an excellent student if only he would apply himself instead of fooling around in class." When he was a sophomore the athletic director at Minnesota told him he wanted him to achieve a 3.0 cumulative average, the minimum for being a Williams Scholar, because no athlete had made it. McHale said okay, got a 3.0, then drifted comfortably back to the 2's in the next two years. He is still about two quarters short of graduating. In the summer of 1981, after his rookie year with the Celtics, he went back to Minnesota to pursue his degree. As he walked across campus bound for his first class, carrying a notebook and good intentions, he ran into an old buddy who was cutting lawns. They talked away the morning, after which McHale decided to bag classes completely. "I tell everyone my educational career was waylaid by a man on a mower," McHale said. "And the next year I discovered golf, so my summers were *really* shot."

McHale claimed that the first time he even thought about the NBA was early in his senior year. "I was at a party with some football players and somebody brought in a *Sporting News* that had me rated as the top forward and the second-best center in college basketball. 'Hey, you're going to be a top-five pick,' someone told me, and I said, 'Really?' People think I'm b.s.-ing them with that story but it's true. I never really cared or took the time to find out if I was good. All I knew was that I had had success at Minnesota and in the Big Ten. I played in all those postseason All-Star games basically for the travel. I had no thoughts of improving myself in the draft or getting more money or anything like that. I remember I picked up the paper and read that Darryl Griffith wasn't going to play in the All-Star game in Hawaii because he didn't want to take the chance of getting hurt. And I thought, 'What's with this guy? Miss a free trip to Hawaii?' I went over there, drank piña coladas and beer, and won the MVP."

Golden State had the first pick in the draft that year and the coach, Al Attles, and a couple other team representatives flew in to Minnesota to interview McHale. Wearing jeans and a sweatshirt, his normal BMOC garb, McHale picked them up at the airport in his 1966 Plymouth with the squeaky brakes. "They must've thought I was a psycho or something," said McHale. Actually, the Warriors proved to be the psychos. They traded the No. 3 pick in the draft, who turned out to be McHale, plus a center named Robert Parish, for the No. 1 pick in the draft, which they used to select Joe Barry Carroll, and the No. 13 pick, which they used to take Ricky Brown. Designed by then-coach Bill Fitch, and not Auerbach, the deal turned out to be one of the most lopsided in NBA history. McHale and Parish went on to be All-Pro. Carroll went on to be All-Enigma, a player, as former Jazz head coach Frank Layden once said, "on a lifetime coffee break." And Ricky Brown played most of his career in Europe.

The first NBA game Kevin McHale ever saw was the first one in which he played, but he earned a championship ring in his rookie season of 1981. By then it was clearly Larry's Team, Bird having been named rookie of the year in 1980 when he led the Celtics to a phenomenal 32-win improvement over the 1978–79 season, still an NBA

record for a one-year turnaround. And like it or not, McHale's entire
career has been colored by being Bird's teammate. He is—eternally—
The Other Celtics Forward. McHale handles the situation about as
well as anyone could, but over the years slights, real and imagined, can
pile up. McHale feels, with some justification, that he has never been
given enough credit for being a gamer. Bird's injuries are always larger
than life in Celtic Land—anyone who didn't already know that found
out in January—but McHale's are always treated rather routinely. If he
is bitter about anything in his career, it was the team's failure to believe
that his foot was badly hurt during the 1986–87 season. The Celtics
thought that the injury was in McHale's head, until a fracture was
found by a Chicago Bulls' team physician late in the season. McHale
immediately dialed Volk. "My foot's broke," he said and slammed down
the receiver. McHale, too, has always been the trade bait, being not
quite as valuable as Bird yet having more trade value than Parish. In
fact, midway through the 1987–88 season, a deal that would've sent
McHale to the Dallas Mavericks was all but completed when Auerbach
flew into town and announced that he would quit if McHale were
traded. After that, McHale says he never worried about his future with
the Celtics.

Certainly, Bird's presence has resulted in McHale's being underrated. Bird is generally considered, if not the greatest forward of all
time, then second only to Elgin Baylor, and, as all-around players go,
his only rivals are Oscar Robertson, Jerry West, Havlicek, Magic Johnson, and, now, Michael Jordan. Such comparisons involving Bird have
been hot-stove league fodder for years. But nobody ever asks where
McHale ranks. Are there ten better players in history? Definitely.
Fifteen? Perhaps. Twenty? Probably not. And considering strictly the
art of setting up, back to the basket, and scoring points from the low
post, McHale has few peers. Kareem Abdul-Jabbar and Wilt Chamberlain for sure. Moses Malone? Maybe, though Malone scored many of
his points on offensive rebounds. Anyone else? No. And certainly for
variety and precision of moves, McHale is number one of all time.
Detroit forward John Salley describes the experience of guarding
McHale near the basket as "being in the man's *chamber*." It's the
perfect metaphor, hinting at both the peculiar form of black magic that
McHale uses to slither through defenders, as well as the Franken-
steinesque aspect to his body—deep bags under the eyes, unusually
long arms, shoulders that appear to be coming off their hinges. He got
his height, six feet eleven, from the maternal, Croatian side of the
family, but he got everything else, it seems, at a variety of body-part
warehouses.

Bird's work ethic has been well documented, but no one seems to wonder how it is that McHale, and McHale alone in today's game, can consistently beat double- and sometimes triple-teaming defenses from the low post while jumping only a few inches off the ground. His long arms are a major advantage—it continually drove Kleine crazy in their postpractice workouts that McHale can simply reach over him for rebounds and followup shots—but it's not the arms that have set McHale apart. It's the feet. No player in history has worked as hard polishing the various stepbacks, crossovers, sudden plants and re-verses, duck-unders, reach-arounds, and "Big Daddy Lipscomb" moves that make him all but unstoppable when he has the ball. Only when he's in a quiet and thoughtful mood, though, will he admit that, yes, it has taken quite a bit of work to perfect them. Whenever he's asked about it in a group, he always says something like, "Tell you the truth, I don't know what the hell I do out there." McHale seems comfortable leaving that impression. Others are not, including Chris Ford. "Kevin's work ethic is just as good as Larry's, if not better," said Ford. "Just the way Larry has presented himself as the serious, dedi-cated athlete, you hear Kevin goofing off and throwing around one-liners, and you tend to think the game isn't that important to him. But I think they've both gotten as much as they could out of their talents. When they step on the floor and the game begins, I think the passion and drive in both of them is equal."

The other thing that has made McHale great is his shooting ability; again, some of that can't be taught, but much of it comes from hard work. "The footwork is important," he says, "but my success begins with the premise that I can shoot the ball. That's where so many big guys get off the track right away. Everything is predicated on my defensive guy thinking, 'If McHale shoots this ball, he's going to make it.' Most low-post guys get the ball, their defender is thinking, 'Come on, shoot the ball, miss, and we can get the hell out of here.' The one thing I know right away is when I'm going to take a jump shot. When the entry pass is in the air, and I feel my guy with just one hand on me, playing off me, there is no way I am not going to shoot. And there's no way he's going to block it." From twelve feet and in, McHale is one of the most reliable jump-shooters the NBA has ever known.

But he's not Larry Bird. How many times and in how many ways has he heard that? Hundreds. And how much does it bother him? McHale says it never bothered him and doesn't bother him now. He's half-right. It doesn't bother him much now, but it used to. Teammates who are close to both players say that it did. "How could it not?" said M. L. Carr. "Kevin's game has been the constant here, the constant plus-fifty-percent shooting, the constant moves, the constant presence down there, night after night. There are times when Larry is off and times when Robert is off, but there are not many nights when the Celtics don't know exactly what they're going to get from Kevin. And if he is off, that means he's going to shoot, say, forty-eight percent instead of fifty-eight percent. But no matter what he did, he wasn't Larry. I know it bothered him. I saw it." Take the 1984–85 season. On March 3, McHale scored 56 points against the Pistons, a franchise record, more than Cousy, Sam Jones, Tommy Heinsohn, or even Larry Bird had ever scored in a single game. Ten days later in New Orleans, Bird scored 60 points and made the cover of *Time*. Top that, Kevin.

Further, Bird has on occasion singled out McHale for criticism. In 1983, after Boston had been swept by Milwaukee in the conference playoffs, Bird privately (but bitterly) criticized McHale after McHale walked out of the locker room, saying, "I can still hold my head up high." During the playoffs in 1988 against the Hawks, Bird made the comment that "Kevin didn't want the ball on the road in the fourth quarter." Most of the Celtics felt that the comment was unwarranted and, even if Bird believed it, should've been kept private. "I confronted Larry about it, but he wouldn't apologize," said Danny Ainge. "That's one thing about Larry—he believed what he said and he wasn't backing down. I couldn't understand it. Here is one of the best forward combinations in the history of the game, maybe *the* best, and something like that happens." There have been countless other times, too, when Bird has been lukewarm on McHale, even as he extolled the virtues of Parish and D. J.

Conversely, McHale has served as somewhat of an unofficial historian for Bird. During Bird's many magic moments over the years, one was much more likely to pick up a kernel for posterity from McHale than from Bird himself. Soon after Bird ripped McHale in the 1988 Atlanta series, for example, the teams came to Boston Garden for a decisive Game 7. It turned out to be so typical of McHale's career that the play-by-play and final statistics should be engraved on his tombstone. In the first half he single-handedly kept the Celtics in the game, scoring 21 points and grabbing 9 rebounds. But in the fourth period— clutch time, headline time—Bird took over. In the final twelve minutes Bird missed only one of his 10 field goal attempts and scored 20 points to lead the Celtics to a 118–116 victory. McHale finished with 33 points, only one fewer than Bird, but as he stood by his locker, all anyone wanted to ask him about was Larry Bird. And that seemed fine with McHale. "Sometimes after Larry plays a game like this it makes me think ahead," said McHale, looking misty-eyed. "I'll be retired in Minnesota and Larry will be retired in Indiana, and we probably won't see each other much. But a lot of nights I'll just lie there and remember games like this, and what it was like to play with him." As locker room moments go, that was about as good as they get.

But why has Bird been grudging in his praise of McHale? It's not like McHale, for all his talent and wit, ever threatened him as a player or even as an object of popularity. "Kevin is the best in the world at what he does," said Bird, not long after McHale passed the 15,000-point milestone. "Turnaround jumpers, shooting on a double-team, blocking shots. If Kevin wanted to, he could be the top defender in the league, too. The things he can't do are dribble the basketball, fall on the floor to get the ball, and not bitch at the officials." He laughed. "But to me he's been most valuable because he's the ultimate bailout. No matter how much trouble I'll be in, I know I can always throw the ball to Kevin, and he'll be able to get the basket and take the pressure off." He thought some more. "You know, Kevin shows you potential and he's so awesome on some nights. Then other nights he's just average. He just makes it look so easy. Kevin reminds me of my little brother, Eddie. He makes everything look so easy, and when you say something about him working harder, he just kind of mopes around."

Still rather lukewarm and vaguely patronizing, particularly that "my little brother" stuff. If there is a consistency to Bird's resistance to his teammate over the years, it seems to be in his perception that, first, things come too easily to McHale, and, second, that McHale won't dive on the floor for loose balls, a category in which Bird is among the all-time leaders. It is also a fact, as both Bird and McHale know, that the night-in-and-night-out burden of being the leader, The Main Man, the player who took the big shots, clearly fell on Bird's shoulders, not McHale's. But whatever negative impressions Bird has of McHale are probably related more to matters off the court.

"The most important thing in life to Larry is basketball," says Ordway. "The most important thing to Kevin is, at various times, family, fun, recreation, friends, and basketball. Basketball is somewhere in the top five, but, frankly, it might be closer to five than one. I think Larry resented it that night after night he's out bustin' his butt for basketball, basketball, basketball, and there is Kevin with a totally different set of priorities. On the court, Kevin is as fierce a competitor as anyone, but at other moments he's always talking about his family or his golf game or his fishing. That got to Larry at times." One could argue that McHale *had* to make priorities for himself outside of basketball, lest he wither away in Bird's shadow. But everything about McHale's life and personality suggests that he would have made such priorities whether or not there had ever been a Larry Bird.

Ainge, who knows both of them well, agrees with Ordway's assessment. "I think they have respect for each other, but they approach the game so differently that it's bound to cause some tension," said Ainge. "I think Larry always felt that Kevin would be so much better if he had the attitude that Larry did about basketball. Myself, I don't buy it. I was a lot like Larry when I first came into the league, tunnel vision about basketball, but I'm a lot more like Kevin now, and it hasn't made a difference when I go out on the court. Basketball has never been Kevin's whole life, and the times when he's made it that way are the times when he's been at his worst."

The basic thing to remember about Bird and McHale is that they would not have been particularly close friends in any situation. They have totally different personalities, totally different perspectives, totally different senses of humor. And there was probably less ill feeling between Bird and McHale during the 1990–91 season than at any other time in their careers. As disillusioned as McHale had been with Bird's gunning during the first half of the 1989–90 season, that's how impressed he was with the turnaround Bird made, i.e., getting back to the *old Bird* over the last half. And Bird has seen McHale play through too much pain to question his being a "true Celtic," something he had done in the past. McHale has always said that, had he been on a different team from Bird, "I would've scored a lot more points and won a lot fewer games. And it wouldn't have been nearly as much fun." Larry Bird could say the same thing. And someday he *should* say it.

During practice at Hellenic on December 22, Bird reached over to pick up a loose ball and fell to the ground. Several teammates began laughing, until they saw that Bird wasn't joking, and, like the old lady in the commercial, had fallen and couldn't get up. Finally, he rose, and spent the rest of practice stretching on the sideline. The sore back that Bird had brought to training camp almost three months earlier had kept him out of the Celtics' final two exhibitions, but he had played in every regular season game. At times he looked stiff and could be seen wincing in pain as he went through the daily exercise regimen prescribed by his physical therapist, Dan Dyrek. But he hated questions about his back, and as long as he was playing and playing well, the Celtics had to assume everything was all right.

Certainly everything was all right with the Celtics as a team. In the final week of 1990, they won the makeup game with Atlanta by 132–104 and destroyed the Indiana Pacers 152–132, before taking the evening of December 28 off, losing to the Hawks in Atlanta 131–114.

But so what? They were home almost throughout the holidays, they were happy and harmonious, and their record stood at 23–5, second best (to Portland) in the NBA. It was, someone said, like the old days with a few new faces. "And you know what?" said McHale. "It's fun again."

CHAPTER 6

The First Sign of Trouble

JANUARY

On the fourth day of the new year, Kevin McHale padded around the Boston Garden locker room in his terrycloth white robe, hair wet from a shower, a dash of shaving cream on his face, a toothbrush hanging out of his mouth. In less than an hour the Celtics were to face a tough challenger from the West, the Phoenix Suns, but McHale appeared to be readying himself for dinner and maybe a late movie with his wife.

"What are you doing?" Ford asked McHale as the coach prepared to convene the pregame meeting.

"I'm brushing my teeth, Doc," said McHale. "What's it look like?"

"We've got a game, you know," said Ford.

"Well, ten years from now nobody will know who won this game," said McHale, "but I'll know if I have cavities."

Ford laughed and walked away. Gavitt, who was standing nearby, just shook his head and smiled. "It's a good thing Chris knows you guys," he said.

What Ford knew was that he had a team on a roll, and anyone who wanted to brush his teeth before the game—hell, *during* the game— would be permitted to do so. The Celtics had opened 1991 by blasting the Knicks 113–86 on January 2 at the Garden. Practices at Hellenic had become spirited, harmonic affairs. In a scrimmage the day before the Phoenix game, Bird had come down on a two-on-one fast break, fired the ball off the backboard, and grabbed his own rebound/pass for a lay-up. The place broke up. When Bird took a breather a few minutes later, Michael Smith kept goading him to come back into the scrimmage to play against him. Smith longed for Bird's respect and frequently asked him for postpractice pointers, and Bird, for his part,

118

seemed to genuinely like Smith and have compassion for his inability to live up to his potential. All that meant nothing, however, when Bird did check himself back in. He posted up Smith four straight times and each time drained a fallaway jump shot. "You okay, Mike?" Bird teased as he trotted upcourt after the third one. "Not hurt, are ya?" Even Auerbach sensed something he hadn't seen in the Celtics in a few seasons. "Come on, put an elbow on him!" he yelled as the ever-talkative McHale scored on Pinckney during a postpractice one-on-one game. Auerbach couldn't understand how Pinckney could fail to be riled up by McHale's taunting tactics. With the newly acquired Derek Smith on the suspended list—the plan was to keep him there until his knee had healed to the point that he could begin practicing with the team—Auerbach and the coaching staff still wanted nothing more than to light a fire under Pinckney.

Newsday's Jan Hubbard was in Boston for the Phoenix game to do a piece on the Celtics, who were fast becoming the NBA's biggest story.

"Tell me about the young guys," Hubbard said to Bird.

"The young guys?" said Bird. "Well, that'd be everybody but Parish, right?" He laughed, then sat down and talked about the positive effects that Shaw, Brown, and Lewis had had on the team.

Bird received quite gleefully the news that high-scoring Phoenix forward Tom Chambers would not be playing that evening because of a pulled hamstring. He looked at Joe Qatato, the Celtics' assistant equipment manager, and laughed. Bird and Joe Q. were quite close—Q. visited him regularly in the offseason, and the only photo that hangs in Bird's cubicle at Boston Garden is a snapshot of Joe Q. from his high school football days. "Knew it," said Joe Q. "Knew he wouldn't play." Chambers is the kind of player against whom Bird loves to measure himself. The Phoenix star is white, yet he has the kind of innate talents of leaping ability and quickness that are usually associated with black players. (Indeed, he is one of the few whites ever to be invited to participate in the NBA's Slam-Dunk Contest.) Furthermore, he has size (six feet ten), outside shooting ability, and, like Bird, almost unbelievable dexterity with his left hand. All things being equal, there is no reason that Chambers should not be *better* than Bird. But all things are not equal, like work habits and heart, and in those areas Bird was clearly superior, knew it, and drew satisfaction from it.

"Chambers has had some big games here, though," a reporter said to Bird.

Bird looked up from tying his sneakers and snorted. "Yeah, but does he ever *win* here?" he said.

It wasn't just the coaches and players who were feeling great in the early days of 1991—the whole Celtics extended family was basking in the team's success and the new "Gavitt way" of doing things. The players' wives, in particular, felt, probably for the first time, that they were an integral part of the operation. Auerbach rarely gave them the time of day, putting players' wives in a classification just above player-agents. Gavitt, however, never failed to stop and talk, and his wife, Julie, was a warm and friendly presence, too. Dana Kleine, for one, appreciated Gavitt's efforts. In Sacramento, where her husband had played before being traded to Boston in 1988, Dana had met ex-Celtic Bill Russell (formerly the coach and general manager of the Kings) on at least a dozen occasions, and each time he looked at her without even a flicker of recognition. Gavitt had scored big points when he approved much-needed renovations to the wives' room in Boston Garden early in the season, adding carpeting, pictures on the walls, refreshments, and even a baby-sitter. Dana's introduction to that room came during her first game at the Garden when, as she changed the diaper of her then-three-week-old son Daniel, a mouse ran across the floor. But nothing was done to change it until Gavitt came along.

The Phoenix game was over almost before it started. In the first period, Bird spotted an opportunity as the ball was passed in to Phoenix forward Xavier McDaniel. He left his man, Tim Perry, and crept over toward McDaniel, actually hunching his body over so he could be seen less easily. He approached from McDaniel's blind side and swatted the ball away. That began a Celtics fast-break, which ended with Bird—the second wave, the heavy equipment—launching, and making, a three-point shot. The success of the play hung on Bird's ability to make a split-second defensive calculation, i.e., *even with his limited speed, he could sneak up and make the play because McDaniel, though a potent scorer, is a player who frequently holds the ball far too long before he shoots*. Bird was especially proud of his off-the-ball defensive abilities, though he admitted that they had slipped somewhat. "I kin still anticipate jist as well, but I'm a little bit slower gettin' there," he said. "I used to be able to anticipate so well that I got there before the ball, even though I'm not real fast. I was one of the best at it, seemed like I was ever'where on the court, always gettin' a hand on somethin'."

The Celtics broke the game open in the third period. The Phoenix bench hollered at Bird as he took a shot and, when it went in, he flipped them the finger as he turned and ran upcourt. Later, as the Celtics went on a 10–0 tear, Shaw scooped up a loose ball, found McHale cutting down the middle, and threw him a no-look pass. McHale gathered it in and with one stride, threw down a vicious dunk that gave the Celtics a rousing 97–75 lead, and forced the Suns to call time-out. The play emblemized everything positive that had happened to that point—the running, the aggressiveness, the teamwork, the inspiration that the young players had given LarryKevinandRobert. The crowd sensed it, too, and remained standing throughout the time-out, cheering at the top of its lungs. Sitting on the bench in street clothes, Derek Smith grabbed Jon Jennings's hand and placed it on his arms. "Feel," said Smith. "Goosebumps." Over in the press section, Milwaukee scout Hal Wissel, who was gathering notes for the Bucks' visit to Boston five days hence, closed his notebook and shook his head. "I'm convinced they're playing *better* than they did in '86," said Wissel, "and that '86 team was one of the best I've ever seen."

As the lead grew to 128–95 Ford cleared the bench and gave Phoenix its first look at Vrankovic. "How big is he?" said Chambers, wandering over to the press table during a time-out. "Can he block shots? Can he play at all?" Vrankovic's periodic appearances never failed to generate such curiosity. In two minutes, he failed to convert an alley-oop pass from Michael Smith, drove the lane and lost the ball, missed a sweeping hook shot, and committed his obligatory two personal fouls.

"Damn," said Chambers as the final buzzer mercifully sounded on the Celtics' 132–103 victory. "I'm disappointed. I wanted to see him score."

The real hero of the night was Shaw, who with 21 points and 9 assists had clearly gotten the best of his Phoenix counterpart, Kevin Johnson, one of the league's outstanding point guards and a longtime collegiate and West Coast summertime pickup game rival. "The Celtics could definitely make it to the Finals," said Johnson. "There are several teams that can, but Boston is definitely at the head of the pack."

"Anything else?" the Celtics beat reporters asked Ford, as the January 7 practice broke up at Hellenic College. The Celtics were leaving in a few hours for New York City and a game against the Knicks the following evening.

"No, that's it," said the coach.

Hours later, the *Globe*'s Jackie MacMullen and the *Herald*'s Mark Murphy were home in bed, listening to the eleven o'clock news, when the beat reporter's worst nightmare boomed out at them.

"Larry Bird did not accompany the team to New York tonight because of back spasms," Channel 4's Bob Lobel said.

Both of them shot up in bed. MacMullen immediately called team physician Arnie Scheller at home, while Murphy got trainer Ed Lacerte out of bed. Both got a confirmation. And both were enraged. How could team officials have failed to tell them the biggest story of the day, maybe of the week, maybe of the *year*? It was a familiar, though nonetheless frustrating, feeling for the print media. They are the ones who dutifully traipse to every practice session and every game, home and on the road, yet the electronic media often gets the story just by taking a phone call in the office. Lobel is a talented and popular personality in and around Boston, but he shows up at Hellenic College about as often as a solar eclipse. Who leaked the story? Why hadn't Ford said anything about it at practice? And, most important, how badly was Bird hurt?

Typically, Lobel's report raised more questions than it answered, for rarely does television news take the time to cover all the angles. Even with the presence of Gavitt, the Celtics had once again bungled their public relations. Explanations started to tumble out the following day, as the Bird-less Celtics prepared to face the Knicks in Madison Square Garden. Bird had experienced back spasms and was put in a brace. He had undergone a series of tests (X rays, CAT scan, flexion extension, etc.) and would undergo more. He would also be missing the following night's game at home against Milwaukee. Ford knew Bird's back had been bothering him but a decision had not been made to keep him home until later in the afternoon, after everyone had left Hellenic. Ford said he did not leak the story (reporters believed him because that was not his style) and didn't know who did. Trainer Lacerte wasn't happy about the leak. He prided himself on his ability to walk the tightrope between being loyal to the team and honest (well, fairly honest) with the media, and he felt that such big news should've been distributed evenly. But Gavitt was absolutely livid that the story had gotten out in such a slipshod manner; he liked the controlled, orchestrated press conference and not the leak, which was out of the Auerbach tradition of playing media favorites. A couple days after the leak, Gavitt convened a meeting that included Volk and the public relations staff and demanded a system of "centralized communications." And over the next month, Celtics communications about Larry Bird's physical condition were nothing if not centralized.

At any rate, the absence of Bird could hardly have made Madison Square Garden, the onetime mecca of basketball, any more moribund than it already was. By January, the Knicks were a defeated and dejected team, and all of the bogus rah-rah-rah tactics of their chamber-of-commerce-style coach, John MacLeod, rang false. (MacLeod landed up at Notre Dame at the end of the season.) The atmosphere was right out of a Nets' game across the river, what with very little noise and half of the crowd cheering for the Celtics. The Knicks had invited boxer Sugar Ray Leonard, who was trying to hype a fight against Terry Norris, to toss up a ceremonial opening tip, and even the shameless Leonard looked embarrassed. Meanwhile, director Spike Lee, a.k.a. Mars Blackmon, bosom buddy of Michael Jordan's, and a

Garden fixture, was a bit disappointed that Bird hadn't shown up. He was scheduled to have his picture taken with the Celtic for a *Sports Illustrated* feature. Lee had made several disparaging references to Bird in his movies, suggesting that he thought Bird was overrated because of his skin color. But others close to Lee said that he actually respected Bird and was looking forward to meeting him. "Ah, he probably wouldn't have done it, anyway," Lee said to photographer Nat Butler when he heard that Bird wasn't coming. He was probably right. Bird had told a friend that he didn't care much for Lee.

In Bird's absence, Ford decided to start McHale—inserting either Pinckney or Smith at the spot would've been almost meaningless—and McHale feigned concern. "You're going to mess up my rhythm," he said. Ford was asked if McHale was serious. "Who knows when Kevin is serious?" said Ford. But McHale was serious when he got out on the floor. The Knicks' Charles Oakley, the muscular power forward who guarded him most of the time, is one of those players who really inspire McHale, primarily because he does not respect Oakley as a player. McHale continually complained that officials were not diligent enough in reducing what he called "the hand-to-hand combat" that went on near the basket, such warfare being Oakley's forte. "Basketball is, by nature, a running game," McHale believed. "That's how players learn. When you're in eighth or ninth grade all you do is run. Very few ninth grade coaches get two guys together in a drill and say, 'Okay, now go kick the shit out of each other.' I think that's one of the league's great problems. Officials allow too much grabbing and shoving. There's not enough low-post creativity anymore, because it's very hard to be creative when a guy has two hands on your back and a knee up your ass. Hey, I'm not saying I'm not guilty of the same thing. When we play Patrick Ewing, some of the things I do to him, grabbing him, practically tackling him, makes me embarrassed to say I'm a basketball player." Ironically, though, the physical nature of the game helped McHale because he is one of the few offensive players creative enough to counteract the gang violence. His prescription for beating Oakley was rather simple, though—turn and shoot quickly before Oakley could rough him up. "No moves, no nothing," said McHale. "And guys like Oakley in that situation have no prayer. I'm just shooting ten-foot jumpers against Eddie Pinckney or Joe Kleine at Hellenic College. It's as simple as that."

And it very nearly was. Oakley had made a potentially bad situation worse by spouting off the day before the game about playing physical and "putting bodies on the floor." McHale was so intimidated that he scored 28 points, grabbed 11 rebounds, and blocked 3 shots in forty-three minutes. The last of those blocks came with two minutes left when he cleanly got all of a Mark Jackson lay-up, the kind of rejection Bill Walton used to call a "smother chicken." The Knicks called time-out right after that and McHale walked off the court, nodding his head repeatedly to his teammates, as if to say, "Yup, this is the way I thought it would be." Oakley must've felt like clocking him.

The Celtics hardly got away unscathed, though. Reggie Lewis collected five stitches via a loose elbow but nevertheless played the type of game that typified the season to date—he made only 5 of his 20 shots from the floor, yet had 3 steals and a team-high 12 rebounds. Kleine's frustrating season continued. With McHale starting, he was due to get significant minutes as backup center, but early in the second period he caught a vicious (though unintentional) elbow in the nose from Ewing and had to leave the game. As Lacerte pulled a bloody cotton ball from his nose in the locker room after the game, McHale started in.

"Ol' Joe thought he was back in Arkansas [Kleine went to the University of Arkansas] for a minute," said McHale. "He's out there in Madison Square Garden yelling, 'Su-eee! Su-eee!'" Later, as Kleine packed his bags, his nose caked with dried blood, he looked over at McHale with something close to envy. "I don't think anyone who ever played, and I mean Wilt Chamberlain and Bill Russell, could ever stop him down low. He's amazing." Then he shook his head. "But, boy, the bitch does talk a lot, doesn't he?"

Larry Bird was going to be out for a while and that meant life in Celtic Land would get a lot more complicated. At the meeting with his staff on the morning of the game against the Bucks at the Garden on January 9, Gavitt announced that all—and he meant *all*—communication about Bird's back would come from him. And so he gathered the assembled media together an hour before the game to tell them what he knew about the situation. Neither team physician Scheller nor trainer Lacerte was present. Neither was Auerbach. Volk was out in the audience, twirling an umbrella. It rained that night.

Gavitt explained that Bird's main problem was an inflamed nerve root in the area of the lower vertebrae on the right side. The disc was not herniated or ruptured, but Bird had been feeling pain all the way down in his right ankle, a danger signal of possible permanent nerve damage. He was put in a cumbersome device called a flexion brace, which did not permit his walking around very easily. (Bird is not fond of advertising his maladies, and no one even bothered to ask if he would be showing up at the Garden.) Also, he was given steroid injections to reduce the swelling in the facet, the inflamed joint in the area of the nerve root. And he would supplement the injections with a daily dose of oral steroids.

"Surgery," said Gavitt, "has never been a consideration."

Gavitt's performance was so flawless that there weren't even many questions. The most obvious was: When would Bird be back?

"Your guess is as good as mine," said Gavitt. "I'm not going to guess and we're not asking our medical team to guess. We've got to focus our coaching staff and our players' attention on the duties at hand. We'd love to have Larry with us and we know that as soon as he can be with us and as soon as he's healthy, he will be.

"What's important here is Larry's good health, both short term and long term. He's been banging and fighting this. We're talking about anything other than a malingerer here. We're talking about a guy who in the past had to have his uniform hidden so he wouldn't play when he was hurt."

The press conference suddenly put a new cast on the Bird injury. It was not a minor setback. The reality of the situation was that the Celtics' captain was home in a cumbersome back brace and would not be back for a while. It was the first major stumbling block in a season that, to that point, had been positively serendipitous. (Indeed, Bird was the first regular to miss a game by injury.) How would the Celtics react? Ford sensed that the Milwaukee game was an important one—if his team came out and promptly fell on its face at home, the coach knew there would be big problems. With a sense of urgency, he implored the Celtics to play defense and get out and run, and they did just that, building an incredible 54–26 lead in the second period. But then it nearly collapsed in the second half. The Celtics suddenly looked tired, and the Bucks cut the lead all the way to 84–82 early in the fourth period. Only some inspired play by Lewis and Brown, plus several calls that went Boston's way, enabled the Celtics to hold on to a 110–102 victory.

It seemed like a successful evening. The Celtics beat a good team without their captain and leader, and, in the process, took possession of the NBA's best record (28–5). But disturbing little patterns were already evident. McHale played every minute of the game and that couldn't continue. He scored 30 points and had 10 rebounds, but he also did not collect an assist in all that time. And ball movement was only one thing the Celtics missed when Bird was not on the floor. Boston grabbed only one more rebound than Milwaukee, one of the weakest rebounding teams in the league. Who would make up for Bird's rebounds, the key to Boston's fast break? Not Gamble, who isn't big enough. Not Michael Smith, who didn't get off the bench. Perhaps Pinckney, but Ford used him for only five minutes. Parish had 15 and

McHale had 10—that burden was predictable but could not continue.

Ford sensed that his team needed a rest and, with the lowly Clippers coming to town two nights hence, he made the following day's practice at Hellenic optional. After the game, Kleine, the Celtics' number-one gym rat, was asked to predict who would be there the next day. He went around the room, pointing at the now-empty lockers. "Stojko will be there. What else does he have to do, go to the museum? Dee. No chance. McHale. Yeah, can't afford to miss the opportunity to bust chops. Chief? Yeah, right. [Parish would be voted the Celtic least likely to attend an optional practice.] Eddie Pinckney. He'll be there. Reggie. No chance. Oscar, he'll be there. Brian. No chance. Popson. Of course. Don't think we'll see Larry. I'll be there. And Michael Smith will show. That's it. I guarantee it."

"Well," said Kleine, turning on the lights at Hellenic College the following morning, "I'm a little disappointed in my man Oscar. Thought he'd be here." Kleine's morning line on the optional practice attendants had been accurate with the exception of Gamble, who decided a day of rest was in order. Derek Smith was at Hellenic, too, continuing to work with Lacerte on rehabilitating his knee.

"Hey, Derek, you ready to play yet?" McHale asked, smiling. "I'm talking to my wife and she says, 'Larry's hurt, so why don't they just start playing Derek Smith?' Guess she hasn't read about how many operations you had."

McHale then turned his attention to Kleine, whose X rays had revealed just a small crack in the bone in the nose, not a full-scale fracture.

"Big nose, little crack, better than little nose, big crack, right, Joe?" said McHale.

"Whatta you sit around at night, smokin' dope and thinking of all this stuff?" Kleine asked.

"Nah, not anymore," said McHale. "It all comes to me now in a flashback."

A variety of newspapers were spread out on the bleachers. With no coaches around, no drills to run, and no film to watch, McHale Standard Time was even more nebulous than usual.

"Hey, Michael Jordan scored his 15,000th point last night in Philly," said McHale, leafing through a sports section. "Did they stop the game?"

"Yup," said Popson. "Ceremony and everything."

"Gee," said McHale, making his point about the Celtics' failure to recognize his milestone, "must be nice."

He perused the NBA box scores. "A bad game for Oakley again. Well, at least he's playing so bad he can't bitch about not making the All-Star team. Nothing I like better than guys in this league who can't play complaining about not making the All-Star team. We need a lot more of that."

He came across an item about Todd Marinovich, the USC quarterback. Like the Piersall character in *Fear Strikes Out*, Marinovich had been pushed to the limit by an obsessive father, who controlled every aspect of his son's training, even his diet.

"Now there is a guy, this Marinovich, who's going to flip out one day," said McHale. " 'DAD! I'M EATING A HAMBURGER, DAD! LOOK AT IT. IT'S FULL OF FAT! IT'S REALLY BAD FOR YOU!' "

Eventually, the noisy three-on-three game commenced but with a different result—the team of Kleine, Pinckney, and Smith, who had begun calling themselves "The Brookline Brothers," actually won. They whooped and hollered on the floor, then ran into the locker room. They stayed for a few minutes while McHale, Popson, and Vrankovic idly shot around, wondering what was going on. Eventually, they reappeared as a Revolutionary War fife-and-drums corps, parading around the gym floor, Pinckney limping and playing an imaginary flute. Kleine held a towel aloft that said: HELLENIC COLLEGE 3-ON-3 CHAMPS, MUD PIE. Mud pie, explained Kleine, was the play used by the Brookline Brothers to win the game. "Everybody runs around until somebody gets open," said Kleine. "That's mud pie." The Brothers hung up the towel, after which Popson went over and drew in a large asterisk.

Adolescent? Silly? Yes. But that's how winning teams act. They were still talking and laughing like children as they left the gym together that cold winter afternoon. Nobody knew it at the time, but the happiest moments of the season were now behind them.

Chris Ford bought his five-bedroom house in Lynnfield thirteen years ago, right after he was traded to Boston, for $110,000, and he and Kathy still love it. It is relatively modest by, say, the housing standards of Bird and McHale, but it is very nice, and it has a fifty-by-forty-foot basketball court in the backyard. Both backboards are glass, and an official NBA rack of official NBA basketballs sits by the double doors leading to the court. Kevin McHale has stopped over to shoot around. It is a nice and comfortable suburban life for the four Ford children, much different from the way their father grew up.

On a Tuesday night in January, the Fords gathered up their youngest son, Michael, and headed for the Lynnfield High School gymnasium for oldest son Chris's game that evening. Though only a freshman, Chris was a regular member of the playing rotation. The Fords are somewhat the first family of Lynnfield and not just because of Chris's celebrity. During the 1990–91 school year, the Fords had a child in each of the town's four schools—Chris in high school, Katie in middle school, Anthony in elementary school, and Michael in preschool. Kathy, a classically trained pianist who gives private lessons, works part-time for the school district as a traveling accompanist. She enjoys it and it keeps her in touch. Until the 1990–91 season, Chris even served as head coach of his son's town team, scheduling games and practices as best he could around the Celtics season. Kathy helped out, too, and also coached her daughter's basketball team. To the extent that the life of a professional athlete and coach can be considered normal, the Fords are just another well-to-do Lynnfield family, centering themselves around family and school activities.

When the Fords arrived at the Lynnfield gymnasium that evening and began chatting with fellow parents, the talk was not of Bird's back and the Celtics' glittering record. It was of candy sales, raffle tickets, homework problems. "Hey," said Chris, grabbing one of his son's friends, "you got a date for the dance?" Chris missed a lot of that bonding during his youth in Atlantic City, New Jersey. He doesn't miss much now. Just before tip-off, Michael Ford suddenly bolted across the court. Chris and Kathy exchanged looks: Who was on duty to get him? Chris got up and called to his son.

Chris Ford, Jr. is something of a prodigy, blessed with above-average athletic ability and basketball instincts. As soon as he entered the game as the first player off the bench, Lynnfield's passing and movement without the ball perked up. Ford's visitor found the evening fascinating, for it was on another winter night, twenty-eight years earlier, that he first saw the father in action. At that time, Chris, Sr. was a high school freshman and a prodigy, too, the best player on the floor as a skinny fifteen-year-old. The comparisons were unavoidable. The form on Chris, Jr.'s one-handed shot was excellent ("He's probably a better shooter right now than I ever was," said Chris), and he played all aspects of the game wisely and calculatedly, almost to a fault. His father, on the other hand, dominated more overtly, with a manic intensity and a will born of desperation. There was grace in the father's game, but there was more hunger, a quality evident in the styles of urban blacks and poor white kids like Larry Bird. Chris, Jr. plays the game because it's always been there and he's good at it. Chris, Sr. played the game because it was his salvation.

* * *

The area of Atlantic City from Arkansas Avenue to Texas Avenue, boardwalk to the bay, used to be known, somewhat pejoratively, as "Ducktown," having been settled by immigrant Italians who kept ducks in their backyard. When the weather was warm, they sat on their stoops day and night, looking out for each other, wary of intrusions from the outside. Chris Ford spent his boyhood in Duck Town, though his precise ethnic persuasion is uncertain. "He doesn't know what he is," says Kathy Ford, "and doesn't want to dig too deep to find out." He acted Italian because most of his friends were Italian. His father, a roofer, died when Chris was eight years old, leaving his mother, who was riddled by arthritis, to support four children. They got by on public assistance and her occasional stints as a chambermaid. The Fords moved from apartment to apartment in Ducktown, but the one above a bar on Atlantic Avenue was the most intriguing—a family of gypsies lived on the first floor, the Fords lived on the second, and a hooker lived on the third. The first house Chris Ford ever lived in was the one he bought in Lynnfield.

The local parochial school was St. Michael's, which was free to parishioners. That's the only way Ford could've gone. It so happened that St. Mike's was *the* basketball school on the island, totally dedicated to the sport, the parish gymnasium always open, CYO coaches always willing to teach, family activities centering around the games. Ford was an average student and had less spending money than most of his friends, but he was an instant success on the basketball court. The neighborhood boys were either hoods or athletes, and Ford became the latter. "Basketball was my out," he said. He could score, but from the earliest age he also saw passing angles and unintentional picks and opportunities for steals, things about the game that no one else could see and no coach could teach. Ford never realized he was poor until he went to Holy Spirit High School in nearby Absecon. Clothes were not a problem at St. Mike's because he wore a uniform (blue slacks, white shirt, blue tie) every day, but at Holy Spirit the boys were free to wear any kind of sportcoat they wanted, and Ford started to feel embarrassed about wearing the same one every day. Fortunately for him, a school letter sweater could take the place of the jacket, so Ford wore the sweater every day.

When he and Kathy began dating, her parents, the Salernos, were not pleased. They were Italian, but Ducktown was the kind of neighborhood from which they had escaped, and Kathy used the word *regressing* to describe their attitude about their daughter's choice of dates. When Chris came over to the Salerno house in Margate, he was so shy that he literally put the newspaper in front of his face so that he would not have to speak directly to her parents, somewhat the Jersey version of the Hoosier hick named Bird who came along a few years later.

Like his son years later, Chris was also a varsity player as a freshman. His team lost every single game, 0–22. But the next year, when Ford felt confident enough to become the team leader, Holy Spirit went 19–3. By the time he graduated and headed for Villanova, he was probably the best scholastic player in the history of south Jersey.

Like Bird and McHale, Ford is sensitive about staying close to his roots. (Perhaps they sense that quality in each other and it helps their relationship.) Ford spends much of the offseason at their home in Margate, visiting the White House sub shop and other old haunts, but like many Atlantic City natives he stays away from the casinos, except for an occasional dinner and show. "It was better the old way," says Ford. He constantly worries, too, about the effects that an affluent lifestyle will have on his children. "It was much better to grow up the way I did," said Ford. "I'm not crazy about the way they're growing up, tell you the truth. I don't think they get to see the real world. Yet, I'm the reason they're growing up that way. I've tried to give them an understanding of the world and the way it works and the way things aren't always handed to you, but it's hard to grasp that unless you've been through it. My childhood made me a better player, sure, but it made me a better person, too. You need some kind of struggle. I don't know whether my kids are getting it."

Lynnfield High was ahead by almost 40 points when the coach put Chris, Jr. and two starters back in the game.

"Jeez, what's he doing that for?" Chris wondered aloud.

"Maybe he saw the Milwaukee game," said a family friend, referring to the night that the Celtics nearly blew a big lead.

"Thanks a lot, Vinnie," said Ford. "I had almost forgotten that."

By seven o'clock on the evening of January 16, everyone in Boston Garden waiting for the tip-off against Golden State knew that the United States had begun an air offensive against Iraq. In a terse, one-sentence statement, the NBA announced that it was going to play that evening's slate of games: "Although tonight's games will not be canceled, we will be seeking additional guidance from the White House and State Department tomorrow." The Garden was unusually quiet as organist Harry played a medley of patriotic songs, like "You're a Grand Old Flag" and "When Johnny Comes Marching Home Again." Still, the mysterious condition of Bird was so much on everyone's mind that

Rookie head coach Chris Ford had to make one thing clear right from the beginning of the season—he would be heard.

Larry Bird speaks rarely, but when he does, everyone listens.

1

Dave Gavitt, the Savior, and Red Auerbach, the cigar-smoking Eternal Prese
appear at a news conference to announce Gavitt's hiring.

Is Reggie Lewis ready to make the
Celtics "Reggie's Team" in the 1990s?

8

Dee Brown kept his eyes closed during this climactic slam dunk at the All-Star
Game, but they were opened wide by events off the court.

9

Bird hits a stepback jumper over Detlef Schrempf during the Indiana series.

10

The Celtics were often helpless when Bird was not on the court.

11

There has been almost no way for opponents—or teammates—to stop McHale from getting off his shot.

12

Dave Gavitt, right, shares a word with young assistant coach Jon Jennings.

13

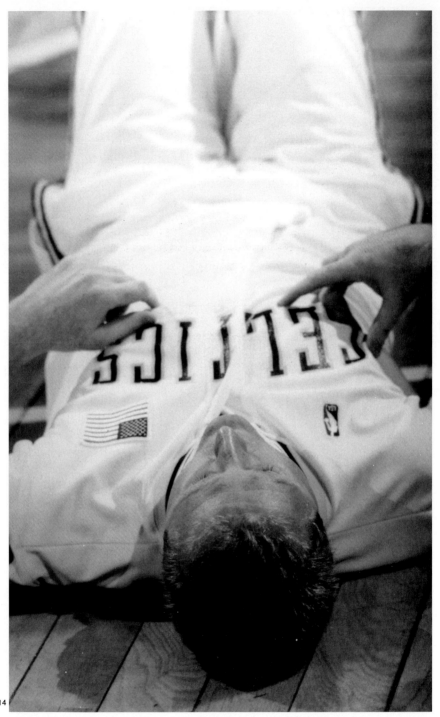

14

Bird did his back exercises religiously, but nothing could save him from postseason surgery.

when Scheller, a major in the Army Reserve, called a press conference to announce that he might be sent to the Middle East, one reporter asked: "Why are you telling us this? What about Bird's back?"

The pregame cheers for Golden State's Chris Mullin, an Irish kid from New York City, were predictably loud. It was just another subtle way that the black player could sense the atmosphere in the Garden. There was nothing racist about it, but it did demonstrate a certain race orientation, for outstanding black players, even Michael Jordan, were not greeted as warmly. Parish went down with a shot to the eye in the first twenty seconds of the game, which prompted Kleine, Parish's backup, to jump off the bench, smile, and say to Ford: "Uh oh, Doc, better get him outta there."

The Warriors game was the fifth that the Celtics had played without Bird and the increase in playing time was starting to wear on McHale. "RUN, KEVIN, DAMMIT!" Ford shouted at him after Mullin scored on a fast-break followup shot. But it wasn't just McHale. Shaw had a nightmare of an evening trying to defense the Warriors' devastating backcourt combination of Tim Hardaway and Mitch Richmond. Hardaway, a lightning-quick six-foot point guard, finished with 37 points and 10 assists, and each of them was an acid-indigestion attack for Red Auerbach. Hardaway had been the player whom owner Alan Cohen wanted to choose in the 1989 draft, but Auerbach had insisted on Michael Smith, whom the Celtics made the thirteenth pick. The Warriors gleefully plucked Hardaway at No. 14 and had themselves an All-Star.

The most electrifying play of the evening was made by Dee Brown early in the third period. After Shaw missed a jumper, Brown, who was lurking near the basket, went up, up, and up, his hand well above the rim, and viciously slammed the ball back down. On the bench, Kleine went crazy, kicking his feet and shaking his fists like he was in convulsions. The play was extraordinary on three levels: It took incredible timing, it required an unbelievable leap, and it also took a great deal of strength to shove a ball back down the hoop with that much force that far from the basket. Several reporters immediately ran to the *Globe*'s Ryan, the unofficial Garden archivist at such moments.

"Never been done by a six-foot guard in this building," said Ryan. "Certainly not by a six-foot *Celtic* guard."

But even that failed to inspire the Celtics. Trailing 107–105 late in the game, Gamble couldn't get the ball inbounds within five seconds, and the turnover helped the Warriors score a 110–105 victory that both Ford and Auerbach found particularly galling. Though Golden State coach Don Nelson shows the proper reverence for his eleven seasons as a Celtic, he is not exactly in Auerbach's good graces. During a

Boston-Milwaukee playoff series in 1983, then-Bucks coach Nelson made what Auerbach considered inflammatory comments about Danny Ainge; worse, Milwaukee swept the series. Then, too, Nelson's reputation as an innovator bothers Auerbach, who liked to keep things basic. Ford was more than a little perturbed because any loss to Nellie carries with it the corollary that the losing coach had been outsmarted. Nelson's specialty is weird lineup combinations that present matchup problems for the opposition, as well as the technique of isolating his best offensive players and letting them play a brand of one-on-one playground basketball. That's exactly what he did with Hardaway, Richmond, and Mullin, and Ford didn't have an answer. But, then, the Celtics hadn't been able to answer anything for a solid week. They needed Bird back, and needed him badly.

"Let's face it," said McHale, "we're just not a championship team without Larry." He was correct. The 1972 Oakland A's won the World Series without star slugger Reggie Jackson, and the 1991 New York Giants won the Super Bowl without their first-string quarterback, Phil Simms. But NBA teams, comprised of only five starters, were much more fragile entities. The Lakers could not win a championship without Magic Johnson, the Bulls could not win one without Jordan, and the Celtics could not win one without Bird. Everyone knew it, but only McHale was secure enough to give voice to the sentiment.

The pall over the team continued the next day at practice. It was a popular theory to blame events in the Persian Gulf, but none of the players was terribly interested in global politics. "The war really puts things in perspective" was the most popular thing to say, but, in point of fact, the Celtics were more worried about themselves than they were about our boys in the Middle East. Since Bird had flown the coop, they had beaten New York handily, slipped by Milwaukee and the Clippers, and lost to Washington and Golden State. The improving Nets were coming to town on January 18 and that was to be followed by a home-and-home series with the Pistons. It was time, as Kleine said, "for a gut check."

The role of wartime philosopher fell, of course, on McHale. He talked quietly to the team after practice, then met with the media. The bags under his eyes were even darker than usual—like Casey, he had been staying up until all hours watching CNN's unprecedented coverage. "I thought a lot about my father last night," said McHale. "He was in North Africa in World War II, and I've got a brother-in-law over in the Persian Gulf right now." His thoughts drifted to the team. "We haven't played well since that first half against Milwaukee. We've been lethargic. Basketball isn't a helluva lot different than a golf swing, you know. You can go out there and know the things you have to do to keep from hitting a fade, yet you still might hit a fade. You have to play your way out of it. That's what we have to do. Play and practice our way out of it."

On the following evening at Boston Garden, they did not, losing by 111–106 to the Nets, a team they expected to beat even on the road. As the final buzzer sounded, more than a few boos reached Celtics ears as they headed glumly for the locker room.

"So, what's the deal with Bird?" Bill Laimbeer asked as the Celtics media visited his locker before the game at the Pistons' Palace of Auburn Hills on January 21. "We hear he's been cut." Laimbeer was obviously enjoying the Celtics' frustration and the cloak of mystery that was wrapped around Bird. Indeed, the hot rumor around the NBA was that Bird had already undergone back surgery and was recuperating in a hospital in Florida. It sounded farfetched, but the Boston media could not even be 100 percent certain that it was not true. No one had seen Bird, and even the players who had visited him, like Kleine, wouldn't talk much about it. Only Gavitt was commenting on Bird and he was saying very little. Boston's call-in radio talk shows were full of Bird speculation, of course, and several callers per evening asked, sarcastically, when "Doctor Gavitt" would have Bird back to health. The media had taken to jokingly asking Lacerte: "Ed, any timetable on Larry?" And Lacerte would remove his watch and set it on a table. "There's your timetable," he'd say. But he would not talk about Bird, who had not shown his face at either the Garden or Hellenic College for two weeks. Jan Volk, sitting at courtside before the game, was asked why the Celtics insisted on the hush-hush approach to dealing with Bird's injury.

Volk breathed a heavy sigh. The mere mention of the words "back" and "Larry Bird" all but ruined his day.

"We've been through this before," said Volk, referring to the 1988–89 season when Bird failed to come back from early-season surgery to both heels. "The eternal questions. 'When will Larry be back? What's the timetable?' We gave estimates before, and when he failed to come back in that time frame, it was such a severe psychological downer that it was really hard for the club and really hard for Larry."

Actually, the point was well taken. The impression was left during that 1988–89 season that Bird had somehow fallen short of expectations because he did, in fact, fail to make it back when everyone thought he would. It was a devastating time in Celtic Land. *Larry is human.* Still, it seemed that some middle-of-the-road position on talking about Bird was possible. Only Gavitt was permitted to answer even the simplest questions about Bird, and Gavitt, by his own choosing, was not around all the time.

The game itself was more like the Kings vs. the Clippers than the Celtics vs. the Pistons. Parish was also out (sprained ankle), and Detroit didn't have its best player, Isiah Thomas, who was contemplating surgery for a damaged right wrist. Vrankovic even found himself in the game early in the second period as a backup to Kleine. Stojko drew a few oohs and ahs when he hit an old-fashioned, sweeping hook shot, but a minute later, as the Celtics brought the ball down on offense, he looked confused and McHale had to wave him to the other side of the floor. (At other times during the season, Stojko wasn't sure when he could go into a game. There he would be, kneeling by the scorer's table, oblivious to the referee's frantically waving him onto the floor.) Stojkos's troubles with the English language definitely retarded his progress as a player. He understood all the plays but sometimes key words were lost in the crowd noise during games, or on other occasions his teammates lapsed into idioms that he couldn't quite grasp. Stojko claimed that his main problem was not comprehension but, rather, doubting himself once he had determined what was said. "My first choice is usually correct, but sometimes I think it's not," he said one day. At any rate, explaining plays to your center in the heat of action was not a recommended way to run an offense.

As expected, the Pistons won the game rather handily, 101–90, but it wasn't a lost evening. In thirty-one minutes of action Kleine had scored 18 points and looked, at times, like a first-string center. However, in the heat of the action he had also received a large bump on his head. His nose was still puffed up, too, and the whole Kleine package suggested a Saturday-night palooka at a South Philadelphia gym.

"What was that boxer's name who was always getting beat up?" said Shaw after the game. "Tex Cobb, that was it. Well, we've got Tex Kleine." As had become their custom on the road, the Celtics took a charter home immediately after the game, so they were at Hellenic College early the following afternoon for a practice session. Ford didn't want to work them too hard, but the Pistons were coming to town the following night in what had taken on the aspect of a "must" game. The record without Bird was 3–4, and two of those wins had been shaky. Sooner or later, the Celtics needed to dig in their heels and beat a credible team, just to show that they were not completely dependent on Bird.

A half-dozen or so reporters were casually watching the practice action when suddenly, from the balcony above the court where the weight machines were located, came the unmistakable sound of a Hoosier twang. All eyes swung in that direction. It was L. Bird. A few minutes later he ambled out on the court in his stocking feet, carrying his sneakers, and paused to watch the action. He continued on to the training room to talk with his friend, Joe Q. The Bird sighting, obviously, put a new edge to the session. What did it mean? Was he back up to snuff? Would he play the following night against Detroit? More to the immediate point, would he talk? The press observed an informal yet nonetheless unwavering protocol at Celtics practice sessions. Obviously, no one interrupted a coach or player during practice. Even after practice, reporters were theoretically not allowed on the floor, but it was standard operating procedure to walk out and collar, say, a Kleine, a Pinckney, or a Michael Smith, even while they were shooting around. It was okay to go get Casey or Jennings on the floor, too, but Ford would eventually come to the sidelines to talk. McHale could usually be counted on to answer questions, but McHale Standard Time being what it was, it often took a while; fortunately, he was usually worth the wait.

Parish and Bird, however, were more complicated. As soon as practice was over, Parish would frequently be gone, like vapor, and a reporter needed quick reflexes to intercept him before he got to the door that led to the locker room. (Reporters were not allowed in the locker rooms at Hellenic.) The routine way to get Parish was to snag him after he was dressed and heading for his car, which was usually about the time McHale and Co. were beginning their three-on-three games. Bird was unpredictable. Sometimes he talked, sometimes he didn't. If a writer had a good relationship with him, that writer could interrupt him as he shot around after practice, but only if he wanted to talk about nonbasketball-related items. There was no shouting, "How's your back?" to Bird unless one wanted to risk being frozen out forever. Now, on this particular day, Gavitt had a chance to show his public relations skills. He should've gathered together himself, Bird, and Ford, set a limit of, say, five minutes of questions, and cleared up a week's worth of confusion. Even if Bird had wanted to obfuscate, the reporters would've at least heard it from the horse's mouth. But Bird didn't want to talk, so he didn't. Gavitt, when asked, would say only that Bird's condition continued to be "day to day." And Ford was annoyed that there were even questions about Bird. The coach was generally given high marks by the press for being direct and fairly honest, but the Bird issue had begun to cause some friction. Ford could not understand why everyone kept asking him about Bird. He felt that Gavitt's "day-to-day" bulletins were sufficient, which, from the perspective of the press, was a plainly ridiculous position. Given the Celtics' poor public relations history, the reporters could not be sure, first of all, that Gavitt wasn't lying, and, second, that Bird wouldn't suddenly materialize at Boston Garden one evening, number 33 on his back, ready to go. And then they would've missed the story again. When it became clear that Bird—so close, yet so far away—would have nothing to say, the *Globe*'s Peter May had something to say to Gavitt.

"I know you think you're clearing things up with those 'day-to-day' reports, Dave, but you're only making things more confusing," May told Gavitt.

Volk would've immediately turned defensive, but Gavitt merely asked, "How's that, Peter?"

"Because when you say 'day to day' it sounds like Larry could come back tomorrow," answered May. "If he's going to be out for a long, long time, why not just say it? Then maybe we wouldn't be asking you every five minutes."

"Because we honestly don't know," said Gavitt. "It *is* 'day to day.'"

"Well, if it's 'day to day,'" said May, "might he play tomorrow against the Pistons?"

"No, I don't think so," said Gavitt.

"Well, then, it's not really 'day to day,'" said May. "You already know he won't play tomorrow."

"Look, I understand your position," said Gavitt. "And I understand that you have to keep asking me. But our position is that we want to make it clear to Larry that he's under absolutely no pressure from the team to come back."

That much was clear: Larry Bird's status was "day to day."

Even if Gavitt understood that they "had to keep asking me," not everyone else did, particularly Ford and the other Celtics, who grew irritated just *listening* to the daily questions about Bird. The exercise could only be described as humiliating for the beat reporters, for it seemed like their entire lives were wrapped up in Larry Bird's physical condition. "Don't you have anything else to do?" Ford said in exasperation one day to a group of reporters. Unfortunately, they didn't. The reporters had to keep plugging away, all day, every day, trying to find out answers for the several million Bostonites whose lives *were* wrapped up in Larry Bird's physical condition. As Steve Bulpett wrote one day, "Out of sight, out of mind doesn't work with Larry."

Out on the court, the usual suspects were working overtime. Casey, wearing a shirt that said ANIMAL EXPERIMENTS ARE A DYING TRADITION, had devised one of his old Catholic League drills for the big men. He set a folding chair down on the blocks near the basket, put a ball on it, and instructed his charges to grab it, turn, and, without dribbling, dunk. McHale looked slow and even a little awkward, but he was the only one able to do it five times in a row. Eventually, only he and Kleine remained, and began to engage in a strange, almost joyless,

gladiatorial game of one-on-one. McHale would get the ball, lean into
Kleine, Kleine would push back, and McHale would go into his retinue
of moves until he worked himself free. Then they'd walk slowly to the
other side of the court and go through the whole process again, no
name calling, no Big Daddy Lipscomb commentary, no Mud Pie plays.
The time for that had come and gone.

"Whoa! Look at this," said Brian Shaw as Derek Smith stepped into the
locker room in an impeccable gray suit, white shirt, gray-and-black tie,
and gray shoes. "Right out of the pages of *Q-G*."

"I believe the magazine is *G-Q*, Brian," said Smith.

The gaffe was apropos. Shaw's play of late, like most of his teammates', had been rather dyslexic. But the Pistons presented an obvious
opportunity for redemption.

Out on the court, ninety minutes before game time, some of the
Pistons were engaging in a popular pregame activity—trashing Boston
Garden.

"You know why it's always cold in here?" said John Salley. " 'Cause
the people in Boston know the brothers don't like it cold, that's why."
Scott Hastings, somewhat of a nonplaying version of McHale, said
after nine seasons in the league he still could not get used to the organ.
"In every other building you hear, like, Vanilla Ice or somebody blaring
from the speakers, and it gets you in kind of a mood," said Hastings,
who, while at the University of Arkansas, used to play endless practical
jokes on his roommate, one Joe Kleine. "Now you come here, and
there's a guy playing a Wurlitzer. You don't know whether you're
gonna see some little monkey dressed in a costume come scampering
out on the court. I'm never sure whether I'm at a basketball game or a
circus."

On that night it was a little bit of both. Laimbeer had taken to
wearing a pair of goggles as a result of an early-season eye injury, and
one Garden fan kept shouting at him, "Take off your plastic mask, you
FAGGOT!" No mixed message there. There was a great and nearly
unnoticed comic moment in the second period when Parish was forced
to retrieve the ball after a Laimbeer free throw. Parish wrinkled his
face, looked down at the ball contemptuously, and quickly handed it to
the ref, recoiling as if he might contract a disease just from touching a
ball that had passed through Laimbeer's hands. In an interview with
Jackie MacMullen some time earlier, Parish had acknowledged the
depth to which his hatred of Laimbeer ran. "I don't see how anyone can
respect a guy like that, a person who doesn't have the guts to accept the
consequences of what he does," Parish said. "He throws people to the

floor, or undercuts them, then when it's time for the moment of truth, he hides behind Mahorn. Well, who do you suppose he will hide behind this year?"

Laimbeer's problem in the final three minutes of the January 23 game was that he couldn't hide from Parish, who not only put the game out of reach but also embarrassed Laimbeer in the process. First, he came out of nowhere to block a Laimbeer lay-up. Then he did his patented spin move on the baseline to go around Laimbeer for a lay-up that gave Boston a 7-point lead. Finally, he faked Laimbeer off his feet, squared himself up with typical Parish precision, and made a lay-up to give the Celtics a 101–89 lead that eventually turned into a 111–94 victory. The Pistons called time-out and Parish limped gingerly off the court to the accompaniment of a standing ovation. And Laimbeer walked off to the accompaniment of the fan. "HEY, LAIMBEER! HEY, FAGGOT! HOW'S IT FEEL, FAGGOT?"

"Tonight you could've played the *Rocky* theme song for Robert," said Ford. Said Shaw, who had played brilliantly with 18 points and 10 assists: "Chief really gave us a lift spiritually."

Parish finished with 16 points and 12 rebounds, four more than Laimbeer, one of the best rebounders in the league. It was clearly his best moment in quite a while, perhaps since the championship season of 1985–86, but when the press entered the Celtics locker room, Parish, as was his custom for home games, was gone.

"At least he's no hypocrite," said the *Herald*'s Steve Bulpett.

"Hey, Dee," Jon Jennings asked Brown an hour before the Celtics' Super Bowl Sunday game against the Lakers at Boston Garden. "Are the Fat Boys [a rap group] still together?"

Dee smiled and considered his response. What the hell, he thought. "Yeah, they are. You, Chris, and Case."

Jennings shook his head. "Case, you hear that?" he said. "A rookie talking like that. That is really something."

"You know why that happens?" Casey said. "You know why he gets away with that shit? Because he got in with the head coach right away. Say this for Dee, he's smart."

"He doesn't even carry the luggage anymore," said Jennings.

"Hey, man, this is the nineties," said Brown. "Rookies are different."

On the surface, the Celtics seemed fine. Under the surface, they were extremely worried. Two nights after the hope-lifting win over Detroit, they had again played poorly, losing by 116–94 at Philadelphia. Barkley, who had a knee injury, hadn't even played, which should've more than balanced Bird's absence. Then, too, it had been impossible not to compare the way the Sixers treated Barkley's injury with the way the Celtics treated Bird's. Barkley had been very much in evidence that evening, sitting on the bench, cheering on his teammates, joshing with the press after the game, answering every question about his injury.

"Everybody's asking about me," Barkley said at one point. "What the hell's going on with Larry?"

"Who knows?" one reporter told him. "It's Operation Larry Shield."

The loss to Philly had put Boston's record without Bird at 4–5. It was still 30–10 overall, which was good enough to capture for Ford the Eastern Conference coaching assignment at the February 10 All-Star game in Charlotte. But Ford knew that the Celtics' quick start was largely responsible for the glittering record, and, though he was proud, he also had the vague feeling that he had more or less backed into the honor. A win over the Lakers, who had just begun to really get rolling themselves, would've been a terrific antidote for that feeling. It seemed possible. James Worthy, the Lakers' most important player besides Magic Johnson, had a badly sprained foot and was listed as doubtful for the game.

"Well, we'll make him feel better," said McHale, lacing up his sneakers. "We're the feel-better team of the NBA right now. If a team came in here with Lazarus, he might start."

In the Lakers' locker room, Magic was ruing the absence of Bird. (No more than NBC, however, which had thought enough of a Magic-vs.-Larry duel to have given it spotlight attention on Super Bowl Sunday.) "It's still two good teams, and it's still a very big game," said Magic. "But I'd be lying if I said I didn't miss Larry. He should be here. He's a leader. He's like me. He can put his foot in your butt and you don't mind him doing it." Johnson had attempted to get in touch with Bird when the Lakers arrived in Boston the day before but never heard back from him. That was typical. Brad Lohaus is one of Bird's five best friends in the world but even he rarely calls him. "Larry's not into the telephone," said Lohaus.

Out on the court, meanwhile, Vrankovic and Vlade Divac, another Yugoslav who was having a much more successful season as the Lakers' starting center, were conversing in their native tongue. They had played together on many Yugoslavian national teams. Kleine walked by and pointed to Divac.

"Serb?" he asked.

"Yes, Serb," answered Vrankovic.

Vrankovic's presence had given some of the Celtics an elementary lesson on the complicated subject of Yugoslavian history. Michael Smith was a particularly avid listener and something of a linguist,

Smith was able to converse with Vrankovic in the Slavic tongue. (Most of the other Celtics were content with learning a few Slavic cuss words.) Yugoslavia was at the brink of civil war (which ultimately broke out) at the time, mostly because of a long-standing conflict between the Serbians and the Croatians, of which Vrankovic was one. "But Vlade and I friends," said Stojko.

Before the game, the Celtics' PR staff announced that Gavitt was giving an update on Bird at 12:05, three minutes after President Bush was scheduled to address the nation on the Middle East situation. Someone asked Mike Arace, the young Celtics beat reporter from *The Hartford Courant*, which spokesman he intended to listen to.

"I'm not sure," said Arace, "how do you tell them apart?"

As for the game, Worthy didn't play but wasn't needed. The Celtics stayed close through the first two quarters but wilted in the third. Magic was all over the place, running the offense, directing traffic, helping out on defense. A Martian could have looked at the game for five minutes and noticed that the best player on the floor was L.A.'s number 32. Midway through the fourth period, he missed a left-handed hook shot, got his own rebound, and put back a right-handed hook that gave the Lakers an 87–75 lead that turned into a 104–87 victory.

"They step up, we back down," said McHale, after the game, as disgusted as he had been all season. "Until we all come together and realize what it takes, how we have to respond to a challenge, we're lost." He shook his head. "Ah, I'm done, guys. I've got nothing more to say."

At his home in suburban Boston, meanwhile, Bird had started to watch the game on television but fell asleep. Anyway, he said later, Sunday was the day all the fishing shows came on, so he probably wouldn't have stayed with it.

Less than twenty-four hours later, McHale was rejuvenated as he lounged on the press table at the Target Center in Minneapolis, seven hours before the game against the Minnesota Timberwolves that evening. He was home, relatively speaking, and he felt good. The Wolves had gotten him forty tickets for the family and friends who would be driving down to the game from Hibbing, though his parents wouldn't be coming.

"My mom finally dragged my dad on a vacation to Las Vegas," said McHale. "She's been talking about it for, like, thirty years. He's probably going crazy."

Don Casey strolled over. "Let's go, Kevin, we've got a big man's meeting."

"Oh, hell, Case, I'll be over in a minute," said McHale. "You know what we were talking about? How overrated coaches are in the NBA."

"Good topic," said Casey. "While you're at it, you ever talk about how overpaid players are?"

"I'll agree with you there," said McHale.

The Minnesota game actually meant a great deal to McHale. Almost a year ago to the day, the Timberwolves, then in their first year of existence, had upset the Celtics by 116–105, sending the entire state into a temporary tizzy, and McHale did not want it to happen again in front of so many familiar faces. It didn't. The Celtics built a huge lead, but when Ford tried to rest the starters, unjudicious and errant shooting by Smith enabled the 'Wolves to climb back into the game. Ford had to reinsert the starters, and the Celtics promptly took command again and won going away, by 108–87. The most notable aspect of the game was Ford's decision to start Pinckney and again bring McHale off the bench. "We couldn't help but notice," said Casey, "that Kevin seems to score 22 points whether he starts or not. That tells us that he's much more effective, on a per-minute basis, as the sixth man." Pinckney, meanwhile, had an interesting game. He totally dominated the boards at both ends, but was absolutely unable to put a shot back in the basket. At one point, he grabbed three straight offensive rebounds and failed to convert each time, though he was shooting from a distance of about two feet from the basket. His stat line was one of the strangest of the year—4 points on 1-for-8 shooting and 15 rebounds.

"Well, Eddie, even though you missed a few easy shots, it must've made you feel good that you did some other things, like rebounding," said one reporter, desperately looking for the bright side.

That was too much for *The Patriot-Ledger*'s Mike Fine. Fine is known for his directness and will go down in Boston media history for the moment a few years ago when he turned to Bird and asked, "How come every time I see you talking on these television commercials you sound so smart and smooth, but in person you sound like such a douche bag?" Fine turned to Pinckney and said: "On the other hand, Eddie, even though you rebounded pretty well, it must make you feel like shit to miss such easy shots, right?" Pinckney, easygoing as ever, could only laugh. Actually, he felt kind of good and kind of like shit.

The Celtics wrapped up an eventful month by routing the Orlando Magic at the Garden 144–102 on January 30. But the big news had happened the day before at Hellenic when Bird returned to practice. He not only completed the Celtics' halfcourt drills but he participated in the scrimmage and appeared to go full tilt. Bird declined to talk to the media, but Auerbach attended the practice and took over Gavitt's role as Birdspokesperson. "The big thing is getting him back in shape as quickly as we can," said Auerbach. "But once he starts practicing, we expect him to be back soon." How soon? "There's no way of knowing. But he looked good. You could see the fire in his eyes."

The following day Bird himself broke his silence after a Celtics shootaround. He said he was feeling much better, though he had to go home and lay on the floor after the previous day's practice. He explained that the reason he did not go to games was because he couldn't sit in a chair for long periods of time. He said he was encouraged but would not speculate when he would return. The last thing he wanted to do, he said, was come back and play for a couple weeks, then reinjure himself.

He made his comments not to Boston's two daily newspapers, but to two local television crews that were at practice.

CHAPTER 7

Bird "Busts" the West

FEBRUARY

On February 5, the day before the Celtics hosted the Charlotte Hornets, Bird was ready to make his return. The brass hadn't wanted to announce it officially, but as Bird went through his practice paces the decision had already been made that he would make a test run against the Hornets, then stay out of the following night's game at New York against the Knicks. Bird wasn't happy that the New York decision had been made before he had gotten the opportunity to see how his back had responded to game conditions, but the delicate art of NBA politics was part of the equation, too. Bird had been chosen by the fans as a starter for the All-Star game in Charlotte on February 10 (McHale and Parish were picked by the coaches as reserves, Dee Brown by the league as a participant in the slam-dunk contest), but obviously the Celtics did not want him to play, not with a nine-day, five-game Western road trip that could decide the fate of the season immediately following. An unwritten but strictly-enforced league rule dictates that any player chosen must participate if he plays the regular-season game *immediately* preceding the All-Star game. The NBA feels that will discourage teams from protecting their superstars and thus denuding the All-Star game of its headline players. Through some skillful planning, then, the Celtics had in one fell swoop gotten Bird a test run for the road trip and also kept him out of the All-Star game. The league was not overjoyed that Bird was staying home from the festivities but couldn't do anything about it.

In Bird's fourteen-game absence, the Celtics had gone .500, and at least three of those seven losses—to Golden State, New Jersey, and Charlotte (on February 1)—were the kind that haunted a team, com-

ing as they did against inferior opposition. One of Bird's great strengths
was his refusal to be dragged down by bad teams, and one had to figure
that, at the very least, the Nets and the Hornets would've fallen had
Bird been in the lineup. "That'll never happen," he told Mark Murphy
flatly when the *Herald* reporter asked him, after his comeback, if the
Hornets will ever beat the Celtics when he is on the floor. It had
become clear the extent to which Bird's absence affected every part of
the Celtics' attack, both offensively and defensively, and how, little by
little, the deficiencies of other players had begun to be exposed. Parish,
for example, did a sturdy job of compensating for the rebounds that
were lost when Bird was out, but he couldn't begin to match Bird's skill
as an outlet passer, and that hurt the fast-break. McHale could do a
better defensive job than Bird on an individual basis, but he lacked
Bird's grasp of the team defensive game, the ability to make gambling
steals off the ball, and so the Celtics had become defensively predictable in his absence. Without Bird's three-point threat on offense, opposition defenses could concentrate more of their efforts on containing
Gamble too, and, indeed, his output had fallen most dramatically over
the last fourteen games. But most of all, the Celtics missed his fire, his
confidence, his energizing *presence*.

As practice ended, Casey wandered over and said to him, quite
seriously: "You know, you did look pretty good out there today." Bird
gave him his contemptuous look: "Shit, well that was only Eddie
Pinckney guarding me. You could score on him." And then it was time
to run quickly through the Charlotte offense. The coaching staff was
somewhat concerned, or pretended to be, about the Hornets' J. R. Reid,
a young frontcourt player who hadn't as yet lived up to his press
clippings. "He might be a little quick for Robert all the time," said
Casey to Bird. "Can you guard him?" Bird flashed another withering
look. "I bin gone three weeks. Has J. R. suddenly become an All-Star
and I didn't hear 'bout it? He'll git his twelve. I'll git my fifty." He was
bustin' chops, and that was a good sign.

Bird had actually made his official return to Boston Garden a few
days earlier, having decided to watch the February 3 game against the
Bullets from the bench. Everyone agreed that, though Bird was a sight
for sore eyes, the brightly-colored cardigan sweater he had chosen for
the occasion was not. "I don't have anything to say about that sweater,"
said Reggie Lewis, laughing. "Larry and I have different tastes." The
elegantly attired Shaw only shook his head. Kleine was the only Celtic
who liked it, "and that probably says how bad it is," said Kleine. Bird
kept a low profile that night, and did the same when he bustled into the
dressing room just before six P.M. on the evening of February 6. He
looked healthy and excited but said he didn't want to talk. His team-

mates gave him space too, although they were greatly relieved that Bird was at last around to answer questions for himself. McHale had devised a standard reply when someone asked him about Bird. "I'd tell them it wasn't my day to watch Larry," said McHale. "I'd tell them that Popson has Wednesday, Joe has Friday, and I'm taking Sunday." Bird did take the time to defend McHale from the sniping of Jennings and Casey, who claimed that only their intense lobbying had gotten him added to the Eastern Conference All-Star roster. "A lot of teams didn't like you, Kevin," Jennings said. "Detroit. Atlanta thinks you're slow. We had to make a lot of phone calls." Bird walked by, carrying his sneakers en route to the training room. "You been makin' calls for Kevin for seven years, have ya?" he said. McHale first made the All-Star team in 1984.

After the thunderous roar that greeted Bird's name in the starting lineup, the Hornets knew they needn't have bothered to show up; the Celtics had about as much chance of losing this emotional game as Bird did of beating Dee Brown in the slam-dunk event. Bird made a clever feed to Lewis on the Celtics' first possession, leading to two free throws. A minute later he got the Hornets' center, Mike Gminski, up in the air with a pump fake and threw a blind pass over his shoulder to Shaw, who hit a jumper from the corner. Shortly after that he grabbed a rebound, outletted to Lewis, hustled down the floor, took a return pass and buried a three-point shot. Within minutes the Celtics led 15–2 (they eventually won 133–117) and Bird was pumping his fist in the air. He played unevenly after that, missing five of his six subsequent three-point attempts and committing four turnovers, and he appeared to be slightly out of shape. (Celtic legend Havlicek had shown up at Hellenic a couple days earlier and told him, jokingly, that he needed to lose weight.) But Bird still finished just one rebound short of a triple-double (18 points, 9 rebounds, 13 assists, 2 blocked shots), and, moreover, he seemed to inspire everyone else. Gamble, freed from double-teams, consistently beat his man and made 10 of 13 shots. Dee Brown, who seemed to need Bird more than Shaw did, played thirty-one steady minutes. Parish, back to being a fourth or fifth option on offense, made five of six shots. And, most tellingly, there was McHale with a game-high 28 points in twenty-eight minutes off the bench. Almost no one noticed McHale's economical output, but then, that was to be expected. Bird was back, and so was the magic.

It wasn't too many years ago that the NBA All-Star weekend was a rather quaint affair—not even a weekend, in fact, just a single game that attracted more or less of a cult following. But the 1991 All-Star weekend in Charlotte, North Carolina, was a full-blown, three-ring, corporate circus, just a couple degrees below the Super Bowl on the hype thermometer. The locale of the event alone was a testament to the NBA's overall prosperity and strength, for the Hornets franchise was thriving and prosperous in just its third year of business despite being in a relatively small market. In 1982, the NBA was in such desperate financial straits that it had actually formed a committee to look into the possibility of folding as many as four franchises or, at least, merging a couple. But just six years later, Charlotte, along with Minnesota, Orlando, and Miami, paid some $32 million to join the league as expansion teams. By 1990, *Financial World* magazine evaluated their net worth between $51.2 million (Minnesota) and $60.8 million (Orlando). And both the Lakers (at $200 million) and the Celtics (at $180 million) were listed among the top ten of all sports franchises. The greening of the NBA under the guidance of Commissioner David Stern was truly one of the sporting world's great turnaround stories.

Some of the traditionalists fretted about the NBA's ever-growing corporate image, however. With some fanfare, for example, the NBA announced during the 1990–91 season that McDonald's "revolutionary" McLean Deluxe had been named "official sandwich of the NBA." There was a corporate tie-in to virtually everything the NBA got involved with—the "Edge" NBA Most Valuable Player, the "Digital" NBA Coach of the Year, the "Minute Maid Orange Soda" NBA Rookie of the Year, the "Master Lock" NBA Defensive Player of the Year, the "Miller Genuine Draft" NBA Sixth Man Award. Casey joked that the league had become so corporate that players and coaches would soon be required to carry official luggage engraved with the initials "D. J. S.," for David J. Stern. The more corporate the league got, the more concerned it became with image, and consequently, the more fines it handed out for fighting on the court and loose talk about referees and casual gambling off it. Many NBA people praised the league's watchdog mentality and were glad that it had not followed the hypocritical posture of the National Hockey League, which was to publicly decry brawling but tacitly endorse it. Others, like McHale, felt that the "corporatization" of the NBA had led to an inevitable dearth of true personalities and characters, and McHale always went out of his way to praise the outspoken and totally unpredictable Charles Barkley, the league's most frequently fined superstar. Barkley was a loose cannon if there ever was one—league officials held their breath when five or six postgame beers began to loosen his tongue— but he was a total original. Several seasons ago, for example, he got involved in a feud with Terry Cummings, a sometime preacher then playing for the Milwaukee Bucks. "Tell Terry Cummings to go fuck himself," Barkley told reporters, "but tell him in a religious fashion." Throughout most of the All-Star weekend festivities, Barkley wore a cap bearing the inscription FUCK IRAQ.

But no one complained too loudly about the spit-shined NBA for it beat the hell out of the state of the league a decade earlier when the Finals were shown on a tape-delay basis and every pro basketball player was a suspected druggie. Now, even the NBA's "Super Saturday" activities (the old-timers game, the three-point shootout, and the slam-dunk contest) were broadcast on national television.

No one begrudged Dee Brown his invitation to compete in the All-Star Slam-Dunk competition, for his leaping ability had already become well known, and his put-back slam against Golden State on January 16 had become one of the season's most frequently replayed sequences. Anyway, qualifying for the dunk competition wasn't like making the All-Star team. One didn't need a long track record or a lifetime of achievement, and wisely, the NBA used the vehicle of the dunk to showcase its new stars, of which Brown was clearly one. Indeed, Brown, who had won four of the previous five dunking competitions he had entered while a collegian, even came into Charlotte as one of the favorites. Brown had worked hard on his dunking routines after practice. He had an "alley-oop jam," for which he stood out of bounds, threw the ball high above the basket, then ran in and stuffed it before it hit the ground. He had a 360-degree maneuver, which he called "Corkscrew" in honor of Joe Q., whose nickname was "Corky." He was open to ideas, too, and spent a lot of time consulting with teammates, particularly Shaw and McHale. And out of those bull sessions came the idea that, on the evening of February 9, set him apart from the other seven dunkers in the competition.

As Brown prepared for his first dunk, he suddenly placed the ball on the floor, knelt down, and used the air pump located on the tongue of his Reebok sneakers. The crowd went wild. Instinctively, Brown had capitalized on the organic connection between shoewear and basketball. It didn't matter that some basketball people considered the Reebok pump to be more hype than anything else. Everyone knew about the pump and Brown had scored major style points by using it. More importantly, Brown followed up his pump with a vicious, backward, two-handed dunk, and, from that point on, the field was clearly chasing Dee Brown. A small portion of the crowd booed when Brown repeated his pumping on each subsequent dunk, but he didn't seem to hear them. If his initial "pump" was merely an honest expression of individuality, a creative way to get a step up on the field, Dee had to have known that he had hit on something and wasn't about to stop. The fact that it might've looked cynical, overly commercial, and a grab for Reebok's money did not occur to Dee, a child of the nineties, the era when all of America is one big marketplace. He was competing, after all, in the "Gatorade" Slam Dunk Championship, which followed the "Sheraton-ITT" Long Distance Shootout, which followed the "Schick-Miller Lite" Legends Game. Soon after the competition, Michael Jordan, the once and future slam-dunk king, himself commented: "He played that a bit too much, that pumping up before every dunk. He went a little too far, but evidently, he was trying to help his situation with Reebok. . . . I'm not saying I wouldn't have done it—I just thought he played it too much." *I'm not saying I wouldn't have done it.*

Charlotte's Rex Chapman, hometown favorite and the only white player in the competition, was a factor in the early rounds, leading reporters to wonder if they should mention his skin color if he won. "Now, how would it look if I did that?" said Shaun Powell, a young black reporter from *The Miami Herald.* Eventually, though, it was down to Brown and Seattle's Shawn Kemp. Before his last dunk, Brown went over to the judges, who included Julius Erving, and told them to make sure they noted the special feature of his climactic effort—he would keep both eyes closed. Which is exactly what he did. As he approached, he put the ball in his left hand, shielded his eyes with his right arm, and jammed the ball through the basket. The crowd went crazy and even Kemp, who is somewhat of a young stoic, stood and cheered and shook his head at the sheer brilliance of Brown's maneuver. Perhaps Kemp could've done it had he thought about it, but he hadn't, and the competition belonged to Brown. So, presumably, did the future.

"I've got your headline for tomorrow," Steve Bulpett said to Powell. " 'Brothers Repel Honkie Dunk Challenge.' "

Ford had elected to take a laid-back approach to Sunday's All-Star game. He let one of his players, Milwaukee's Alvin Robertson, skip part of the opening warm-ups so he could watch his alma mater, the University of Arkansas, take on the number-one-ranked team in the nation, UNLV, and whatever x-ing and o-ing he did he referred to as "Offensive Ideas" and "Defensive Thoughts." Jennings, meanwhile, was delighted whenever one of his players even knew who he was; Detroit's Dumars made him feel particularly good because he knew that Jennings had gone to Indiana University. The presence of McHale and Parish on the Eastern team actually made life easier for Ford— neither cared much about playing, and Ford, thinking ahead to the Celtics' remaining thirty-five games, didn't want to play them much. Early in the fourth period, in fact, McHale told Ford to take him out and put Barkley back in the game so that Barkley could go for the game's

MVP award. Ford gladly complied, and Barkley did win the award in the East's 116–114 victory.

Ever the coach, though, Casey couldn't help but notice that Jordan was not terribly good at coming off picks and mentioned something about it during the game to Jennings.

"Why don't you write out a drill for him, Case," said Jennings. "I'm sure you could turn him into a much better player."

The Celtics' contingent chartered back to Boston after the game, just twenty hours before they would be leaving again for the long trip. As Dee Brown and his wife (he and Jill had been married at Wellesley Hills Congregational Church on December 29) said good-bye, a crowd of people rushed them screaming, "DEE! DEE!" Jill broke into tears. Their life together, she realized, would never be the same.

The Celtics' trek West after the All-Star game was a long-standing tradition dictated by scheduling conflicts in Boston Garden. Each February, the Celtics and Bruins had to vacate the premises for a couple weeks, while management leased the building to various ice shows; in February of 1991 it happened to be "Disney on Ice." The trip was an obvious downer if the team was playing poorly, but at times it had its salutary effects too, if only because it got the Celts out of Boston in midwinter and into some warmer weather. In seasons past the Celtics, Bird in particular, had played some of their best ball on that trip, and despite the questions about Bird's back, there was a good feeling in the air. The team was excited about traveling on its own plane, for Gavitt had convinced the owners that the additional cost (about $600,000 over an entire season) of chartering a private plane from MGM Grand was outweighed by the benefits. There would be no more lost time in out-of-town airports, no more cholesterol-laden airport food, no more early-morning wake-up calls in strange hotels, and no more traffic jams en route to Logan Airport in Boston—the charter departed from the more conveniently located Hanscomb Air Force Base in the suburbs. There were things to get used to, though. The night of the trip to New York for the Knicks' game, for example, both Gamble and Lewis had parked their cars in a fortified lot at Hanscomb, and it took them ninety minutes to find the right person to let them out when they returned at about one o'clock the morning after the game.

Ironically, Bird's injury probably made up Gavitt's mind about the plane. There's nothing worse than commercial travel for a person with a bad back, but on the charter Bird had his own queen-sized bed, a medical area where he could get attention, and the luxury to walk around and stretch without being bothered. At least a half-dozen teams had begun chartering on a full- or part-time basis before the Celtics, but it was doubtful that Auerbach would've ever given the okay. He remembered, after all, the days when one Celtics road trip consisted of jumping on an all-night train at Rochester, New York, getting dropped off near a cornfield at dawn, and either hitchhiking or walking the rest of the ten miles into Fort Wayne, Indiana. And that's when his Celtics were world champs.

The plane and Dee Brown's newfound stardom were the major topics of conversation when the Celtics landed in Seattle on February 11 and immediately bused to a local high school for a workout. As Brown and Bird walked in together, a local TV crew immediately mobilized. "There he is!" shouted one, and Bird no doubt inadvertently winced. But, no, they wanted to interview Brown.

"Git ready, Rook," Bird said, laughing. "It's only jest beginnin'."

McHale, meanwhile, said the only one who didn't like the charter flight was ex-Celtic Tommy Heinsohn, the Celtics' broadcaster on SportsChannel. "Five hours without a cigarette and Tom is devastated," McHale said. "His eyes are rolling around in his head by the time we get off the plane. He wanted them to land in, like, Kansas, so he could get a butt." McHale shook his head. "After about the tenth meal on the flight, I turned to a couple guys and said, 'Man, this is really decadent, isn't it?' And they said, 'Why? What's wrong with it?'"

Out on the court, Bird was shooting without visible pain. He claimed to have watched only one quarter of the All-Star game on TV before losing interest and falling asleep. He had, however, seen Chicago's Craig Hodges convert 19 straight three-point shots to win the Long Distance Shootout. Bird had won that event in 1986, 1987, and 1988 and once took great pride in calling himself "The Three-Point King." Bird was asked if he had ever made 19 in a row from three-point range.

"Sheet, you kiddin'?" he said, genuinely offended. "Fifty or sixty maybe. Easy. Many times. Although most of 'em, usually, from the corner. What Hodges did under those circumstances was big time, no doubt about it." He couldn't resist a subtle dig, though. "Kinda tough to shoot like that from the bench, idn't it?" Hodges at the time was getting very little playing time.

After practice, Bird walked over to his physical therapist, Dan Dyrek, who had come along on the trip at the Celtics' expense primarily to work with Bird on a daily basis. Dyrek slipped a cumbersome-looking back brace around Bird's shoulders. So much of the Celtics' hopes and dreams for the season were resting on a guy, who, when not in uniform, wore a back brace. That was how fragile the Celtics' chances for a championship really were.

When the team walked into The Coliseum the following morning at ten A.M., they found that the SuperSonics had just taken the court for their own shootaround and wouldn't be finished until after eleven. Casey had already sent the bus driver to 7-Eleven to get coffee, so the Celtics had nothing to do but stand around the hallway and bust Wayne Lebeaux, the equipment manager/traveling secretary who was responsible for scheduling. Actually, it probably wasn't Lebeaux's fault—The Coliseum was a poorly managed facility and screwups were common—but the facts didn't really matter.

"Actually, I think Wayne's pulling a smart one, Doc," Bird said to Ford. "See, each time you give him a little shit, and you think he's just takin' it, he gits back at you in all these little ways."

The bus finally returned, and after a few phone calls, Lebeaux found out that the Celtics could shoot around at a nearby mental health facility.

"Mental health facility," said Casey, sipping his 7-Eleven coffee. "Thought I was through with this when I left the Clippers."

Ford wanted to get the subject away from Lebeaux and bad scheduling. He wasn't above bustin' the manager from time to time, but it was still early on the trip and much more could go wrong.

"You know who started shootarounds?" asked Ford. "Bill Sharman, with that '72 Laker team that won thirty-three straight."

"A dark day in the NBA," said McHale. "A very dark day."

"Hey, Kevin, I've been meaning to ask you," said Casey, "what did it feel like to have some real coaching during the All-Star game?"

"Gee, real exciting, Case," said McHale. " 'Course I been there seven times before. Whereas it was like the highlight of your life to date."

Casey ignored him. "Yup, first time it's been more than a playground game," he said.

"I really didn't notice, Case," said McHale, " 'cause it's really not that important. Somehow I don't think my gravestone will say: 'He was a member of a victorious Eastern Conference All-Star team.' "

The mental health facility was adequate, though the side walls were extremely close to the court. During the postpractice shootaround, Smith and Gamble glanced at Ford, then immediately began trying to bank shots off the wall and into a side basket. Smith took pride in his ability to convert trick shots; it was about all he had left to distinguish himself as a Celtic. The players were still bustin' Lebeaux when they boarded the bus to return to the hotel.

"It's all right, guys," said Ford, trying to smooth things over. "We're right about on schedule."

"I tell you what, Doc," twanged Bird from the back. "You're gittin' awful mellow in half a year. Bill Fitch woulda chewed his ass out good."

The team, said Ford when he got off the bus, seemed awful loose. "I think that's a good sign," he said. "We've had an awful tough three weeks."

McHale was in a reflective mood as he sat down on the Celtics bench an hour before the Seattle game. He asked a reporter for his impressions of Bird's physical condition based upon the previous night's practice session.

"Thought he looked okay," said the reporter.

"I think he looked a little stiff," said McHale. "But you know what? He'll be all right. He knows all these people are here to see him. He has a sense of that, even if he'd never admit it. It motivates him. I think we look at the road the same way—as a chance to come into somebody else's building and bust 'em. I know I still feel that way. And when you do it, it's the greatest feeling in the world."

McHale's opinions on Bird were, as usual, right on the money. The constant mental burden of *being Larry Bird* bothered Bird at home, where he stayed away from commitments and quite frequently ducked out on the press at Boston Garden, but the road seemed to liberate him. There were new faces, new routines, new hotel coffee shops, maybe a Tony Roma's rib house around the corner. Bird would frequently stiff the press at home, then talk for an hour to a reporter from a remote newspaper in the state of Washington during a road trip. He was generally in better spirits out on the road, too, sometimes going to elaborate extremes to pull off a practical joke. When Quinn Buckner was with the Celts in the early eighties, everyone would kid him about looking like an ape. (It went over only because Buckner was an extremely popular player.) During one road trip in Los Angeles, Bird arranged for the team bus to take a detour past a local car dealership. There, wearing a CELTICS 28 jersey, Buckner's number, was a giant plastic ape. Working with Lebeaux, Bird had set the whole thing up.

"Something's really going to go out of this franchise when Larry leaves," continued McHale, bouncing a ball at his feet. "And, I guess, to a lesser extent, Robert and me, too. But mostly Larry. They're really going to lack a guy like that, somebody who's got that something special, you know? Every good team really has to have one. Magic in L.A., Larry here, Charles in Philly. I really believe Reggie, Brian, and

Dee are going to be good. Real good. But they're going to need that other element, that element of toughness, something special."

McHale's dark eyes scanned the court, stopping to focus on Vrankovic.

"You know who it could be?" he said. "Stojko. Maybe. I'm completely serious. There are so few guys in this league potentially—and I emphasize 'potentially'—who can do what he can do. Seven three with jumping ability and an all-around athlete? Come on. But he needs to play a lot more minutes than we can give him if he's going to improve. What we need to do is trade him to Orlando for a couple years, then get him back, like a farm system. He's got one unstoppable move—that sky hook." Just then Stojko launched a hook from short range that clanged against the rim.

"Well," said McHale, "it might not happen, after all."

He looked over and saw Shaw and Brown schmoozing with Seattle rookie Gary Payton, a point guard against whom they would both soon be testing their skills.

"We never used to talk to guys before the game," said McHale. "Yeah, I'm known for being friendly and all that, and I do some talking, but not when I was young and never to a guy I was going against. You kind of went by and maybe said, 'How ya' doin'?' to kind of psyche him out."

He pointed at Dee. "That dunk contest will be great for that kid because the one thing he lacked was confidence. I know Dee looks confident on the outside, but you can tell the way he hangs his head out there once in a while that he isn't completely confident. He talks it, but he doesn't walk it. I don't know what it was with guys like Larry and me—maybe we were sick or something—but we didn't go through that. I know Larry didn't and I know I didn't. I felt like every single night I was out there, I was better than the other guy. Even when I was a rookie. I remember the first time I went up against Wes Unseld, a true legend, an all-timer. Now, he was at the end of his career, so maybe he would've thrown me around like a sack of feathers a few years earlier, but he meant nothing to me. Nothing. I respected him as a player, but I didn't feel for one second like he was better than me. And you know what? He wasn't."

Casey ambled by and McHale's mood lightened. "You know how they shot in Case's day?" he said. "Like this." He dribbled out to the court and released an awkward-looking two-handed set, kicking up his left leg in the process. "That's a Don Casey set shot." Casey shook his head. "What I want to know is," said Casey, "you ever give up?"

Lebeaux, meanwhile, was reading a strange note that a fan had just handed to him. " 'Kandy Johnson, Section 24C, Row 13, Seat 1, would like to meet Larry Bird and the team before tonight's game,' " Lebeaux read. " 'If this is possible, please get a message to that section. Thanks for your help.' " Lebeaux had never seen the man before and didn't know a Kandy Johnson. It was an extraordinary request, presented as it was so matter-of-factly, as if total strangers were routinely ushered in to meet the team. Bird was in the locker room getting pregame treatment from Dyrek when he read the note. "Sure, no problem," said Bird. "Bring her on in. Maybe her whole family, too. We really got nuthin' else to do."

Late in the third period McHale suddenly emerged from a pack of players, hobbling pell-mell across the court toward the Celtics bench, having turned his left ankle badly. Lacerte led him into the dressing room—"Oh no, not again," was Ford's initial reaction—and McHale's absence in the fourth period stalled Boston's attack. The Celtics led by only one point with a couple minutes left when Bird took a typically nervy three-point shot that went in and put the Celtics up by four. But Eddie Johnson, a one-on-one specialist who is sometimes without peer in putting points on the board rapidly, hit two improbable three-point shots in the final minute and the Celtics led by just 112–111 with twelve seconds left. Boston inbounded to Bird, who was immediately fouled. The place was a din. Johnson stood behind Bird and waved to the crowd, imploring them to yell even louder, which they did. They were wasting their breath. Bird swished the first, then the second, and the Celts held on.

"I learned a long time ago to drain out crowd noise," said Bird after the game. "I don't hear it. I didn't feel that comfortable at the line because I hadn't shot many free throws recently. But I'd rather have me at that line than anybody else." He smiled, but he meant it too.

Lewis and Shaw, meanwhile, discussed an awe-inspiring Shawn Kemp dunk, on which he had taken off from just in front of the free-throw line, soared over several players, and jammed the ball into the hoop.

"Never saw anything like it," said Shaw. "Absolutely big time."

"Yeah," said Dee slyly, "about three days too late, though."

Spirits were high as the Celtics boarded a bus at their Fisherman's Wharf hotel on February 13, the day before Game 2 of the trip, for a workout at the University of San Francisco. Most NBA teams stayed in San Francisco even though the Golden State Warriors played their games across the bridge in Oakland. Besides the difference in ambience, NBA officials shied away from Oakland hotels, where many a player had fallen off the cocaine wagon in the eighties. A few seasons ago, when one NBA team had a game against the Lakers in L.A. on Saturday night and a game at Golden State on Tuesday, the coach elected to spend all day Sunday and Monday in L.A. "I'd rather have my players screw themselves half to death in L.A. than spend a couple extra hours in Oakland," he reasoned.

The $20,000 Dee Brown earned for winning the Slam-Dunk contest had become the hottest topic of conversation among team members.

"Dee, you get that money yet?" Parish shouted at him as Brown made his way down the aisle. Whether bound for practices or games, Chief was customarily in his seat, all the way in the back, at least ten minutes before anyone else. Generally, he sat quietly, but if he had anyone to pick off, he was in prime position to do so.

"No, not yet," said Dee. "They might've sent the check home."

"Sheet," twanged Bird. "I always made sure I got mine. Pick it up right there, so they don't go sendin' it someplace else."

"Well, I'm gonna call home today, see if it got there," said Brown.

"Uh oh," said Chief. "Check went home. Check went to the crib. Call off that party, boys, check went to the crib. It's over. Done. Spent."

Up in the front of the bus, meanwhile, Lebeaux was in trouble again—the bus driver was having a hard time finding his way through the confusing streets of San Francisco to the gym.

"Wayne, oh, Wayne," shouted Bird. "I think I've seen every part of San Francisco. Is this a tour, or we goin' to practice?"

Finally, Shaw, a native of nearby Oakland, went to the front of the bus and directed it to the gym. Lebeaux's face was red.

"Uh oh," said Bird. "Wayne's losin' his power."

Later, Lebeaux brought coffee to the coaching staff (which Bird was starting to call "the brain trust"), and Bird spotted him.

"Hey, Wayne, we could use some orange juice," twanged Bird. " 'Course we're only players, not the brain trust."

"Orange juice?" said Lebeaux. "That's why they have a coffee shop."

"Listen, better wipe that stuff off your nose, Wayne," said Bird.

"Don't answer him," interrupted Casey. "That's what those country hicks want you to do."

"Hey, watch it now, Case," said Kleine. "We got a couple country hicks here." Kleine hails from Slater, Missouri, which Kleine described as a *"Last Picture Show* type of town."

After practice, the two country hicks adjourned to the coffee shop of the Celtics' Fisherman's Wharf hotel for lunch. The weather was warm and sunny, and Bird's back felt terrific. He ate Mexican food and talked about his disappointment with the Celtics' play in the home game against Golden State nearly four weeks earlier. "Won't happen agin," he said. He glanced outside and spotted Shaw, bag slung over his shoulder, heading to his parents' house in Oakland for a brief visit.

"Hey, Brian!" shouted Bird out an open window. "Goin' back to Italy?"

McHale's ankle sprain was a lot worse than everyone originally believed. "The Lord giveth," said Ford, glancing at Bird, then at McHale, "and the Lord taketh away." McHale had spent almost every minute of his time in San Francisco getting treatment from Lacerte, then slipping into an awkward-looking compression boot that alternated ice, electrical stimulation, and intermittent pressure to try and reduce the swelling. "*Quigley Down Under,* with Tom Selleck, on the in-room movie service was the highlight of my trip so far," said McHale, lying on the training table in the visitors' locker room at the Oakland Coliseum Arena. Dyrek energetically manipulated the ankle, literally trying to massage the blood out of the area, and McHale winced. Dyrek called the process "tissue mobilization." "Well, I call it pain," said McHale. "Reminds me of the time Walton insisted that we go get rolfed, that painful, deep-muscle massage. It hurt so bad I almost rolfed myself."

The Warriors' Hardaway, the coulda'-been-a-Celtic point guard, gave Shaw fits early in the game and Ford really went after him. "You're backing down!" Ford shouted. "You're being a pussy!"

Shaw came back at him during a time-out. "I'm not backing down. I'm no pussy!" The normal Shaw composure was gone, and Ford loved it. Shaw played better from then on, getting key relief help on Hardaway too, from Brown's lower-to-the-ground defensive posture. Even Eddie Pinckney helped out with a hellacious brand of defense on Mitch Richmond. In shredding the Warriors' halfcourt trap, the Celtics moved the ball better than at any time since the 1985–86 championship season, zipping it from one player to another without even a dribble, and at one point Bird shook his fist in the air, shouting, "Attaway, Pinckney!" It was meaningful, for Bird rarely directed praise at him. A big three-pointer by Bird with 6:15 left gave Boston a 106–93 lead and they coasted to a 128–112 victory from there. Ford still hadn't cleared his bench late in the game, and the Warriors' Mullin, mildly irritated, asked Casey, as he took the ball out of bounds near the Celtics bench: "How many you guys want to win by?"

"Sorry, Chris," said Casey. "We have a clause in our contract for margin of victory."

After the game, Parish just couldn't let the Ford-Shaw exchange go by. The veterans had taken to calling Shaw and Brown "Chris's sons," for they believed, halfheartedly anyway, that Ford was easy on them.

"One of your son's talking back, Doc," said Parish, his deep bass cutting through the locker room noise. "Either take his car keys or ground him, one or the other."

Shaw smiled. Ford smiled. The Celtics were 2–0 on the trip, 37–12 overall, the second best record in the NBA behind Portland's 40–9. McHale was hurt, but Bird was healthy and happy. It was easy to smile.

It was Jon Jennings's assignment the day before the Lakers game to hoof it from the Los Angeles Airport Marriott over to the National car rental booth at the airport. Casey was determined to take Ford down to the Little Tokyo area of Los Angeles for a massage. Jennings wanted no part of it. "More of that L.A. shit," he said. Nevertheless, he was glad that Ford was getting out of his room. "He's the Howard Hughes of coaches," said Jennings. "One day he's going to show up with his hair down to his shoulders and start drawing plays on the board with his fingernails." Jennings's decision not to make the trip was a wise one— Casey got lost driving around Little Tokyo and, when they showed up a half hour late, the masseuse told them they were out of luck. Boston Celtics? She didn't care.

Schedules, schedules, schedules. The Celtics' bus bound for the Forum and that night's game with the Lakers sat in front of the Marriott, idling away, while everyone waited for Pinckney.

"All right, who was supposed to bring Eddie down?" Ford said.

Actually, Pinckney was usually the least of the coachs' worries. It was SOP on the road for Pinckney and Kleine to cab it over to the arena a couple hours before their teammates to get in some extra work. But Pinckney had decided to take a nap before this game and he had overslept.

"One-fifty, Pinckney," said Bird, when Pinckney sheepishly ambled onto the bus, ten minutes late. "Cash."

Ford was trying to be angry, although his heart really wasn't in it. "Did you hear me this morning in the meeting when I said five-thirty?"

Before Pinckney could respond, Bird yelled from the back of the bus: "I'm sorry, what was that, Doc? We couldn't hear you back here."

"I said, 'Did you hear me in the meeting when I said five-thirty?' "

"Yes sir," said Bird in a schoolboy tone. "We all heard you. I don't know about Eddie, but we all heard you."

With the trading deadline fast approaching, NBA news was a hot topic.

"I was talking to my agent, and he heard a deal on his speaker phone," said Smith. "Milwaukee sent Ricky Pierce to Seattle for Dale Ellis."

"I can't believe that," said Bird.

"What? The trade?" said Smith. "I can't believe it, either."

"No," said Bird, "I can't believe *your* agent has a speaker phone."

Though they were in enemy territory, the Celtics were obviously more prepared for the Lakers than they had been without Bird two weeks earlier in Boston Garden. McHale was again out of action, but Bird took such an obvious joy in playing the Lakers that the feeling seemed to be contagious. Everyone was up. Steve Bulpett recalled a sublime moment a few years earlier when Bird, dressing alone in the Forum locker room, suddenly sang, almost to himself, "We're playin' the Lakers, we're playin' the Lakers." Though his rivalry with Magic had lost some of its appeal to the fans, Bird seemed to appreciate it, or, at least, enjoy it, more than ever. Early in his career, the competition with Magic and the Lakers had been so intense that Bird was never really able to step back and objectively consider what their joint effect had been on the game. He tired of the subject quickly, just as, say, Chris Evert and Martina Navratilova never enjoyed talking about each other while they were the two best players in the world. But time had provided perspective, and when he was asked about Magic before the Lakers game, he warmed to the subject.

"I've never seen nobody as good as him," said Bird, ungrammatically but sincerely. "And there'll probably be nobody down the road as good as him. There's other guys who will come along who can score and rebound. But there probably won't be anybody who can control a game like he does.

"It's amazing when you think back to the years when it was always us and them in the Finals. We kind of took it for granted. I don't think it's that way anymore. I think we appreciate what we had. The Finals is what we're working for. It would be a big accomplishment for us, no matter who we got in against. But it'd be sort of nice to get to play the Lakers agin. That'd be fun, me and Magic agin."

Bird and Magic sensed that they were the only two members of a very, very special NBA club—those players who had won championships and MVP awards throughout the eighties and were still active and productive. Julius Erving was gone, Kareem Abdul-Jabbar was gone, and Michael Jordan still hadn't won the big one. Membership in that club mandated praise of the other member. It was part of the ritual. Their mutual admiration society was not phony in any way, because Bird and Magic could still play the game, but it was not without its nostalgic element, either. The best player in the NBA was clearly Jordan, not Magic, but Bird would not admit it. Magic was his choice, he said. And why not? Together they had forged an identity for themselves and for the NBA that bound them together for eternity. Bird and Magic, Magic and Bird. A few weeks before the second Celtics-Lakers game, *Sports Illustrated* had been working on a story about the NBA stars who would be playing for the United States in the 1992 Olympics. Magic would not consent to pose for the cover photo unless Bird was also on the team. Informed that Bird had said he had no interest in playing in the Olympics, Magic still insisted on a few dozen rounds of phone calls to determine that Bird would not be offended if he, Magic, appeared in the photo. Bird could've cared less— and Magic probably knew that—but club ties were strong, the ritual inviolate.

The story of the Celtics-Lakers game on February 15 was not Bird or Magic, however. It was Parish. Written on the blackboard in the Lakers' locker room before the game was the Celtics' starting lineup with "Parish" spelled as "Parrish." ("Pinckney" was spelled as "Pickney," too.) "Some things never change, do they?" said Chief when a reporter stopped by to tell him. He didn't seem angry or upset—he had seen his name spelled with two r's about a thousand times over the years—but inside he was indeed unusually fired up for the game. The Lakers' Divac had been quoted a couple days earlier as saying the game against the Celtics was "an exhibition," and he made a few other comments suggesting that the Celtics did not present the stiffest of opposition. Jennings made sure that the team, Parish in particular, was aware of the story. Such motivational gimmicks were usually pooh-poohed by Bird, McHale, and the other veterans, but they were, in fact, quite common in the NBA. Teams in need of firing up often turned the most innocent comments into fierce challenges, altering the context and scope of mildly negative articles so drastically that, by game day, no one had any idea what was actually said but they knew it was *real bad*. Then, too, Divac, was a great target. He was young, unproven, foreign, and he had his own commercial to boot. Parish had a terse response when Jennings told him about Divac.

"Well, *fuck* Vlade Divac," said the Chief.

And then he went out and did it. Parish scored an incredible 21 points in the first period, forcing Lakers coach Mike Dunleavy to remove Divac halfway through the period and install backup Mychal Thompson, who fared no better. Considering Parish's age and disinclination to carry the scoring load, the performance defied belief. It was like Bird scoring, say, 35 in one period, or McHale getting 30. It did, in fact, take something out of Parish for the next two periods, but he returned with a vengeance in the fourth, grabbing key rebounds and shutting down Divac, who, besides a spectacular reverse dunk off a fast-break pass from Magic, had just an average game. "Vlade got his reverse dunk," said McHale after the game, "and Robert got 29." Bird had his troubles with Worthy, an underrated defensive player, and took at least a half-dozen of the worst shots known to man, off-balance left-handers, leaning half-hooks from eighteen feet, trash that even Bird couldn't convert into points. Yet with 4:56 left, he came down on the left wing, stopped at least a foot and a half behind the three-point line, and launched a high rainbow set shot that swished. It gave the Celtics a 10-point lead and, in typical fashion, the L.A. crowd began to file out.

"They're flying out of here like it's the Ali Rashad Hotel and air raid sirens are going off," said Don Greenberg who covers the Lakers for the *Orange County Register.*

Actually, the star of the 98–85 victory was Lewis, who had 26 points and zero turnovers, but after the game all he could talk about was Bird. "How about that three-pointer Lahr-ree took?" said Lewis, using his rather strange pronunciation of Bird's first name. "Like all great ball players, he always does something. No matter how bad he's been shooting, he does something." Inside, perhaps, Lewis wondered if he could be that type of player someday. Bird was not, in the strictest sense, a "pure shooter," a term that described more of a standstill, practice-time shooter. Former Indiana University great Steve Alford was a pure shooter, for example, but only a marginal NBA player. To be a "great shooter" in the NBA was kind of like being a "great putter" on the PGA tour; it was less a compliment than a veiled critique, a description of a player who didn't do the difficult things, like scoring off offensive rebounds or hitting a 230-yard two iron into the wind. To Lewis, Bird was respected not because of his shooting ability but because of his *cajones*, his insistence on taking the big shot and making it when the game was on the line.

Working the room after the game were a number of Hollywood types, Kevin Costner foremost among them. With a slew of Academy Award nominations for *Dances With Wolves,* Costner was absolutely the brightest star in the Hollywood sky at the time, yet one sensed his shyness when he went over to introduce himself to Bird. They shook hands and talked for only a moment before Bird got up to leave.

"Hey, Kevin!" McHale shouted to Costner.

"Oh, hi, Kevin," Costner said, making his way to McHale's corner.

"Saw 'Dances,' man," said McHale. "It was great."

"I appreciate that," said Costner.

"I've never seen a better cinemagraphic depiction of South Dakota," said McHale.

The conversation continued in that vein for ten minutes, by which time Bird was sitting impatiently on the bus, ready to return to the hotel and a postgame meal in the coffee shop.

"Let's get this going," Bird said. "If we lost, we'd a been outta here a half hour ago." He got to his feet and looked out the window. "Sheet, even Joe Kleine's out there, looking for stars. Joe Kleine!"

McHale climbed on the bus just as Ford was saying good-bye to Sister Filomena Conte, his fifth grade teacher back at St. Michael's, who was now living in L.A.

"That's your old teacher, Doc?" said McHale. He ran to a window and began banging on it. "Whoa, Sister, hey," McHale yelled. "You should hear all the cussin' Chris does on the bench. You'd be ashamed of him now."

The good sister continued walking. Perhaps she had heard about McHale.

"I guess you were really impressed with that movie," Ordway said to McHale as the bus headed back to the hotel.

"What movie?" said McHale.

"Costner's movie, *Dances With Wolves*," said Ordway.

"Oh, that," said McHale. "Tell you the truth, I didn't see it."

Casey took a large contingent, including his family, Ford, and Jennings, to Spago, the trendy West Hollywood restaurant presided over by celebrity chef Wolfgang Puck, whom Casey had gotten to know during his Clippers years. They ate and drank and ogled celebrities far into the night, as Casey proclaimed: "We're at the power table, the *Streisand* table." Dining nearby was *Chicago Tribune* critic Gene Siskel, best known for his syndicated movie-review show with Roger Ebert.

"I remember you with the Clippers," Siskel told Casey. "I thought you did a great job."

"Hey, I appreciate that," said Casey. "Thanks." Casey then turned back to the table and whispered, "Which one's he?"

Dee Brown walked into the Marriott hotel in Denver to find his wife waiting for him. Larry Bird walked in to find "the Golden Girls" waiting for him. It had only been a week since Brown had won the Slam-Dunk contest, but Jill had already felt the strain of Dee's sudden fame. Dee was glad to see her. Ford was not, for wives on the road were considered a taboo in the NBA. But Ford considered the circumstances—their age, the changing circumstances, and the fact that the Celtics were playing well—and decided not to get on Brown about it.

Bird checked in, put his bags in his room, and came back downstairs to see the Golden Girls—Bonnie Brown, Donna Rossow, Lenore

Goehring, and Joyce Tisdall, all of whom were pushing sixty. They had
first gotten interested in Bird through Brown's son, Scott, who lived in
Indiana and worshipped Bird from afar. One of them lives in Denver, so
the other three decided to make the 650-mile drive from Mobridge,
South Dakota, to see him play against the Nuggets six years ago. As
they checked into their downtown hotel, they ran into Bird and basically, according to Bonnie, "just attacked him." It was one of those
happy twists of fate for the Golden Girls, because they caught Bird in a
good mood, and he stayed and talked to them for an hour. Actually, it
was not so far out of character. Just as Bird was friendlier with Joe Q.
than with McHale, and more likely to hang out with Brad Lohaus than
Magic Johnson, so was he more inclined to give his time and friendship
to a foursome of older women than to the retinue of glad-handers and
autograph-seekers who hounded the Celtics on the road.

Bird and the Golden Girls shared a table in the downstairs lounge for
over an hour, talking about Larry's fishing, Larry's favorite grandmother, and Larry's wife, who just a few days earlier had mailed each
of them a new pair of sneakers in anticipation of their visit to Denver.
Dozens of other fans came by and hung at the periphery of the group,
wondering if they would be asked in, then drifted away when it became
obvious that Bird was paying them no mind. Finally, he got up to leave.

"Gotta do some runnin'," said Bird. "I'll see ya all before the game."

"Okay, Larry," they said. "Get a good night's sleep, and we'll see you
tomorrow."

By this time a group of male Celtics fans sitting nearby was absolutely apoplectic with jealousy. Two of them, Neal Carlson, a farmer,
and John Krivohlavek, an elementary school principal, had driven
seven hours from Minden, Nebraska, to get to Denver for the Celtics
game, a ritual they had observed every year since Bird came into the
league.

"Why does he talk to you?" said one of the men. "He won't even look
at us. We're big fans too."

"Because he likes us and we don't threaten him," said Donna
Rossow. "And you know what he said? When he's through playing we
can visit him in Indiana too."

About the only reason to have been watching the Denver Nuggets on
February 17, 1991, was to see their waterbug point guard, Michael
Adams, in action. And when the Celtics came to town he was sidelined
with an injury.

"I don't care if he plays or not," said Dee Brown, when someone
mentioned Adams's quickness and three-point shooting ability.

"Hey, I admit I'm glad he's not playing," said Shaw.

"Well, I know three people who's glad he's not playing," said Bird. He pointed to Lewis and Shaw, who would've had to guard Adams, then to Ford, who would've had to figure out a way to stop him. "I know they don't pay me enough to chase him around."

Bird was antsy to get going. He sensed a big game coming, which was only logical, since Denver didn't have anybody to guard anybody, far less Bird. With the Golden Girls cheering him on from their prime seats under the basket, Bird came out firing. He hit his first four shots and finished the first period with 17 points. It was a joke. Half the time he looked over at the bench while his shot was in the air, his disdain for his opponents evident in the smirk on his face. The Nuggets were so bad that in the third period Michael Smith took a Nuggets free throw out of the basket and pitched it the length of the court to Pinckney for an uncontested dunk, a defensive lapse rarely made even by elementary-school teams. All that remained was comic relief and, true to form, Kleine provided it when a loose ball that was batted around at least five times ricocheted off his face. Everyone cracked up. By that time, McHale, in street clothes, was eating a slice of pizza at the end of the bench. "When I saw that," Adams said, "I know they were showing us a lack of respect." The final score was 126–108. Bird had a game-high 24 points in just twenty-five minutes. The Golden Girls had a good time. And the Celtics were 4–0 on the trip. Without Kevin McHale.

The following day, McHale's attention was fixed upon a sign in the Jewish Community Center gymnasium in Phoenix, the Celtics' final stop on the trip. It said: NO HANGING ON RIMS.

"Hey, Mike," he called to Mike Fine, who is Jewish. "See what you make of this sign." Fine read it. "Now, Mike, is this a big problem?" McHale asked. "Somehow I think The Springing Jew is somewhat of a dying breed, don't you? Can't you hear them out there saying, 'Oy, vay, how the boy can jump.' "

Ford was trying to keep the Celtics focused on a fifth straight win, which was almost unprecedented on an NBA road trip, and so he worked them hard. Popson started the scrimmage by hitting a hook shot over Bird, which prompted Bird to demand the ball, dribble back upcourt, and immediately launch a three-point shot over Popson.

"Three-two," shouted Bird, as he released the shot and watched it settle into the basket, "I'm up." Over the next five minutes the "white team," the starters, punished the "green team," and Brown grew frustrated over his inability to get anything going. Ford hollered at him and Brown came right back.

"Uh oh, father-son," said Bird. "They're at it agin." He dribbled over to the assembled media (Ford had stopped closing practice, a sure sign that the trip was going well) and said: "This is why they don't want you guys in here. To see this ass-kickin' we put on 'em every day." He looked at Kleine, who was changing from a green into a white jersey. "See, Doc's feelin' so sorry for Joe that he had to put 'em on the other team."

It was a bad day for the autograph hounds outside of the JCC too. Most of them were adults and Bird was feeling frisky.

"Excuse me, but don't you have a job?" he said to one, who tagged along, demanding that he sign after Bird first refused.

"You know, the Marines are looking for a few good men," he said to another, "maybe yer one of 'em."

He finally made it onto the bus and flopped down on his seat. Obnoxious autograph-seekers have become an increasing problem in sports, particularly to athletes like Bird, whose signature is valuable on the open market. It had become nearly impossible for Bird to distinguish the young fan who sincerely wanted his autograph from the money-hungry trader, who just wanted to collect as many "Larry Birds" as possible. When Brad Lohaus was with the team, he would sign many of Bird's autographs because Bird would insist, "No, I'm telling you, *he's* Larry Bird." Bird had an excellent memory for faces, too, and would often surprise a traveling autograph-seeker with a refusal. "I jist signed for you in Denver," he'd say, and the hound would stare at him wide-eyed. His favorite off-the-court moment of the trip had occurred while he was talking with the Golden Girls in Denver. A group of autograph pros whom Bird had already turned down enlisted the help of a female guest to get Bird's autograph. It was a common practice, and Bird had detected it. So when the woman asked him to sign, he did so but convinced her to go out a side exit and keep the card for herself. Lately, Bird had taken to signing the name of "Pete Rose" on his cards from time to time. "But Doc made me stop when I signed it on the team photos," he said.

Bird hated the hypocrisy of the whole autograph game.

"These guys, most of 'em, will say, 'Hey, Larry, you're the greatest,' and when I don't sign three of 'em, they'll turn around and say, "Motherfucker. Asshole. Piece of shit. Hey, what an asshole Larry Bird is.' I hate it when somebody comes up to me when we're out of town and I sign for him, and then he says, 'You know, we're gonna' kick your ass tonight.' Why does he say 'we'? I always ask the guy, 'How many baskets did you score?' "

When the Celtics arrived back at the hotel, a contingent of Smith, Pinckney, Popson, and Vrankovic left for a nearby arcade for a round of miniature golf and various other time-killing recreations. Kleine, who was waiting to go for ribs with Bird, watched the group with amusement.

"McHale and I figured out why Michael is so good at games," said Kleine. "Miniature golf, shooting games, video games, things like that. See, Mormons had to spend all their dates in places like arcades and amusement parks because they were afraid to be alone with their girlfriends in case things got, you know, out of hand. That's why they're always real good in that stuff. Anyway, that's our theory, and we're sticking with it."

Later that afternoon, Bird sat—or "set," as he would put it—in the lobby of the Westcourt Hotel in Phoenix, enjoying the day off, enjoying being Larry Bird, enjoying being the sine qua non of a potential championship team, something he had not been in a few years. He adjusted himself repeatedly on a couch, trying to find a comfortable position. His back felt relatively good on the court, particularly after a few minutes of action had warmed it up, but in his private moments, at home or in a hotel room, he constantly had to change positions, lying on the floor for a few minutes, then standing, then sitting, then leaning against a wall. He had stopped going to the movies on the road because he couldn't sit comfortably and didn't want to keep getting up. By the stop in Phoenix, it seemed as if Bird had turned a corner with his back problems. No longer could he hope that they would work themselves out. He had been through a month of hell, and there was no guarantee it was over yet. When the word "surgery" was mentioned, he didn't pooh-pooh it, as he used to. He knew it was a definite possibility, both to continue playing and to have a productive life after basketball.

"There were a couple days there I wanted to quit 'cause it hurt so bad," Bird admitted. "The pain was gone on down my right leg, and I said, 'The hell with it. Ain't worth it.' I was settin' there at home, jest thinkin' and thinkin', 'Why are you doin' it?' But, then, I also started thinkin', 'Look, yer prolly gonna have this thing the rest of yer life, in some form, anyway.' " Bird used to joke that he wanted to be the fattest man driving out of Boston when he stopped playing, but like many athletes near the end of their careers, he had had a change of heart. Injuries and wear and tear had made him feel more like a normal human being, a mortal, and he didn't particularly enjoy it. He liked his body when it was in tune and humming, and he wanted to keep that feeling in civilian life.

"I think I wanna be active," said Bird. "What I might do, though, is git in shape, git outta shape, then git in shape again. I won't do it like I used to, though. It's gittin' tougher. Three years ago I could lose fifteen pounds like nuthin'. Now? I don't know if I could." He had put on a few pounds when he was out of action, but he wasn't sure how many. "I was so bored, I'd set around the house, drive my wife crazy, and eat and eat. In two and a half weeks I was off I ate ten gallons of ice cream and seven weddin' cakes. Why them? I ate weddin' cakes 'cause you knew they was gonna be good. I mean, who would fuck up a weddin' cake?" That was Bird philosophy at its most crystalline.

The conversation turned to his future. "Never thought about coachin', and I'm not sure I'd be patient enough for it. The one thing I know I'll do is go on a fishing tour for a year. Maybe play some golf, but that's it. Let my body heal up and figger out what I wanna do with the rest of my life." He smiled. "I already know that, though. I'd like to fish every day. I'd never git tired of it. Why would I have to do anythin' else? I bin playin' basketball for twenty-some years, and that hasn't changed. It could be the same with fishin'. Exactly the same." Bird's only other summer activity besides fishing and golf was home repair. The preceding summer he had built fences, helped on a tennis court addition, laid brick, did some concrete work and some roofing. "I couldn't lay everythin' out, but I could do jest about all the work," he said. "I enjoyed it. I don' live for it, like I live for fishin', but I like it."

His reverie led him to a familiar subject—the respect he had for Parish and the departed Dennis Johnson. He began talking about them with emotion that was, for Bird, close to outright passion. "Ever'body knew when we needed a basket D. J. passed me the ball and I came off a pick set by Robert, who sets the best pick in the world. I don' know how he does it. Now I don' come off those picks as much because that's not our offense. But if it wasn't for Robert, I wouldn't have scored half the points I have. Does he resent me? I'm sure pret-a-near ever'body has a lil resentment toward me. Jesus Christ, they're out there working their asses off and all you hear is, 'Larry Bird's in town' or 'Larry Bird and the Celtics are here.' I never talked about it with 'em, but what kin I do about it? I'm not gonna quit playin' as hard as I kin because I git publicity." He smiled widely. "Robert and I are talking about playing in Europe together. That'd be pretty neat, I think. Be a change, make a little money, have some fun." Imagine Larry Bird in Europe, a man of simple tastes, searching for a thick steak, a baseball game on the tube, teammates who moved without the ball. But he seemed serious.

Dee Brown had had an interesting trip. Virtually every day his agent, Steve Zucker, had called him with some offer that had come in since that fateful day when he pumped up his sneakers. "It was just like the first morning after Jim McMahon and the Bears won the Super Bowl," said Zucker. Someone wanted him to run a dunking clinic in Spain. In Denver, the Nuggets mascot, a mountain lion, put on a blindfold to simulate Brown's blind dunk and splattered himself on the blackboard. The night before the Phoenix game, a man awakened him at three o'clock in the morning to ask if he could have his sneakers after the game. Later that night, Brown had to laugh as he watched Phoenix's nonpareil mascot, The Gorilla, pump up a pair of Reeboks for still another impersonation.

The team that the Celtics met on February 19 was one with serious chemistry problems; the day before, the Suns had held an unprecedented four-hour meeting. The Celtics found that rather amusing, particularly Bird, who had a quick diagnosis of their condition: "Shoot, Kevin Johnson is the point guard, and he's takin' all these shots, and that means Chambers ain't gettin' his, and he's mad, and then McDaniel wants his, and, shoot, there you are. The only sane one on the team is [center] Mark West." The Suns' Kurt Rambis, an NBA veteran, was a little sheepish about the length of the meeting, and later described it as "a half-hour meeting and three-and-a-half hours of porno films." Nevertheless, the Suns did approach the Celtics game with a playoff-type intensity and erased an early 12-point Boston advantage to lead by 107–105 with about one minute left. At that point, Bird came down on a controlled fast-break, pulled up at the three-point line, missed, and the Celtics went on to lose 109–105. It was the eternal debate with Bird. On the one hand, he should not have shot the ball. On the other hand, he had made clutch three-pointers against Seattle, Golden State, and the Lakers, as well as three others in the Denver game. What is a bad shot for Larry Bird, one that doesn't go in? "It's a real, real tough call," said Casey, who generally had an instant opinion on everything. "He's done it so many times, but certainly you wouldn't want anyone else shooting that shot. There wasn't anyone under the basket. It wasn't a best-case scenario, put it that way." Actually, Bird had had an atrocious evening all the way around, making only 5 of 23 shots from the floor. All that had stood between the Celtics and a perfect 5–0 road trip had been Bird's shooting. "What do I think?" said Bird with a shrug. "I think I shot bad. But who knows? Maybe next game I'll take 25 shots."

How quickly things could change in the NBA. Jennings stood at courtside before the Celtics' game against the Bulls at Chicago Arena on February 26 and considered the circumstances. McHale was still out. Bird's back was starting to bother him again and was obviously affecting his shooting form—he had averaged only 30 percent from the field over the last three games. Two days earlier the Celtics had blown a 17-point lead in the last eleven minutes at Indiana and lost

115–109, hardly the mark of a confident team. The Bulls, on the other
hand, had won 9 in a row, 18 straight at home, and were just one-half
game behind the Celtics for the best record in the East. And who the
hell was going to guard Michael Jordan? Outside the arena, it had
started to snow.

"Can you win, Jon?" Jennings was asked.

"Tonight?" he said. "No way."

It was simply life in the NBA. Some games are losers from the
moment a team checks into a hotel, and this was one of them. In the
locker room, there was a kind of let's-get-it-over-with feeling. Shaw
was laughing about a skit on "In Living Color" in which comedian
Tommy Davidson talked about the proclivity of black singers to offer
overly long and stylized renditions of the national anthem before sporting events. A half-hour later, Shaw was nearly paralyzed with laughter,
as a young, black female singer took three minutes and forty seconds,
possibly a world record, to get through "The Star-Spangled Banner." It
was the last humorous moment for the Celtics, who were never in the
game. In the first period, the Bulls' Scottie Pippen saved a ball from
going out of bounds by throwing it directly into Parish's groin area.
"Boools-eye" is the way Chief later described the shot. Chicago led 74–
48 at halftime, 105–69 late in the game, and 129–99 when it was all
over. Ford worried about the effect the loss might have on his young
players. "Our young guys are very fragile," he said. "Chicago stepped it
up a notch, and we weren't ready. We didn't respond. They might think
they're ready to contend for a title, but they're not." But it wasn't only
the young guys—Bird and Parish had played poorly, also, and Ford
admitted he didn't quite know how to handle the Bird situation. He felt
that Bird needed intermittent rest, but he also needed Bird's presence
on the floor, no matter how poorly he was shooting. But Bird wanted to
play most of the game. He felt that he needed minutes to increase his
stamina, and that the most difficult thing for his back was sitting out,
then coming back, sitting out, and coming back. The Timberwolves
were coming to town the following evening, the Celtics' first game at
Boston Garden since February 6, and perhaps an expansion team
would be a needed antidote.

Shaw was visibly excited as he laced up his sneakers ninety minutes
before the Minnesota game on February 27. For weeks he and some of
the other younger Celtics had been complaining that it was hard for
them to warm up at Boston Garden, partly because of the cold temperatures but mostly because of the old-fashioned organ, which Shaw
referred to as "Lawrence Welk music." So, Gavitt, ever the diplomat,

had consented to let each of the players record an hour-long tape of their own musical selections that would be played between six and seven P.M. Then, promptly at seven, as the majority of the fans were starting to take their seats, Ron Harry would take over at the organ, lest the traditionalists think the Garden had gone to hell in a handbasket. It was a Solomon-like plan, a Gavitt plan. Shaw had selected mostly rap music for his tape, with artists like MC Hammer and CNC Music Factory. Speculation centered on whose tape would be the worst. Shaw figured the honor would go to Kleine, who had promised a tape heavy on country music, or Bird, a Kenny Rogers fan.

"Nah, I think it'll be Stojko," said Dee Brown. "He'll choose Julio Iglesias."

When the big moment came at six P.M., Shaw eagerly went out to warm up. But when the tape started it was barely audible. "Where's the bass?" he said, dribbling in place near the foul line. Actually, the sound was so tinny that even a Garden traditionalist would not have been offended. "I guess the next step is a sound system," said Shaw, disappointed. "Can't win for losin' around here." Gavitt was quietly miffed, his efforts at change and accommodating the players having been defeated by the resolutely ancient Garden. At precisely seven P.M., Harry took over, the sound clear and strong on "The Mexican Hat Dance."

Bird had kept himself out of the music discussion but instantly got himself into the game. His shooting was deadly from the outset and just before halftime he let loose with a three-point shot right in front of Ford. It went in and beat the buzzer. Ford looked at Casey and Jennings and spread his hands in front of him, as if to say, "Look where he shot the damn thing from." But despite Bird's brilliance (35 points, 7 rebounds, 6 assists), the Celtics could not pull away, and Ford could not buy Bird much rest. Boston finally prevailed 116–111 to lift its record to 41–15. For all the success of the Western trip, the Celtics were pretty much the same team at the end of the month that they had been at the beginning—one capable of lofty highs and decumbent lows, following a proven but aging and wounded warrior into uncertain battle.

CHAPTER 8

Highs and Lows

MARCH

Kevin McHale sat in the bleachers of Loyola Marymount College in Los Angeles, trying to adjust McHale Standard Time to West Coast time, which was not easy. He was reading the morning edition of *The Los Angeles Times,* though not for information about that night's opponent, the Clippers, first of five on a nine-day trip that was the last extended road swing of the season.

"See this story here?" said McHale. "This guy caught a twenty-one-pound, twelve-ounce largemouth bass in Lake Castaic. That's a bogus weight, I'd bet. Probably full of spawn." McHale liked to fish almost as much as Bird; moreover, he even enjoyed reading about fishing.

"Kevin, I know that's far more important," said Casey, "but we were wondering if you'd like to join us for practice."

"Truthfully?" said McHale. "Not really."

McHale had returned to action a week earlier at Boston Garden in a 108–98 victory over the Spurs, and had scored 31 points in a 126–117 win over Miami the night before the Celtics left on their trip. But the ankle was hurting him more than he liked to admit, and so was Bird's back. Furthermore, Shaw had badly sprained his right ankle in a disappointing 116–107 loss to Portland at the Garden in a nationally televised game on March 3, and was unavailable for the Clippers game, which left the offense in the hands of a rookie, albeit the estimable Dee Brown. Everything about the Celtics suggested a team in trouble, yet their record of 45–16 was still second best to the Trail Blazers, and they seemed once again glad to be out on the road. That was particularly true of Bird, who busted Steve Smith, Mike's thirteen-year-old brother, in a one-on-one game after practice. Bird repeatedly muscled the youngster down low, howled when he blocked his shot, and finally won the game in a shutout, 10–0.

No one was taking that night's game more seriously than Casey, who had been unceremoniously dumped by the Clippers a year earlier. Ironically, a viral condition had kept Casey at home for the Celtics' first game against the Clippers, the poorly played 109–107 victory on January 11 at Boston Garden. It was the first game that Casey had missed in eight years of NBA coaching, and several of the Celtics suggested that the illness was psychosomatic. "Clipper-itis," Ford called it. Casey tried to pretend that the rematch was just another game, but it wasn't, for the pain of having been fired at age fifty-two stuck with him. He felt as if he had been hung out to dry by the Clippers brass, particularly general manager Elgin Baylor, who was never comfortable with Casey in the first place. The Clippers hadn't even called a press conference when Casey was first hired, in fact; ever the history buff, Casey compared it to John F. Kennedy's announcement that he had appointed his brother as attorney general. "JFK ran out of the house and told everybody, 'We're hiring Bobby,' then ran back inside," said Casey. The part of Casey that wasn't stigmatized by the firing was elated to be free of Clipper Land, one of the acknowledged insane asylums of the NBA. The Clippers are owned by a peculiar fellow named Donald Sterling, a lawyer and real estate magnate who quite often seems bereft of common sense. Sterling once hosted a Christmas party to which he invited Clippers employees and their families, along with an exotic dancer, who removed her halter top during the party and walked around, breasts swaying, for most of the evening. Most of the guests found the ambience more than a bit bizarre, but Sterling seemed to think it was perfectly normal.

Casey's nervous state became obvious on the bus back to the hotel after practice when, after the driver asked for directions for that evening's game, Casey started to tell him how to get to the Forum, where the Lakers play, instead of the Sports Arena, home of the Clippers.

"You know what this shapes up as, don't you?" said Jennings. "A willie whacker." It did, too, for the Clippers usually play the Celtics tough. The previous season, under Casey, the Clippers beat the Celtics 114–105 in Boston Garden, and should've won against them at home too. Only a controversial foul called on Charles Smith that gave Bird two free throws at the buzzer enabled the Celtics to escape with a 112–111 victory. A large framed photo of the play, clearly showing that Smith did not initiate contact, hung in the Clippers executive offices.

As the Celtics bus pulled into the Sports Arena that evening, a young man held up a placard that read: "NO. 1 MICHAEL SMITH FAN." He actually ran alongside the bus for a quarter mile, anxiously scanning the Celtics faces for a glimpse of his hero, then waving his arms like a madman when he spotted him. The fan looked like a carbon copy of Smith too—a tall, thin, handsome fellow with dirty-blonde hair—and at first no one believed Smith when he said that the man was no relation.

"Well, he *must* be a Mormon, then," said McHale. "All that inbreeding." When the Celtics disembarked, McHale yelled to the hundreds of fans who were waiting behind restraining ropes: "There he is! There's Michael Smith!" Of course, Smith never got off his seat during the game.

Jan Volk was along on the trip, reportedly to make sure that the Los Angeles–based Jerome Stanley did not steal Kevin Gamble away from Ron Grinker, as had been rumored. Two Stanley clients, concluded the Celtics, was a scary enough proposition. Stanley was in the crowd waiting for Lewis and Shaw when the Celtics entered the building, but he denied that he had even talked to Gamble.

Casey was the number-one angle for most of the Los Angeles reporters, who had very little else to write about at that stage of the season. The Celtics discussed how Casey would be introduced before the game. "Shoot, what's the difference?" said McHale. "They don't know whether he's Don Casey or Don Chaney." The announcement of his name drew a generous round of cheers.

The Clippers demonstrated their utter lack of a basketball IQ by failing to exploit six-foot-ten Danny Manning's five-inch size advantage over Gamble; time after time, Manning had Gamble locked in near the basket but his teammates failed to give him the ball. "Look at the Celtics," said Cleveland Cavaliers scout Ron Meikle during a time-out in the first half, "they're all looking at Ford. Now, look at the Clippers. Most of them are looking at the Bud Lite Daredevils." Nevertheless, the Celtics played just poorly enough to keep the Clippers in the game, particularly Bird, who repeatedly passed up shots to throw ill-advised passes that resulted in turnovers or blown opportunities. At one point early in the fourth period, a point-guard-less lineup of Gamble, Lewis, Bird, McHale, and Parish produced three disastrous possessions, and Ford quickly hustled Dee Brown back into the game. "Boy, that was tirrible, wadn't it?" Bird said later of that particular interval. The art of bringing the ball upcourt against even token pressure is underrated at any level of basketball, and indeed, one of the glaring weaknesses of both Lewis's and Gamble's games was their inability to dribble around and through congestion. Though he respects Lewis's talents in general, Bird feels, in fact, that Lewis is not skilled enough as a ball handler to be in the backcourt and should be strictly a small forward.

With 2:47 left in the game and Boston leading by 4, Bird, moving awkwardly to his left, stepped back and swished an outrageous three-point shot that gave the Celtics a 96–89 lead, and, ultimately, a 104–98 win. As he trotted back to defensive position, Bird extended his hand to Clipper Ken Bannister, a muscular backup frontcourtman who is widely known as the homeliest player in the league. Bannister looked at it and looked at it, but Bird kept it extended, and finally, Bannister slapped it. "La-REEE! La-REEE!" chanted the crowd as the Clippers called time-out, leaving coach Mike Schuler, GM Baylor, and owner Sterling to ponder the depressing tableau that spread out before them: Their fans were cheering, and their center was slapping palms with the enemy.

Jim Paxson, who lived in San Diego, was a postgame visitor to the Celtics' locker room. He shook hands with everyone, no hard feelings evident, and settled down for a long conversation with his buddy, McHale. He glanced anxiously at the shower room and, finally, when Bird emerged, Paxson edged toward him, a wary look on his face. He extended his hand and said hello. Bird shook and looked away. The exchange lasted about two seconds, and Paxson went back to talking with McHale. No matter how vehemently Paxson denied that he had trashed Bird behind his back in the previous season, Bird, obviously, did not believe it.

As McHale rode the bus back to the hotel, he remembered another postgame ride in L.A. a few seasons ago when he and Walton stopped at a minimart and bought a case of beer. They drove around aimlessly like a couple of college freshmen, drinking beer and talking the night away.

"That seems like so long ago," said McHale. "Now, you know what I'm going to do the rest of the night? Stay in my room wearing Das Boot. Glamorous life, isn't it?"

"No way," said Bird. "Doc, you in awe of Michael Jordan or something? I can't practice here. Reggie?"

"Nope," said Reggie Lewis. "Can't do it."

The Celtics team bus was pulling into the sparkling new multi-million-dollar Nike facility in suburban Portland, the night before the game against the Trail Blazers. Though Shaw was the only Celtic who endorsed Nike—Bird is a longtime Converse man, Lewis is one of Reebok's bright new stars—the marketing-savvy company had invited the team to use one of its several gymnasiums, and a number of executives, including president Phil Knight, were on hand to greet the team. Converse once held the prominent position in the mega-bucks game of sneaker endorsement, and Reebok is a comer, but Nike's aggressive marketing strategy, built around the magnetism of Jordan, had catapulted the Oregon-based company to the top. The Celtics, in fact, were heading for practice at the Michael Jordan Center.

"Think Converse will ever have a Larry Bird Center?" Bird was asked as he got off the bus.

"Shoot, I'm jest worried about gittin' my check," said Bird. Interco Inc., the owner of Converse Inc., was having severe financial problems at the time.

Michael Smith's eyes lit up when he entered the dazzling gymnasium. He immediately dribbled behind the backboard at one end and looked up at the basket support.

"See those two rails up there," said Smith. "Bet I could shoot it over the second one and make the shot on the other side."

"No way," said a reporter. "Ten bucks."

Smith made the first shot but wouldn't take the money. There was definitely a place for this guy, though possibly not in the NBA.

Former Georgetown guard Charles Smith had just been added to the Celtics' roster as a ten-day player to replace Dave Popson, who had been hurting from a degenerative bone spur in his left foot. Popson was, to be sure, not 100 percent healthy, but like most NBA teams, the Celtics were playing fast and loose with the injured list. With Shaw's ankle iffy, Ford had decided that point-guard insurance was more necessary than frontcourt-reserve Popson. The NBA office rarely took a close look at the list, realizing that the physical grind and excessive travel schedule forced teams into some burdensome personnel situations. Later in the season, for example, the Pistons announced that rookie guard Lance Blanks had been put on the injured list due to a groin injury sustained during a Monday practice.

"But you didn't practice on Monday," a Piston reporter said to public relations director Matt Dobek.

"Well, Tuesday, then," said Dobek.

For his part, Blanks, when asked, couldn't remember which groin was supposed to be injured.

Smith, who was one of the Celtics' last cuts in the preseason, was the classic Georgetown product, a poor outside shooter who compensated for a lack of offensive finesse with aggressive, physical play, characteristics that his teammates never hesitated to bring to his attention. "At Georgetown they don't have shootarounds," pronounced McHale.

"They have foularounds." "No surprise you got a scholarship to Georgetown," added Bird. "You're the perfect John Thompson player. Can't shoot it in the ocean, and you chop ever'body when they walk by." Smith just smiled and took it. He was part of a little-known breed, players who would probably never be NBA regulars, but who nevertheless leapt at any opportunity, however brief, to stick with an NBA team.

On the bus back to the hotel, McHale was focused not on the prospect of playing the NBA's top team the following evening, but on the historical ramifications of "The Beverly Hillbillies."

"Just think how good you'd feel," said McHale, "if you were the one to have thought of the concept of the 'cement pond.' Now, *that* would be something to be proud of in fifty years."

The Trail Blazers were coming off a quirk in the NBA schedule— they hadn't played since the preceding Sunday afternoon victory at Boston Garden. During that game, Auerbach and owners Cohen and Gaston repeatedly protested calls made by the crew of Ed T. Rush, Jim Kinsey, and Steve Javie, the latter one of the most oft-criticized referees in the NBA, proving, if nothing else, that the brass was taking the Celtics' title hopes seriously. After the game, a fuming Cohen told reporters: "That was the worst officiated basketball game I've ever seen. And you can quote me. That game was stolen from us." Such a tirade would not have been atypical from Auerbach or Gaston, who wears his heart on his sleeve, but was unprecedented for the businesslike Cohen. He seemed to be inviting a confrontation with the league, and indeed, a few days later he was fined an unspecified amount. Ford had shown his dissatisfaction with the referees in a different and only slightly less subtle way—with the Celtics out of the running late in the game, Ford nevertheless called all of his remaining time-outs, forcing the refs to work the maximum. That is called "ref busting."

In the exciting, well-played Sunday night game before the parochial crowd in Portland, however, the Celtics got more than their share of calls. With 3:12 left in overtime, the Blazers' Jerome Kersey was whistled for a touch foul, sending Bird to the free-throw line; Kersey then protested so vehemently he drew a technical. That gave Bird three consecutive free throws, and he might as well have been standing alone in Hellenic College for all the effect the crowd noise had on him. After he made all three, the Celtics led 105–103. But it still took some clutch play by Dee Brown, who had come into the game late in the fourth period when Shaw fouled out, to win the game. First he made a spectacular feed to Parish for a dunk that gave Boston a 108–107 lead with thirty-seven seconds left. Then he forced a jump ball by leaping between Portland's All-Star backcourt duo of Clyde Drexler and Terry Porter. As they lined up, Brown noticed Lewis open directly to his right, but it was more natural for him to tap it with his right hand to Bird on the left. Bird and Lewis, meanwhile, caught each other's eye, so, when Dee tapped it to Bird, Bird tapped it back across the lane to Lewis. Lewis got it to Brown, who, after being fouled, drained both free throws. "It's free is all I kept thinking," Brown said after the 111–109 victory. "It's free. In many ways it's an easier shot in that situation than a lay-up because you have the time to block everything out." McHale was right—the dunking contest had done wonders for Brown's confidence. And the win over Portland did wonders for Boston's as a team too. With a 46–16 record, the Celtics had every reason to believe that they were once again a legitimate championship contender.

After the game, the Celtics set up camp in the hotel bar, coaches and broadcasters at one table, small groups of players divided among the others. There was no written rule against coaches drinking with players but it just wasn't done very often. Players like McHale, Bird, and Kleine drifted by the coaches' table once in a while to trade insults or steal some nachos, but in general, the subtle segregation rules were observed. Anyway, the hard-drinking days of the NBA, when teams took over hotel bars until dawn, were largely a thing of the past.

At the Ford-Ordway table, the conversation turned, as it often did, to Most, "Johnny stories" being a staple of every road trip. Half the males in Boston did a credible impression of Most at the mike, but few realized how downright surrealistic life with Johnny had been for his broadcast partners and the team. There was the time during Bill Fitch's tenure as head coach, for example, that the Celtics were taking on Milwaukee in a preseason doubleheader at Madison Square Garden in New York. In the pregame show Most continually asked Fitch questions about the Knicks, while Fitch tried gently to guide the conversation to the Bucks, that night's opponent. Finally, during a commercial break, Fitch said: "Johnny, we're not playing New York." Most took an angry puff on his cigarette and said: "Well, what the fuck are we DOING in New York then?"

The great "Johnny wedding invite" story was legendary. As Most prepared for his third marriage in the spring of 1989, he mistakenly sent the invitation intended for his boss at WEEI to another "Mike Wheeler." As the days wore on, and the station GM wondered why he hadn't received an invite to Most's wedding, the putative Mike Wheeler believed that he and his family had somehow won a contest and an invitation to Johnny Most's wedding. He immediately RSVPed for him and three members of his family.

Finally, days before the wedding, GM Wheeler said to Most: "Uh,

Johnny, how come I haven't been invited to your wedding? Are you mad at me or something?"

"What the hell you talkin' about?" said Most. "There's four of you coming, right?"

When the mess was finally straightened out, Most had to call up the "other" Mike Wheeler and "un-invite" him. The man was crushed.

Ordway had always walked a fine line as Most's partner, never quite sure when to cut in and correct Johnny for the sake of accuracy, and when to remain silent, let a tangent run its course, and try to patch up the damage later. Usually he chose the latter course. During a game in Indiana several years ago, Most repeatedly berated the Pacers for not playing Clark Kellogg, who was broadcasting the game for the home team just a few chairs away from Most. He had retired the previous season. During another pregame show, Most hammered away at how important it was for the Celts to control Jamaal Wilkes, though the Lakers had released the jump-shooting forward weeks earlier. Saddest of all was the night a few seasons ago when Most, after catching a glimpse of a number 6 flashing across the lane, temporarily spaced out and started going on and on about the play of Bill Russell. This "Russell," however, was Michael Holton, a reserve guard for the Trail Blazers.

Bird's dealings with Most were particularly comical. During a tirade one evening, Most screamed at Ordway, "I'M THE SHOW! I'M THE SHOW!" When Bird heard about it, he said to Most: "No, Johnny, you're wrong. I'M the show!" One of Bird's favorite little tricks was to slide Most's omnipresent pack of cigarettes a few feet down the scorer's table when he checked back into a game, leaving Most to fume and fuss, sometimes into a live mike. Bird's finest moment occurred several years ago in the Westcourt Hotel in Phoenix when Most was forced to occupy a nonsmoking room. Bird knew, as everyone else did, that Most would light up as soon as he got in the room, so Bird waited a few minutes, then rang him up.

"Uh, sir," he said, disguising his Hoosier twang. "We know that you're smoking in there."

"Who the hell is this?" hollered Most. "How do you know what I'm doing?"

"It's the front desk sir," said Bird. "Look above you at that red light. It's a hidden camera. You have to put out your cigarette."

"What?" hollered Most. "That's an invasion of privacy!"

He never realized the identity of his caller, nor that the red light above his head was the smoke alarm.

* * *

There was a fair amount of history between the Celtics and the Sacramento Kings, Boston's opponent in the third game of the trip on March 12. Back in 1987, in a move that was as bold as it was boneheaded, Kings general manager Joe Axelson put the future of his team in the hands of Celtics legend Bill Russell. He gave Russell a multi-year contract that started him as head coach with the provision that Russell would move up and become general manager after a few seasons. Russell had been a head coach twice before, for three seasons in Boston (1966 through 1969) and for four seasons in Seattle (from 1973 through 1977). At the latter stop he had earned the entirely deserved reputation for being distant from his players and lazy in his professional work habits. Russell's answer was to brand his critics as either racist, jealous of his success, or both. Russell lasted about five months as coach of the Kings before he was kicked upstairs to become vice president of basketball operations. He remained in that job until December of 1989 before he was eased out. As an executive, Russell made an honest attempt to spend more time in the office instead of being out playing his beloved golf. But, ultimately, he was ineffective because he treated people like dirt and because he had lost touch with a league that had become ten times more sophisticated than when he was last involved. There is no doubt that Russell was victimized by racist attitudes in Boston while he was a player, but there is also no doubt that he, and he alone, was responsible for his subsequent NBA failures.

The Kings' director of player personnel, the wise-cracking Jerry Reynolds, had drafted Joe Kleine, traded for Eddie Pinckney, dealt both of them to the Celtics, and released Derek Smith. Moreover, his claim to fame was being, as Reynolds put it, "the third most famous citizen of French Lick, Indiana." "Larry's first, of course," explained Reynolds, "and Eddie Bird [Larry's youngest brother, and the only other Bird to have achieved a reputation as a basketball player] is second. Then me." The ex-Kings had different feelings about Reynolds. Smith was extremely bitter, feeling that he had been unjustly maligned by the organization after injuries had kept him from living up to his reputation. Smith's antipathy toward Kings trainer Bill Jones had led, in fact, to a near-fight with Kleine, a close friend of Jones's when both were Kings. Smith's harshest feelings were reserved for Reynolds. "He's a master con man," Smith told Steve Bulpett during the trip. "He's manipulated everyone, and it shows, because they've still got a terrible record and he's still around." Kleine was not publicly critical of Reynolds, but felt that Reynolds, who had also been head coach for all of one season and parts of two others, had undervalued him as a player and belittled his skills around the league. Pinckney kept his personal feelings about Reynolds, if he had any, to himself.

But Bird and Reynolds, though personality opposites, are friends, owing entirely to their common roots. Bird called Reynolds when he got into town and Reynolds invited him to dinner at his house. They spent most of the evening discussing common acquaintances, who include just about the entire citizenry of French Lick, men with names like Jargo Jones, Catfish King, and two of Bird's former high school teammates, Boob Qualkenbush and Beezer Carnes. "Next to those names," said Reynolds, "ol' 'Larry Bird' sounds pretty normal, doesn't it?" The mentality of French Lick is such, says Reynolds, that when he comes back into town most of the folks figure he's looking for a job.

"You know, that Logotee High School post is open, Jerry," someone would say to Reynolds.

"Well, I don't know," Reynolds would say. "I got a job."

"Well, bet you could get that high school job."

"Thanks," Reynolds would say, "I'll think about it."

A certain element of the population is strongly anti-Bird, too, says Reynolds. He hears a lot of, *I could've been like Larry if I was six feet nine*, or *I could've been like Larry if I played college ball*. Reynolds felt it came down to simple jealousy or, rather, the unspoken feeling of: *Hell, he's got all that money, why don't he give me some?*

Bird seemed looser than usual at the game-day shootaround, providing commentary on his high-arching one-handers. "Look at that thing!" he'd say as he released a skyball. "Look how beautiful! High, arching . . . good!" The coaching staff tried to keep everyone's mind on business, but it wasn't easy. As Jennings ran through one Sacramento offensive play, Bird raised his hand.

"Yes, Larry?" said Jennings.

"Now, will they run that play," deadpanned Bird, "before or after we're up twenty?"

Sacramento was still relatively unsophisticated about the NBA game, the franchise having moved there from Kansas City in 1985. The biggest problem for Julie Fie, the Kings' capable director of public relations, was making sure that no bogus press credentials were granted; in the past, a visit by the Celtics, the Lakers, or Michael Jordan found several "reporters" clamoring for autographs after the game. The man who called the shots for the Kings, owner and managing general partner Gregg Lukenbill, showed his professionalism by refusing to sell the *Sacramento Union* newspaper at the downtown Hyatt (which he also owned) because he felt the Kings' coverage by its reporter, Don Drysdale, was too negative, a triumph for the small of spirit.

The young and inexperienced Kings were not good enough to qual-ify the game as an out-and-out "willie whacker"; rather, it was what Jennings called a "T. C. B. game," a "take-care-of-business game. Get in, get out, get the job done." Of course, the Celtics had been in the same situation during the 1989–90 season and barely escaped from Sacramento with a 115–112 overtime victory. The lackadaisical Celtics performance had so angered Jimmy Rodgers that he drove his fist into a blackboard at halftime. To commemorate that moment, an unknown prankster drew a fist on the blackboard before the game that bore the inscription, "Jimmy Rodgers Was Here One Year Ago."

The Celtics did their best to "stay focused" (Ford's new pet phrase) and were in control most of the way. At one point late in the game, though, Shaw suddenly pulled up on an uncontested lay-up and shov-eled the ball back to Dee Brown so that Brown could uncork a more spectacular slam-dunk. Brown was covered and just managed to con-vert the lay-up. On the bench, Ford leaped to his feet and screamed at Shaw. Over on press row, Steve Bulpett summed it up: "Doc just can't identify with that mentality at all." It was true—the way Chris Ford learned to play basketball, one never passed up a sure thing to get a more spectacular thing.

For one Celtic the game was much more than a T. C. B. affair. And the longer Joe Kleine sat on the bench, the more frustrated he became. Kleine felt that the Kings' brass might as well have branded BACKUP CENTER on his buttocks with a hot iron, so entrenched was that tag around the league. He emphasized that he did not object to backing up Parish—"Chief's a better player than I am," said Kleine. "I wish he wasn't, but he is."—but steadfastly believed that he should be a starter somewhere else, and *would've* been had he not been undersold in Sacramento for the better part of three and a half seasons. Kleine was ambivalent whenever his name surfaced in trade talk, as it had earlier in the season when Seattle rejected a deal that would've sent Xavier McDaniel to Boston in exchange for Kleine and a first-round pick. Kleine liked the Celtics organization, his teammates, and the city of Boston, and he was cognizant of his not insignificant off-the-court roles: He pushed Parish and McHale hard and diligently in practice; he was friend to both Larry and Kevin; he was a motivator and a spark plug; he was a human landing area for darts of abuse launched by teammates on all sides. Playing second fiddle—second?: eighth or ninth fiddle—to the better-known Celtics was an accepted part of life and, most of the time, rather amused him. One day he showed a visitor a large stack of Bird's autobiography lying around his apartment in Brookline. "Get this," said Kleine, "fans don't want my autograph.

They send me Larry's book and want me to get *his* autograph." Kleine once stopped to sign an autograph for a young fan, then noticed the youngster crying; it turned out that he had mistakenly signed the boy's only Larry Bird basketball card. Kleine immediately gave the boy his practice jersey.

Kleine even held his tongue on the Vrankovic situation. It hurt him a little bit that the Celtics, by dint of bringing on Cowens to work with Vrankovic, seemed to be anointing the Yugoslav as center of the future. What made it even tougher was that Cowens and Bill Walton, red-headed centers like himself, were his favorite players growing up. Kleine worried that he was not taken seriously enough as a player. He was used to success—he was, after all, the top scorer at the University of Arkansas in both his junior and senior seasons, a member of the gold-medal 1984 Olympic team, the sixth pick in the 1985 draft—and he once had to talk the townsfolk of Slater, Missouri, out of erecting a big sign that said HOME OF JOE KLEINE. ("I was flattered, but I really didn't think it was right.")

Kleine desperately wanted to play well against his old team, but Ford didn't put him in until just 4:48 remained, by which time the Celtics had all but wrapped up the game. Sentiment has little place in the NBA, but it did seem that the coach could've done better by him than that. Kleine immediately shot a jumper that didn't hit the rim or the backboard and the crowd hooted. Kleine looked grimly determined and tight as a big, bass drum. With 2:04 remaining, he hit a left-handed hook shot and raised his arm to the crowd. Then, as the final buzzer sounded on a 110–95 Celtics victory, he swished a jump shot, raised his fist again, and mouthed the words: "Take THAT, motherfuckers!" After the game the Sacramento writers clustered around Kleine's locker, trying to get at the root of his anger. Back to being good ol' Joe, Kleine explained that, yes, he had a good relationship with the fans when he was here, but, yes, he was a little annoyed when they hooted at him, and, no, he holds no lasting animosity toward them. He smiled. The writers smiled. And when everyone had gone, Kleine, enjoying his moment of small triumph, turned to Parish with a big grin on his face and said, "But fuck 'em, anyway."

Parish laughed deeply as he knotted his silk tie.

"Right on, Joe," he said. "Right on."

The Marriott hotel in Salt Lake City is located directly across the street from the Salt Palace, so the players can walk to the game, a happenstance that brings mixed blessings. A couple hours before the Celtics' game against the Jazz on March 13, Parish strolled out the front door of the hotel, wearing a gray suit and carrying a Celtics' bag. "Stroll" is the only verb that fits Parish's very distinct form of locomotion, ground eating yet very, very controlled. Impeccably dressed, seven-foot black men tend to stand out in mostly white Salt Lake, and Parish quickly drew a large crowd of autograph-seekers. He couldn't stop lest he be held up for a half-hour, but neither did he alter the pace of his stroll, for that is not Parish's style. And so the strange assemblage moved out of the hotel, across the wide expanse of West Temple street, onto the sidewalk on the other side and, finally, up to the players' entrance at the Salt Palace—Parish strolling stoically and deliberately, eyes focused dead ahead, blithely ignoring those underfoot who were scurrying backward and thrusting pennants, balls, and wads of paper into his face. Only when he reached the safety of the arena lobby did he even indicate that he knew the fans were there.

"Whew!" said the Chief. "Long walk."

The game was something more than that. Two clutch Dee Brown free throws, reminiscent of the pair he converted to help beat Portland, sent the game into overtime at 99–99. With 3:21 left in OT, Bird nailed a big three-pointer, but, as had become a pattern, he came down on the next possession and launched another one when logic dictated a more conservative offensive approach. That three-point shot missed, and the Jazz rebounded, scored, and went on to win 112–109. No one knew it at the time, but Bird's ill-advised shot would not be soon forgotten.

In the coffee shop after the game, McHale returned to what had become a familiar theme for him—the good, ol' days of 1985–86. He admitted that something went out of him after Walton and Jerry Sichting (another player who had managed to be both "a Larry guy" and "a Kevin guy") departed. The three of them, along with Ainge, used to play a lot of chess on road trips, and McHale said a typical stratagem was to take three moves in a row while Walton sat implacably, spaced out at the board. Finally, Walton would raise his head and say: "I gu-guess making like three m-moves in a row, Kevin, would put you at a dis-distinct advantage." As McHale finished that story, a woman dressed in full Celtics regalia tapped him on the shoulder and intro-duced herself as his biggest fan. "I'm the point guard for my basketball team," she said proudly. McHale nodded politely but continued his conversation. She rambled on for a few minutes about her basketball team and her prowess as a point guard, but, eventually, she got the message and left.

"Now what should I have done?" McHale wondered. "See, a couple years ago I would've stopped and said, 'Oh, a point guard, huh?' and next thing I knew she would've pulled up a chair and kept me there for an hour. So now I just try to be sort of polite but not encourage anyone."

Back in Boston after beating Washington 94–86 to complete a success-ful 4–1 road trip, the Celtics prepared for a nationally televised St. Patrick's Day game (March 17) against Philadelphia. Up in the press room, there was something new—milk being served along with the usual soda and coffee. Everyone agreed it was a good idea until Mike Fine found that his was stamped with a March 2 date and Jackie MacMullen found alien black particles floating in hers.

Right before the game, the Celtics announced that McHale would not be playing. The original sprain of his left ankle was no longer a problem, but he was feeling intense pain from inflammation and fric-tion around the joint and the ligaments that had been torn. Imme-diately, the press summoned Eddie Lacerte and asked him about McHale.

"Operation Kevin Shield," said Lacerte, with mock formality, "has officially kicked in."

The prospect of meeting Charles Barkley (who had averaged 36 points in the three previous games against the Celtics) without McHale was not a pleasant one, and, indeed, in the first two minutes of the game Barkley blocked a Parish attempt at a dunk, forced an illegal defense call, was fouled by Lewis, drew an offensive foul on Gamble, and found time to jog to the Celtics bench and shake hands with Ford, Casey, and Jennings. "We became pretty close friends during the All-Star game," Jennings explained later. Auerbach looked over from his seat across the court and glowered; if there was one development about the modern game that drove him to distraction, it was the increased fraternization between teams. Behind Parish, who finished with 28 points and 18 rebounds, the Celtics eventually came back to win, 110–105.

McHale didn't make the following day's trip to Atlanta, either, and as it turned out, most of his teammates could've stayed home, too. Casey mistakenly brought along a pin-striped "suit" that consisted of blue trousers and black coat. "I'm a little color blind," he said when he noticed the mistake. (The burden of keeping up with the impeccably dressed Ford and the neat-as-a-pin Jennings, who wrapped his clothes in plastic even when he carried them in a garment bag, was not easy on Casey. "Every night's like the fuckin' prom," Casey would complain good-naturedly as he left for the arena, carrying that evening's suit in a clothes bag so he would not get chalk all over it when he began scribbling on the blackboard. He generally wore sweaters to the game, and some of the players had taken to calling him "Mr. Rogers.") The problem was resolved when Casey borrowed a blue pin-striped coat from Steve Reilly, the Celtics' vice president of sales who was along on the trip. En route to The Omni, Gavitt looked over at Casey and said: "Next thing you know, Case, you'll be one of those guys on the street corner dressed in striped pants and polka-dot shirts."

In the locker room before the game, Ford was in his most familiar position—eyes scanning a videotape, hands reaching into a huge tub of popcorn.

"Can you believe this?" he kept asking incredulously. "You listnin' to this?"

On the screen was a replay of a Chicago-Atlanta game during which NBC commentator Mike Fratello, in response to questions from play-by-play man Marv Albert, went on and on about his controversial tenure as coach of the Hawks, which had ended the previous season. "Just talk about THIS game," Ford railed at the screen. Ford's impatience with Fratello said a lot about his no-nonsense approach, his belief that the media should take a just-the-facts-ma'am style of reporting. A few days later, his feelings on that subject became even more public.

On the blackboard Casey had written "Pay-Back Game," in response to Atlanta's 131–114 rout at The Omni on December 28. But it turned out to be anything but that. Shaw's ankle still bothered him and he couldn't keep up with the Hawk waterbug, Spud Webb; Dee Brown didn't fare much better when he had his chance. Kleine got into the game in the second period and immediately missed an easy stickback that drove him batty, if only because the Hawks' Jon Koncak was on the floor at the time. Koncak and Kleine are longtime personal rivals dating back to their tenure as top college centers in the Southwest Conference, Koncak with SMU, Kleine with Arkansas. Koncak often directed his quick and razor-sharp wit at Kleine, lampooning, in particular, Kleine's rural background. Kleine, for his part, thought that Koncak came off "as an arrogant asshole" in college, and had not done much to alter that opinion during his pro career. Bird continued to shoot so poorly from the floor (7-of-21) that Ford couldn't be blamed for praying his back *did* hurt; at least that might explain Bird's misdirected shooting.

Midway through the fourth period, Atlanta's war-horse of a center, Moses Malone, got out on a fast-break and dunked, an embarrassing punctuation mark on an embarrassing 104–92 defeat. Moses rarely got out and dunked on anyone anymore. One of the league's dominant players from 1976 through 1985, Malone was a throwback to the unpopular NBA of the seventies. He was a selfish, complaining, nearly unintelligible brute of a man, who seemed to speak in a language decipherable only to himself, although the word "Moses" could be picked up quite often. Imitating "Moses-speak" was a staple of NBA humor and had, one supposes, an element of racism to it. But even many black players participated in it and took pains not to be associated with Moses's distinctive form of communication. Several years ago, when his NBA stock was at its highest, Moses somehow landed up on the television quiz show, "Hollywood Squares." One question directed at him asked: "Does the average American spend more money on food or health care?" Keeping in mind the scripted response that had been given him earlier, Moses mumbled something that sounded like: "Fomeisfoo, butI'monna'say hefcare."

Charley Eckman, a former referee and coach in the NBA of the fifties, once said: "There are only two great plays—put the ball in the basket and *South Pacific*." It was Eckman's way of commenting on the simplicity of the game, that any shot that goes in is, by definition, a "good shot," and any shot that doesn't is not. Any further discussion was, to Eckman, useless rhetoric. To an extent, Eckman was correct. Many NBA coaches would watch in horror as an unlikely shooter let loose with a three-point bomb, only to nod his head if the shot somehow went in. Did that make it a "good shot?"

Still, the subject of "shot selection" was one that was never far from the Celtics of 1990–91. The *Herald*'s Steve Bulpett wrote a detailed story about it on March 15, after the loss to Utah, which had included the ill-advised Bird three-pointer. Ford told Bulpett that the Celtics offense had a tendency to "get into a frenzy." The coach insisted that "we just have to be patient" and utilize the "several different options" that are on the floor. All of those comments speak to "shot selection." Parish even mentioned the word "shot selection" outright and said, "We have to do something about it." Bird begged to differ. "Whenever we miss some shots, everyone says it's our offense gone wrong," Bird told Bulpett. "But I don't think there's anything wrong." That pretty much summed up Bird's Eckman-like philosophy—if a shot goes in, it's a good shot. By extension, he seemed to be saying, *And I will continue to take shots that others might consider bad shots*. McHale said: "You've just got to take the shots when you feel them. That's part of basketball. We made a few bad decisions on the offensive end [he was speaking of the March 13 game at Utah], but that's basketball." His position seemed closer to Bird's than Ford's. At any rate, the entirely fair-minded story came out, was dissected, and went away.

When the road trip was over, Mike Fine wrote an opinion piece for his paper, the *Quincy Patriot Ledger,* that said Bird's shot selection had grown increasingly questionable. Fine didn't suggest that Bird was selfish, or that he should be kept out of the Hall of Fame, or that he should be pilloried on Bunker Hill. He said Larry Bird was taking some bad shots, an opinion that had been expressed many times before. Channel 4's Bob Neumeier read Fine's piece and wondered if the team felt the way that Fine did. Neumeier began asking them specifically about Bird's shot selection and found that, publicly at least, none of them had any problems with it. (The best guess is that some of them did think Bird was taking some bad shots but, with the team still in contention for a championship, would not risk saying it.) Neumeier went with the story on the March 20 evening broadcast, just before the Celtics played the Bullets at the Garden. It was not exactly the stuff of Watergate: He did show graphs about Bird's sinking shooting percentage (43.6 percent since his return on February 1), but he included the comments of his teammates that Bird's shot selection was definitely *not* a problem. All in all, it was more yogurt than ice cream. In fact, the argument could be made that it wasn't even a story, except that, in Boston, *any* story about Bird, even a nonstory, is a story.

That same night, Ford did a pregame stand-up interview with another local station during which he was asked about the "rumors" that some team members were upset with Bird. That was the final straw for Ford, who felt that he had heard entirely too much about something that had no basis in fact, and he exploded after the game. "This TV thing about a rift in the team, Larry Bird's shot selection, is a bunch of garbage," Ford told reporters. "If you continue messing up my team, I'll have to take appropriate action." Whatever he meant, it was a clear overreaction.

The story wouldn't die. In the March 22 editions of the *Herald,* Mark Murphy wrote a story about Neumeier's story that carried the headline: "Bird mum, C's numb, over Ch. 4 bombshell." Like Neumeier's report, Murphy's story basically consisted of several Celtics vehemently denying that there was any problem with shot selection, Bird's included; the word "bombshell" was unfortunate but typical in daily journalism, i.e., an editor blowing a story completely out of proportion with a single, ill-chosen word. Murphy did make one small error, however, when he implicated McHale in the controversy. "The Ch. 4 report apparently stemmed from comments made by Robert Parish and Kevin McHale after the Celtics' overtime loss in Utah on March 13," wrote Murphy. Yes, Parish did think the Celts had a problem with shot selection, but McHale, the record indicates, did not.

In point of fact, shot selection was a problem for the Celtics. Bird's pattern of hitting a big three-point shot, then missing a more outlandish one in an even more crucial point of the game, had been repeated too often. Lewis was sometimes too content to use his patented move—dribble right, crossover left, pull up, and take a jumper—and many of his defenders were becoming more familiar with it. Shaw was overly proud of his ambidexterity and took far too many left-handed shots. And McHale, obviously, took countless shots that he shouldn't take, insisting that he could more easily outmaneuver three defenders than pass the ball back outside; Casey referred to that mentality as "the mulely disposition that made him great." The one Celtic who could rarely be accused of taking bad shots was the one who didn't hesitate to voice his opinion about it—Parish.

Predictably, the Ford-media rift involved other elements, however. Ford was feeling extreme pressure, perhaps for the first time all season. The Celtics were still a contender with fewer than twenty regular-season games left, but Ford sensed their vulnerability. Backs and ankles, ankles and backs. Bird was hurting, but no one knew the magic formula of when to rest him, when to play him. With much less attention and fanfare did Lewis suffer from an aching back too, and Ford knew that he had to buy him some rest somewhere along the way. McHale's ankle hadn't responded and he was still out of action. Shaw was playing on his bad ankle but not playing particularly well. A gnawing personnel problem had surfaced, also, concerning the relative merits of Shaw and Brown. Brown's popularity had continued to soar since the All-Star game, and many fans believed he deserved to start. The topic was beginning to surface on local radio shows, and, as luck would have it, the *Herald* chose the week of the shot selection controversy to ask, in its "Question of the Week": Who deserves to be the Celtics' starting point guard, Dee Brown or Brian Shaw? Brown won the voting, and Ford had fits about that too, another overreaction that led *Herald* columnist Gerry Callahan to skewer the coach in a March 24 column. Callahan suggested that perhaps Ford would prefer more innocuous "Questions of the Week," and he provided a few examples: "Are the Boston Celtics the neatest bunch of guys in the NBA, or what?" "How big of a raise should the Celtics give coach Ford for the wicked awesome job he has done this year?" "Don't you just hate those yucky Bulls and icky Pistons?" And so on. If Ford found it humorous, he did not say so.

Privately, the Boston media was almost relieved to have a reason to criticize Ford. Though the public perceives the press as overwhelmingly negative in its reporting, most reporters fret more about being overly *positive* toward a particular individual or institution. Demonstrating "negativism" was wrong, but not as wrong as demonstrating "favoritism." And there was absolutely no doubt that from the moment Chris Ford's name had been mentioned as a candidate for the job, his press had been overwhelmingly positive. As Callahan pointed out, the most unified front presented by the Boston media in a long time occurred when it supported Ford, not Mike Krzyzewski, for the head job. Perhaps Ford deserved the positive press, because his steering of the Celtics' ship had been sure and confident. But no one who occupied the spotlight was right all of the time, and Ford's number, to the silent glee of some, had clearly come up.

One postscript to the controversy: On the afternoon of March 25, McHale emerged from the locker room at Hellenic College, wearing a pair of awful red sneakers, in honor, he said, of the Chicago Bulls' Easter afternoon visit to Boston Garden on March 31. Still bothered by the bad ankle, he had spent most of the morning practice session riding a stationary bicycle and commenting loudly on the scrimmage. But he looked serious as he approached Mark Murphy. "For the first time there's something about Larry and my name's not involved," he said to Murphy, hurt, not anger, in his voice, "then, suddenly, there it is again." Before Murphy could respond, McHale turned and went into the locker room. He was referring, of course, to Murphy's passing reference to him in the "Bombshell" story. Obviously, McHale read the newspaper carefully, and just as obviously, his sensitivity at being "anti-Larry" was never far from his mind.

Bird laced up his sneakers in front of his locker and pondered the question of why so many highly rated college players had lately failed to make much of an impact in the NBA.

"I think it's pretty simple," said Bird. "The college season's so much shorter than the NBA to begin with, and then guys don' play hard all the time in college. So they git here and it's like they hadn't even played a quarter of a pro season, maybe less. They're jist not ready for it at all."

Bird said he didn't know if that was the case with Danny Ferry of the Cleveland Cavaliers, that night's opponent, but Ferry, the No. 2 pick in the 1989 draft, had been a bust to date. Like a few others before him, Ferry carried the tag of being "another Bird," a player who dominated with a smorgasbord of skills and court smarts rather than with exceptional athletic ability. But Ferry, like the others, lacked Bird's confidence and killer instinct, and he seemed to be another indication that

NBA general managers would be wise to abandon the search for another Bird. There wasn't one.

The Celtics needed this March 29 home game badly, for the preceding week had been an unmitigated disaster. Early on the morning of March 22, several hours before the Celtics departed on their charter flight for a game in Indianapolis that night, a Dodge Caravan driven by Charles Smith, the quiet backup guard, struck and killed two Boston University coeds, An Trinh and Michelle Dartley. In the car with Smith was a former teammate at Georgetown, Ben Gillery. The disaster occurred as the women crossed Commonwealth Avenue at Granby Street at about one-forty-five A.M. Smith was arrested and charged with vehicular homicide, driving under the influence of alcohol, and leaving the scene of an accident. About the time the Celtics landed in Indianapolis, Smith was being released on $100,000 personal recognizance after pleading innocent to the charges in Roxbury District Court. Unlike the war in the Middle East, the Smith news was most definitely the kind that affected a team. Smith had no close friends on the team, but he was well liked and respected, for there was no pretense about him. He just wanted to play in the NBA and would scratch and claw for every opportunity to do so. His second ten-day contract period was officially over the following day, and the Celtics had not decided whether or not to sign him for the remainder of the season. The incident made the decision for them.

Boston hardly needed another reason to play poorly in Indianapolis, for Market Square Arena, where the Celtics had lost 17 of their previous 19 games, had become a Celtics graveyard. There was a definite pall in the locker room before the game. The Celtics stayed in the game for three periods but wilted under frantic Pacers pressure in the fourth and lost by 121–109. A rare break in the schedule gave the Celtics nearly a week to lick their wounds, but, on March 28, they lost to the lowly Heat in Miami by 90–88, the expansion team's first victory over Boston in 11 attempts. "What else could you expect," wrote the *Globe*'s Peter May in his account, "on a day that Ronald Reagan came out in favor of gun control?" Before the game, Bird was told that another famous Indiana native, Yankee star Don Mattingly, was excited about meeting him for the first time. "He should be," drawled Bird. "A lot of people are excited to meet me." He was kidding, though not completely. When Bird was brought over, he and Mattingly exchanged handshakes, brief conversation, and mementoes (baseballs for Celtics shirts). And Mattingly, like Kevin Costner before him, did appear much more excited than Bird. Bird's performance in the game, though, was dull. He scored just 9 points, and there was no longer any doubt that he was playing in pain. McHale wasn't playing at all. "I can jog," he said before the game. "If they have a jogging league, I could play."

And so the Cleveland game was a must. It wouldn't be easy, even with Cavalier center Brad Daugherty out with an injury, for the Celtics faced a tough matchup at forward, where Bird had to check the athletic Larry Nance. Bird made just 6-of-13 shots and had only 3 assists and 3 rebounds to go with 7 turnovers. "For the first time in Danny Ferry's career, he *is* playing like Larry Bird," said Steve Bulpett at the press table. Ferry made only one of 10 shots and finished with two points, an altogether humiliating experience for the onetime All-American. But Bird, being Bird, probably won the game for the Celtics. With the score tied at 104–104, the Cavs' Craig Ehlo drove the lane and was whacked across the arms and face by Bird. No call, no basket. With the Celtics trailing by 107–106 at the other end, Bird drove ponderously but decisively across the lane and put up a left-handed shot as four Cavalier players converged on him. At least two of them had their hands on the ball, but a foul was called, and Bird made both free throws to put the Celtics on top 108–107. Cleveland then tied it with a free throw, but Parish won the game with an awkward buzzer-beating line-drive jump shot that was actually blocked from behind by John "Hot Rod" Williams. No one was sure how it managed to go in, but it did, and the Celtics knew they were lucky to escape with a 110–108 win. For the Cavs, there was not a more classic example of an NBA road game—bad calls, bad karma, bad everything.

But the key to the game from the Celtics' standpoint was Pinckney. It was almost as if an alien being had inhabited his body, so fierce and spirited was his play. Jennings jokingly credited his performance to "Final Four Fever"—the NCAA championships were being contested that weekend and Pinckney was far better known for his performance in that memorable Villanova victory over Georgetown in 1985 than for anything he had done as a professional. But against the Cavs he made all 7 of his field goals and 5 of his 7 free throws, grabbed 14 rebounds, blocked 3 shots and shut down both Nance and Williams in thirty-five inspired minutes. Five times during the game, the Garden crowd let loose with a chant of "Eh-DEE! Eh-DEE!" Like Bird ("La-REE!") and Muhammad Ali ("A-LEE!"), he had the kind of name, the hard "e" sound on the last syllable, that lent itself to the two-syllable chant. Beyond that, the savvy Garden crowd knew, having heard various Celtics say it from time to time, that an aggressive Pinckney could mean the difference between a playoff also-ran and a champion. Perhaps that was stating the case too strongly, but that long-sought-after X-factor, the element of defensive toughness and rebounding tenacity, was still missing. And since it was still unclear whether or not Derek Smith was going to make it back, Pinckney was the man to supply it.

Eddie Pinckney fought a daily battle with his image. His nickname said it all: "Easy Ed." His background paralleled Brown's and Shaw's in that he was the product of a strong, two-parent family—"I wasn't the stereotype," said Pinckney. "I saw my mom and my dad every single day."—but what set Pinckney apart was that he was brought up in the projects of New York City. The Pinckneys lived on the fifth floor of a ten-floor high-rise called Monroe in the heart of the Bronx. His father, Edward, worked construction and dreamed of fishing, and his mother, Celeste, was a nurse who stressed education. Seven Pinckney children, six girls and Eddie, came into the world and all seven graduated from college, from good schools, too, like Columbia, CCNY, and Montclair State. Eddie played basketball and softball in the inner city, got good marks at P.S. 100 and Adlai Stevenson High School, and stayed out of trouble. "I was too afraid of my father to mess up," said Pinckney. "He was about six three and very muscular, and I didn't even want him *looking* at me cross-eyed." When the funny, little Italian coach named Massimino showed up to recruit him, he told Pinckney: "I'll tell you right now, you're very talented, but you don't work hard enough." After a particularly stellar game in his sophomore year, Massimino sat him down and said: "Do you want to become an NBA player?" And Pinckney said he didn't know. Massimino couldn't believe it. A six-foot-nine kid from the New York projects who had pro talent and he *didn't know* if he wanted to play in the NBA?

Pinckney was just different from most. He was conditioned by his parents to believe in education and the percentages that worked against a kid becoming a pro athlete, and not to put his eggs into one basket. He took those gospels to heart, not the rave reviews about his basketball playing. "I knew if I didn't make basketball my life, I could've found something else to do," reasoned Pinckney, who, unlike McHale, did not play in all-star games after his senior season at Villanova because he had too many papers to finish.

No one ever accused Pinckney of being lazy exactly, for, like Kleine, he put in countless hours off the court. But at one time or another his intensity, his competitiveness, his toughness, his concentration, and his confidence had all been brought into question. Casey studied him one day and mused: "Hmm, I wonder if the NBA would allow us to use a cattle prod." Pinckney was probably as bright as any Celtic with the exception of Michael Smith, but he rarely came back at anyone with a snappy retort. During a time-out in one game, Casey hollered at him for missing an easy pass, and Pinckney just stood there, nodding his head. Casey suddenly realized that he would've preferred Pinckney to turn on him and say, "Screw you! The pass was lousy, so get off my back!" Despite his size and athletic ability, Pinckney sometimes seemed to diminish physically. He hung at the back of team huddles, shuffled unassumedly onto the court, and constantly put his hand to his mouth and coughed, even, on occasion, in the middle of a play. His wife called it his "basketball cough," and swore that he never did it in the offseason.

Pinckney felt that the "Easy Ed" tag was unfair. "I think coaches put guys in a mold, and say, 'This is how he *should* be,'" said Pinckney. "They think if I play this wild, crazy, out-of-control style that I'll suddenly reach my potential. But I don't agree. I have to play under control. It's ME." His family and friends agreed with him to an extent, but they too sometimes urged him to be more aggressive. His wife, Rose, an outgoing, emotional, and thoroughly engaging woman who had been a Villanova cheerleader, sometimes confronted him after games. "How could you let that guy do that to you?" she'd say. Or she'd take a negative comment made by a broadcaster and challenge her husband. "You have to go out there and prove these people wrong." Quite often Rose got so wrapped up in a game that she couldn't watch it and had to adjourn to the wives' room. But for some reason she was in her seat, cheering and clapping, on the night that cheers of "Eh-DEE!" boomed through Boston Garden.

"I won't play thirty-five minutes every night," said Pinckney after the game, humility in every inflection of his voice. "But if it has to be done in the playoffs, hopefully they'll look down at me and say, 'He can do it.'" The Celtics' coaching staff fervently hoped they would be able to do exactly that.

Parish had joked that Pinckney's performance would make him exempt from Casey's postpractice drills, but the afternoon of March 30, the day before the Easter Sunday that the Bulls came to town, found Pinckney, Kleine, and Vrankovic standing thirty feet apart and catching wildly-thrown balls. "Helps their hand-eye coordination," said Casey. Jennings stood by and shook his head—he called the threesome "Casey's Slaves." "Now, if their legs are gone tomorrow late in the game," said Jennings, "we'll know the reason."

Though the decision was not made public, McHale planned to return to action against the Bulls. He was asked when he would be showing up at the Garden for pregame treatment the following morning.

"Probably about seven A.M.," he answered. "That's the only time to beat Derek."

He made the comment good-naturedly, but it had an edge to it too. Smith was a popular player, and the team truly wanted him to recover, but the feeling among some of the Celtics was that Smith's rehabilitation consumed a little too much of the training staff's time, considering that his return was, at best, iffy.

Jeff Twiss, the Celtics' director of public relations, circulated a release from the Bulls stating that Jordan would do no one-on-one interviews that afternoon and would talk to the press only between ten-forty-five and eleven-forty-five A.M. on game day. Steve Bulpett crossed out Jordan's name and replaced it with "Pinckney." When a reporter approached Jennings and asked him an innocuous question about the game, he put up both hands, smiled, and said: "Sorry, I'm adhering to the Jordan interview policy. Maybe tomorrow between ten-forty-five and eleven-forty-five." The feeling about Jordan around the league was mixed. When pinned down on the subject and asked to talk on the record, almost every NBA player had to admit that he was an exceptional talent, probably the greatest the game has ever seen. But at the same time almost everyone resented the lucrative endorsements and generally positive press that he received. How could they not, for Jordan was easily the best-known player in the NBA, probably the best-known athlete in the world? Every dollar he received from Nike or Coca-Cola was one dollar that someone else would not get. The problem was, there wasn't one clear thing to hold against him. He had a large ego, sure, but he played in a league where everyone—well, Eddie Pinckney notwithstanding—had a large ego. He criticized his teammates in public, but so did Bird and, on occasion, so did Magic Johnson. He could be selfish on the court, but he was still one of the most creative passers in the game. Sure, his righteous, cooperative attitude was a little bit of an act, but he pulled it off well.

But it was de rigueur to bust Jordan whenever possible. And so when McHale entered the locker room on Easter morning (not at seven A.M. but fairly early) and found Jordan's picture on the cover of *Hoop* magazine (the official NBA publication), he picked up a pen and went to work.

"Now why are we autographing these?" he said. "I think Michael needs a little work." He colored in Jordan's eyes, added a beard, then finished up with a pair of nerdy-looking spectacles. "There," he said, pulling back and admiring his work. He tossed the pen to Joe Kleine.

"Kevin, is Will Perdue invited to your coming-back party?" Kleine asked. Perdue was the Bulls' backup center.

"Will is definitely on the guest list," said McHale.

One of the stories in the morning paper concerned the troubled Roy Tarpley of the Mavericks, who had been charged with driving under the influence in Dallas. Tarpley, who was out for the season with an injury, had already been a two-time loser to the NBA's drug policy and was facing a lifetime suspension if he tested positive for cocaine again.

"Does the DUI put him out?" asked Shaw.

"No, only drugs are a third strike," someone said.

"What a league," said McHale. "There's no penalty if you get in a car drunk. That's a 'Hey, how to be, big guy.' "

Commissioner Stern wouldn't have put it quite as cynically as McHale, but Stern had lately expressed concern that the NBA's much-admired drug policy, instituted nearly a decade earlier when cocaine use threatened to ruin the league, did not address the problem of alcohol.

The Boston-Chicago game was played with postseason intensity from the first minute. Reggie Lewis was determined that Jordan was not going to embarrass him like he did in their first meeting in Boston Garden in November, and he relentlessly pursued the Bulls superstar, tugging at him, pushing him, anything just to contain him. Jordan finished the first half with only 7 points. McHale returned to loud cheers at the beginning of the second period, replacing Bird, who, as had become his custom, spread out a towel in front of the Celtics bench and stretched out to ease the tightness in his back. McHale imme-diately blocked a shot by Scottie Pippen, then drew a foul at the other end. Each time he got the ball in the low post, Derek Smith hollered at Chicago's Horace Grant, "Seatbelt, Horace! Seatbelt, baby!" Transla-tion: "Kevin's gonna take you for a ride."

With 10:29 left in the game, the Celtics led 91–80 and the Garden was louder than it had been since that nearly flawless performance against Phoenix some twelve weeks earlier. The lead reached 96–82 when a McHale shot bounced on the rim six times before finally going in; as it did, he raised his arms to the sky. But Jordan finally broke out of the prison Lewis had built around him and brought the Bulls back to a 108–107 lead with just over two minutes left. At that point, the Celtics missed a shot and Jordan went up to grab a rebound between three of the greatest rebounders ever—Bird, McHale, and Parish—then had the presence of mind to call time-out before he was tied up. The Bulls scored again to go up by 110–107, but Lewis hit an unlikely three-point bomb with nineteen seconds left to tie the game. He had been 0-for-11 in three-point attempts to that point, and, indeed, some observers be-lieved that his weakness as a long-range shooter would keep him from being an All-Star. The ensuing sidecourt throw-in by the Bulls resem-bled a game of Pac-Man, with Jordan scurrying around the court, trying desperately to elude various and sundry Celtics and receive the in-bounds pass from Bill Cartwright. Lewis pulled and tugged and bumped him until, finally, Cartwright threw the ball away. Chicago coach Phil Jackson complained in vain for a foul, as he should have. And the referees kept the whistles silent, as *they* should have. Unless Jordan were out-and-out wrestled to the floor, experienced NBA officials do not call a personal in such game-deciding situations. At the other end, Bird missed a three-point attempt and the game went into overtime.

The situation looked grim for the Celtics when both McHale and Parish fouled out in OT. (Both college basketball and the NBA should grant players an additional foul in overtime games—it's only logical.) Three of McHale's six personals were offensive fouls called by veteran referee Mike Mathis as McHale battled for position near the basket. Mathis is one of the league's most highly respected officials, but the Celtics firmly believe that he has it in for McHale, and his calls on that afternoon seemed to reflect it. (Other teams believed McHale was one of the most protected players in the league.) But the Celtics hung on and the score was 118–118 when Jordan got the ball near the sideline by the Celtics' bench and threw in a twenty-five-footer as he fell into Chris Ford's lap. Immediately, Mathis signaled that it had come after the buzzer, a decision verified by TV replay. And so it was on to a second overtime.

"I have to take a leak so bad," said Jennings to Casey, "we might have to concede it."

"You guys outta paper yet?" Ford asked press row with a smile.

There was tension, but it was positive tension, tension that evolved naturally out of the battle, tension that inspired, instead of paralyzed. Certainly it inspired Bird. He hit two step-back jump shots, then got Grant up in the air, drew the foul, and bounced in a jumper for a three-point play. "Don't send a boy to do a man's job," Pippen teased Grant later. Key baskets by Shaw and Brown helped the Celtics hold on to the lead that Bird gave them, but Lewis missed 4 of 6 free throws down the stretch that would've clinched the victory. "Why the heck don't you make one, Reg, so we can git the hell outta here?" Bird said to Lewis at one point. But Jordan, with Lewis all over him, missed two three-point shots that would've tied the game and the Celtics walked away with a 135–132 victory that was either invigorating or enervating, no one was sure which.

Bird's stat line was astounding for a thirty-four-year-old man with a bad back. He played fifty-two minutes, one more than Jordan, one fewer than Lewis, and scored 34 points. They came on 36 shots, leading someone to quip that his shoulder probably hurt him more than his back. But he grabbed 15 rebounds, had 8 assists, and time after time made the clutch shots. "Damn," said Grant after the game, "I thought he was old and lame." Jordan had taken 36 shots, too, but, thanks largely to Lewis's tenacity, made only 12 of them.

The epitaph on this outstanding Easter Sunday game was left to Johnny Bach, Chicago's assistant coach, a handsome, nattily attired gentleman whose personal philosophies lie somewhere to the right of Ronald Reagan's but whose gift for poetical analysis is nonpareil in the NBA.

"What did I think of the game?" said Bach. "It was an exquisite test of will, endurance, stamina, and pride."

That it was.

CHAPTER 9

Limping Home

APRIL

Meadowlands Arena, hard off the New Jersey Turnpike in the least appetizing area of New Jersey, generally brings out the worst in the NBA, and the April 2 game between the Celtics and the host Nets was no exception. A few nights earlier, Charles Barkley had tired of the abuse being heaped on him by a fan sitting near the court—insults are easily picked up at the Meadowlands because there isn't much crowd noise—and directed a stream of spit at the man. Unfortunately, Barkley missed and hit an eight-year-old girl, the definite nadir of his controversial career. As Sam Bowie, the Nets' oft-injured and oft-maligned center, pursued a ball into the first row of seats early in the Celtics game, a fan stood up less than two feet from him and screamed, "Bowie, you're GARBAGE! Absolute GARBAGE!" During a time-out, a recording of "The Mexican Hat Dance" played over the public address system. Kleine and Pinckney, seated side-by-side on the bench, clapped in unison. Another night of fun at the Meadowlands.

With little more than a half-hearted effort, the Celtics built a 21-point lead midway through the third period that promptly shrank to 13 early in the fourth. Ford gathered his troops around him during a time-out, shrugged his shoulders, and said, "Look, either you want it or you don't." They did, winning by 94–77. Near the end of the game, the Nets' Reggie Theus was hammered as he drove to the basket but didn't get a call. When Ford subbed for Bird a few seconds later, Bird said to referee Ronnie Nunn as he walked off the court: "Purty bad when the refs don't even wanna work. Theus got hacked right in fronta ya." Nunn shot him a look. "What did you say, Larry?" he asked. Bird shook his head. "Nuthin', nuthin' at all," said Bird.

Pinckney's hot streak continued unabated. At one point a fast-break pass bounced off his hands directly to Reggie Lewis for a lay-up assist, and a little later a Celtics shot inadvertently tipped in by the Nets' Derrick Coleman was credited to Pinckney because he was closest to the play. That gave him 12 field goals in a row without a miss. "Shhh," he said when someone brought it to his attention. His buddy Kleine, meanwhile, was on the other end of the seesaw. He had performed poorly (0-for-5 in just five minutes of action), and worse, he had to listen to Bird and other teammates talk about how the Celtics reserves had briefly let the Nets back in the game. Bird wasn't singling out anyone, but that didn't ease Kleine's frustration. "Why doesn't anyone talk about the [March 28] Miami game?" said Kleine. "The subs got the big lead, and the first team let them back in the game."

A night at the Meadowlands could bring out the bear in anyone.

Sitting courtside at the Celtics' game-day shootaround in Milwaukee on April 11, the *Globe*'s Peter May and Eddie Lacerte sparred for a few rounds, hardly an unprecedented occurrence. Bird had been kept home from the April 6 game in Orlando (won, not coincidentally by the Magic, 102–98) because of back spasms, and he still wasn't with the team a week later.

"Give me *something*, Eddie," said May. "Just some idea of when he'll be back."

"Day to day," said Lacerte. "That's all I know."

"Well, it's not as serious as last time, right?" said May. "I mean, he won't be out a month, right?"

"Day to day," said Lacerte. "That's all we can say." Lacerte smiled. "I have a new hero, by the way," he said. "Pete Williams." At the time Williams was the Pentagon spokesman charged with giving noninformational press conferences about the Middle East.

With seven games remaining, the season had clearly reached the automatic-pilot stage. Things were going poorly on the injury front. Bird was hurt and absent. Reggie Lewis was hurting but playing. Ditto for McHale. The long-awaited activation of Derek Smith on April 4 (during a 123–104 rout of the horrific Nets at Boston Garden) had been, rather than a cause for celebration, a public relations defeat. During his ten minutes of action in the Nets game Smith had looked stiff and tentative. He was disappointed, having wanted to make a much grander entry into Celtics lore. Maybe it was frustration or maybe it was his honest feeling, but after the game Smith indicated that the Celtics had rushed him back into action before he was ready. Ford and Lacerte were angered by the comments, believing, quite correctly, that the Celtics had been patient and diligent in Smith's care, and that his main problem was overcoming the fear of further knee problems. They understood that that was no small psychological barrier, but neither did they appreciate being the scapegoat for those fears. Strangely, Smith then complained two nights later when Ford didn't play him during the Orlando game. The Celtics still felt they needed him, but his attitude was wearing thin in some quarters.

On the other hand, the mood of the team was not all negative. The collection of disappointing losses—to teams like the Nets, the Heat, the Hornets, the Pacers, and the Magic—had all but cost them a chance at the best record in the Eastern Conference (even though the Bulls, too, were showing the lack of a killer instinct). But second place was probably secure, owing to Isiah Thomas's long-term absence from the Pistons lineup. True, the Celts were essentially dog-paddling in one place, but that was better than drowning altogether.

As the Celtics walked off after shootaround, they ran into an old friend and teammate, the Bucks' Fred Roberts, a wacky, good-natured Mormon who is known league-wide for his unpredictable offensive play as well as an extremely bad crewcut that makes him look like a serial killer from the 1950s. Roberts and McHale chewed the fat for fifteen minutes, after which McHale recalled Roberts's tenure with the team during the 1986–87 and 1987–88 seasons. "Fred would miss his first jumper and everybody on the bench would say, 'Uh oh, Freddie Krueger's here tonight,' " said McHale. "If Fred got off to a bad start, it was usually *Nightmare on Elm Street* from there on in." Bird always joked that he never wanted to make physical contact with Roberts, fearing that his unpredictable shooting touch was contagious. Roberts would run up to Bird to enthusiastically high-five him, and Bird would reluctantly stick out his left pinkie. Or Bird would hop out of Roberts's path, feigning fear, when he walked toward them. Roberts had left on good terms with everyone, but sometimes that kind of team humor backfired. Bird became fast friends with Brad Lohaus, another ex-Celtic and current Buck, and besides calling him "Toys R Us" because of Lohaus's proclivity to buy model airplanes and the like, rarely got on him. But McHale had targeted Lohaus for abuse as soon as he showed up in camp in 1987. After Lohaus got a perm, McHale began calling him "Fifi." It drove Lohaus to distraction and, he claimed, right out of Boston. "Kevin likes to have a good time," Lohaus said, "but I think he crossed the line." When McHale and Lohaus found themselves isolated at one end of the court during the game that evening, neither acknowledged the other.

The endless ankle-injury cycle was beginning to depress McHale—receive painful pregame treatment, play a relatively mediocre game in pain, endure pain after the game, show up tomorrow for more pain. "I saw all these young Milwaukee players warming up and feeling good," said McHale, as Lacerte manipulated the foot before the game, "and I felt like walking up to them and saying, 'You know how lucky you are to feel good like that?' 'Feeling good' makes all the difference in the world, and you know, until this ankle thing started in Seattle, this had been one of my best seasons for just plain feeling good. Now it's turning into one of the worst." Someone asked him how the years of playing on damaged feet and ankles would affect him in the future. "I'll tell you exactly how," said McHale. "I'm going to be lying on a beach somewhere, and I'll say to my wife, 'Lynn, remember all those games when I played hurt? Well, my ankle's really killing me today. Could you bring me another mai tai?' "

WEEI producer Doug Lane came into the locker room to coax someone onto the pregame show. It was not easy—there wasn't much to say and it had already been said, anyway.

"Chief, how 'bout it?" asked Lane.

"NO way, Lumpy!" said Parish. "Lumpy" was the nickname hung on Lane by Bird, who compared his fashion sense to the oafish Lumpy Rutherford character on *Leave It to Beaver.* And "No" was Parish's customary initial response when someone asked him for a favor or when an out-of-town reporter asked him for an interview. It saved him a lot of time, for only the experienced knew that Parish could be worn down in time.

"Come on, Chief," said Lane, halfheartedly. "Only take a minute."

"Why don't you get Larry?" said Parish, smiling. "He's not doing anything."

"Yeah, just call him up at home," said Bulpett. "He'll appreciate that."

McHale cracked up. "You could get the pope easier at his villa than you could get Larry on the phone."

After a few more minutes, Parish dutifully trudged out behind Lane to do the interview.

Milwaukee was not exactly a wild-and-crazy place—the Bucks' conservatively dressed dance team, after all, was sponsored by the Milwaukee College of Business—but the Bucks themselves could be a highly aggressive bunch, particularly their guards, Alvin Robertson and the underrated Jay Humphries. Ford knew he was in for a struggle if he wanted to keep the game respectable. He even went to Michael Smith early in the first period, hoping (against hope) that Smith could light a spark. Smith's defensive limitations being well known around the league, the Bucks immediately isolated over-the-hill forward Adrian Dantley on Smith and Dantley scored. Lewis was late in double-teaming Dantley, too, which caused Ford to yell: "Reggie, you taking a picture? GO HELP!" During a time-out after the Celtics fell behind early, Ford said, exasperatedly, "What in the hell are you guys doing? You tell me." What they were doing was unconsciously coasting, unwilling or unable (or both) to push the throttle in a game that, without Bird, probably could not be won, anyway. Tempers were frayed. Just as Kleine turned to run downcourt, Ford screamed at him: "JOE! GET DOWNCOURT!" And Kleine hollered back, "I know, Doc, I know. Jeez!" Frustrated by the Bucks' aggressive double-teaming and slap-happy defense, Kleine was whistled for a foul and gestured angrily at Robertson, a former teammate and friend from the University of Arkansas. Robertson stood at the line for at least fifteen seconds grinning at Kleine, a reaction that made the Celtic even more furious. The Bucks won going away, 111–92. Freddie Krueger made 12 of 15 shots and scored 26 points.

"We're coasting right now and we've got a week to straighten out," said Ford after the game.

"We've got to take a look inside, improve individually," suggested Parish.

"We were soft," said Kevin Gamble.

They were just things to say, comments to make as they packed their bags for the trip home. What the Celtics needed, everyone knew, were two small miracles—painless, healthy feet and ankles for McHale, and the return of Bird with a strong and supple back.

During a time-out early in the April 14 home game against the Knicks, Casey suggested a way to defense New York's Kiki Vandeweghe, a sometimes-devastating, sometimes-catatonic offensive player who had shredded the Celtics defense early. When Vandeweghe came off a pick set by Ewing and drove toward the basket, Casey wanted Parish, who was guarding Ewing, to fake—"hedge" in NBA terms—toward Vandeweghe, but have Pinckney slip off his man and pick up Vandeweghe.

"Won't work," said Parish. "Eddie won't be able to get there in time, and Vandeweghe will get a dunk."

Casey and Ford considered it for a moment and decided that Parish was correct. They did it his way and Vandeweghe was shut down.

If there was an underrated aspect to Robert Parish as a basketball player it was his knowledge of the game. He was that rare NBA center, too, with soft hands and the ability to dribble himself into shooting position, even if he sometimes looked awkward doing so. No one in the league so forcefully conveyed a strong and silent image as Parish, yet Bird, for one, always praised Chief as the best "talker" on the defensive end, someone who could always be counted on to communicate where the picks were coming from and whether or not a teammate was going to be caught. And whereas no one was in a bigger hurry to leave practice than Chief, no one, including McHale and Kleine, got a bigger kick out of being there than Parish. He was happiest, it seemed, when he was sitting out of a scrimmage, hollering encouragement and insults at equal volume. Almost anything Bird did, particularly if he did it against Michael Smith, would get a rise out of Chief. "BUST 'EM, CAP!" he'd yell at the top of his lungs. "BUST THAT CHUMP!" He was an expert at making a player look ridiculous with just a little twist of a name. "Nice play, Pic-NIC!" he'd yell at Pinckney, or "Way to go, Pop-SICLE!" he'd yell at Popson.

But these things, like so much else about Robert Parish, were not particularly well known. His desire for privacy was no more intense than Bird's, yet he had been much more successful than Bird at achieving that privacy. Unlike Bird's boyhood in the hoop heaven of Indiana, where basketball is engrained in the collective consciousness, Parish was born, raised, and college educated in Shreveport, Louisiana, no basketball hotbed that. He unburdened some facts of his life reluctantly, and others remained steeped in mystery. When he did talk, he invariably revealed an extremely sensitive man with a long memory. In one of the few in-depth features ever written about him, Parish told Jackie MacMullen that he never forgot the pain and torment he felt by being so much taller, and, at first, so much clumsier than his peers. He never forgot the times he heard the word "nigger" whispered down the halls after his high school was closed and he was bused to a more integrated one. He never forgot the anguish of missing two free throws that cost Centenary a victory over its arch-rival, Houston.

Other reporters had detected this sensitivity too. Back in 1987, a Sports Illustrated writer informed Parish that the magazine wanted to do a story on him. Parish was taken aback. "You want to do a story on me?" he said.

The writer said yes, and added, as a joking aside: "We've done our story on Kareem for this week."

Parish took it as an insult and refused to do the interview. When a different SI writer, Alexander Wolff, showed up to do a cover story in February of 1991, Parish at first refused to sit still for the interview, until friends and advisers convinced him it would be good for his image. Predictably, Wolff's story was overwhelmingly positive, as were almost all written about Parish. Interviewers invariably found it fascinating that a heartbeat and a mind clicked under that impenetrable exterior.

Chief finished with 23 points and 13 rebounds in the 115–102 victory over the Knicks, outplaying, as usual, Ewing, ten years his junior, who had 33 points but only 4 rebounds. After the game, Knicks' coach John MacLeod engaged in his obligatory gushing. "Boston played well, and if they continue like this, they could be the NBA champions," said the chamber of commerce president, who probably had something good to say about the lettuce from Chernobyl. "Today they continued to show why they should be favored to win the NBA championship. When you look at a club that is this deep, with veterans and quickness, you know it's a really good team." On and on.

"They did a good job. We double-teamed them today and they still rotated the ball and ran. They have the best of both worlds, and that's why I think they're as good as anyone who has come down the road this year." On and on some more.

"Every time I've seen them, they've been awesome. This is legitimate, not whimsy. They've been on a long-term run. With Bird they're strong, and without Bird they're strong. I'll be surprised if they don't win the championship, to be honest with you."

Evidently MacLeod did not want to consider the other alternative—that his own club was so weak and dispirited that *any* reasonable team would look good against it. At any rate, MacLeod's analysis was so faulty, so blatantly one-sided, that hardly anyone subscribed to it.

Certainly Bill Laimbeer did not. The Pistons' center was waiting to deliver his own ratiocination about the Celtics, when Boston, Bird-less again, journeyed to Auburn Hills on April 16. The Celts had by this time clinched second place in the conference, meaning they would have home-court advantage on the Pistons should they meet in the second round of the playoffs. Laimbeer professed not to care.

"Boston has some obvious question marks," said Laimbeer. "Bird's health. Dee Brown has been good, but his outside shooting is still unproven in the playoffs. No one's sure how Gamble will play in halfcourt situations. Brian Shaw's ability to handle pressure in the postseason is unproven. The Celtics have had a real good season, but all those are legitimate questions." They were, too. The Pistons had struggled all season, but Thomas had returned, and they could count on their experience being worth 5 or 6 points a game in the playoffs.

Casey had written the words "Message Game" on the blackboard. If it was, the message for the Celtics was: Forget It. Thomas and Dumars unnerved Shaw and Lewis immediately, their backcourt pressure helping to forge a 15–2 lead. Parish picked up two quick fouls, exited, returned, and immediately got another, for a total of three in forty-six seconds, reminiscent of an ex-Celtic named Greg Kite, whose proclivity to collect fouls in bunches was legendary. "Musta been some kind of record," intoned Chief after the game. At halftime, with Detroit leading by 23 points, Pistons TV switched to an important NHL play-off game involving the Detroit Red Wings. "You know," Ordway told his listeners on WEEI, "that's not a bad idea. Let's go to the Red Wings, too."

Michael Smith entered the game in the third period to play his obligatory disastrous few minutes. He committed a foolish foul as John Salley, a poor outside shooter, tried a jump shot, then he got whistled for traveling, then he fouled Salley again as he fought to get through a pick. Smith's future as a Celtic, he knew, was not bright, and the knowledge frustrated him. He had been an athletic marvel his entire life, the kind of kid who could catch a football over his shoulder when he was five years old, a high school All-American in football (as a quarterback), volleyball, and basketball. Sports came easily to him because of his formidable hand-eye coordination. He was a smart player, a finesse player, the guy who always had more touch, softer hands, more feel for the game than his opponents; in volleyball, for example, his specialty was setting the ball rather than spiking it, even though he was six feet nine. Unlike Bird and McHale, Smith im-mersed himself in the literature of sport too, reading all the magazines, studying the daily blotch of agate type, constantly comparing himself to other top athletes in New Jersey and Texas. His matriculation at Brigham Young University was a given—he was a high-profile athlete and a Mormon, and BYU was the only place for him. He left college after his freshman year for a two-year mission to southeast Argentina, during which he played pickup basketball only a few times. But he was older and more mature when he returned and he had three good years, finishing as BYU's second all-time leading scorer behind Ainge.

His Celtics teammates found it hard to believe but Smith once had the reputation for being somewhat the campus rebel, which did not require much at BYU. He wore his hair in a semispike cut, he rarely donned socks, he frequently had a three-day growth of beard, and he did not get along with his college coach, the extremely low-key Ladell Anderson. The reputation bothered Smith. "I never did anything that was against school policy or church standards," he said. "Take my beard. Frankly, I hate shaving. The real reason is that my skin is extremely sensitive, and if I shaved every day I'd break out, get all splotchy with acne. But I shaved when I had to. At BYU, you couldn't take a test unless you were clean shaven and I always was."

Smith traced his problems in Celtic Land to the summer before his rookie season. He says he received the message that he should get stronger, so he reported at 237 pounds, fifteen above his most comfortable weight. He got injured almost immediately, the extra weight being the primary cause. While he was on the injured list, he missed a bus to a Celtics exhibition game by one minute. "They waited *twenty-two* minutes for Kleine and Pinckney!" said Smith. That was classic Michael Smith—he remembered exactly how many minutes Kleine and Pinckney were late. He felt that his slow start had given him the tag of being both an undependable space cadet and a poorly conditioned player, and that he hadn't been able to disprove either of them.

Smith's bigger problem, however, was that his type of athleticism was not necessarily the athleticism that succeeds in the NBA. One day at Hellenic College he stood at the free-throw line with a football, and, on his first attempt, tossed it into the basket at the other end; there just wasn't much call for that sort of thing during the game. He lacked strength, and his arms were quite short for a man of his height, thus limiting his rebounding ability. In addition, the Celtics brass thought he was a selfish player, and that didn't help his stock, either. One NBA scout watched a particularly cloddish Smith performance in one game and said, "You know, the Celtics probably wish this kid still had to go on his mission."

But Smith hadn't played any worse than anyone else (with the exception of McHale, who scored a game-high 26 points) in the 118–90 drubbing to the Pistons, and Ford tried a different tack after the game. Behind closed doors, he told his team that *they*, not he, would have to explain their desultory performance to the press. Ford wasted little time getting rid of the reporters after the game. "They made us look foolish as far as handling the ball goes," he said. "But, look, I'm tired of answering the questions, okay, guys? Ask the players." Then he walked away, disappearing behind the door leading to the "team only" section of the locker room. That left only Joe Kleine and a half dozen or so reporters.

"So, Joe," said Peter May, "whatta you say?"

Kleine looked up with a wicked smile. "I have no idea what's wrong with us," he said. "You'll have to ask the coaches." Then he picked up his bag and strode out of the room. "I stood tall, didn't I?" he said.

One by one, the other players filtered out and mumbled a few responses, but no one's heart was in it. A Detroit radio broadcaster had the misfortune to ask McHale how the 28-point margin would affect the Celtics down the road, should they meet the Pistons in the playoffs. McHale stared at him incredulously.

"You're kidding, right?" he said.

"Well, no," said the broadcaster.

"We lost a game in the Finals once by 45 points," said McHale, "then came back to win the championship." (Actually, the margin of defeat

was 33 points (137–104) to the Lakers in Game 3 of the 1984 Finals.)
McHale breathed a heavy sigh. "Look, tomorrow's another day, and
we're planning to assemble for practice as usual." The reporters
walked away, and McHale added under his breath: "And after we
assemble, then we'll dissemble."

On his way out the door someone offered a box score to Parish.

"No thank you," said Chief, who kept walking.

The Celtics played even worse, if possible, two nights later against
the 76ers in Philadelphia. They were without both Bird and Lewis, who
had decided that his ailing back needed a rest too, although, unlike
Bird, he had come along for the ride. The staff was not particularly
happy with Lewis's decision, and Lewis, for his part, was not particularly happy that his efforts in playing with pain had been somewhat
overlooked, at least in relation to the attention that Bird's injury received. But the playoffs were a week away, and his decision to rest was
probably a smart one in any case. Once again, though, the mere
presence of Barkley seemed to taunt the Celtics—he unexpectedly
decided to return to action despite a sprained left knee. "I can hurt it
worse, but I can't worry about that," he said. "Just think, if I tear up my
knee and can't move anymore, I can become a reporter."

The Celtics might've realized what kind of night it was going to be
when Jennings was introduced as *Jan* Jennings before the game.
Parish made a basket, and the organist played "Ol' Man River." Parish
threw a pass away at the other end, and the organist played "What Kind
of Fool Am I?" Pinckney made a basket and the organist played the
theme from "Mr. Ed." Gamble was the only Celtic who seemed to have
a pulse, collecting 16 points in the first period and finishing with a
game-high 33. Otherwise, the mediocre 76ers' pressure gave Shaw
and Brown fits. Michael Smith came into the game and contributed
two turnovers and two personal fouls in two minutes. Boston was so
passive under the basket that Manute Bol, the seven-foot-seven human two iron, easily the least-skilled player in the league, looked at
times like Bill Russell.

"At exactly what point," asked Steve Bulpett on press row, "did we
begin covering the Clippers?"

In the second period Barkley extended his hand to Shaw, and Shaw
high-fived him, a move reminiscent of Ken Bannister's slapping five
with Bird. That gesture of fraternization so incensed the *Globe*'s Dan
Shaughnessy, who was home watching the game on TV, that he wrote
a column about it two days later. "Have the Celtics gotten so soft that
now they congratulate the other team in midgame?" asked Shaughnessy. "Is this how you get ready for the playoffs?"

Not ideally it wasn't. But the Celtics—without their leader, and with McHale and Lewis far from 100 percent—couldn't do anything else. Ford reached back into his past for a metaphor. "We looked like a CYO team out there handling the press," he said. Jennings chose one from the Middle East war accounts in *The New York Times* that he read as he sat dejectedly on a bench in front of an empty row of lockers.

"You know what we are?" said Jennings. "We're Kurds. We keep getting attacked and attacked, and all we can do is run."

Bird and Lewis missed the following evening's game in Cleveland (a 124–117 loss), but both returned for the final regular-season game of the season on Sunday, April 21. Clearly, Bird had to come back to test his skills, lest they be totally rusty for the playoff opener against the Pacers on Friday, April 26, at the Garden. He had missed the Celtics' previous seven games, five of which were losses. For the season, that put the Celtics' record in games played without Bird at 10–12; when he was on the floor, by contrast, the Celtics were 46–13. That was not merely an *indication* that the Celtics were a far, far better team with him; it was abject proof. Bird's performance against Atlanta was fairly strong. He had 17 points, 7 assists, 4 steals, and 4 rebounds in thirty-four minutes. The bad news was that his return really didn't alter the trance-like play of most of the other Celtics in a 117–105 defeat. Parish, around for a rare postgame interview, said: "This was a game where we should not have had to ask anything from Larry. He needs a chance to get his timing back. I wasn't concerned about him at all. It's the other guys that didn't step forward. It's the other guys that are out of sync."

Bird was reluctant to talk, and already had his overcoat on when he faced reporters. Derek Smith, dressing next to him, joked that he was stealing all the reporters away. "You can have them, believe me," said Bird. His analysis of the Celtics' problems was cryptic. "We need something right now because we're not playing good basketball," he said. "You'd better ask the coach what that is, because if I tell the truth, tell you what I think, then everyone will get ticked off."

What he thought, privately, was not all that surprising. He thought that the young players—Shaw, Lewis, Gamble, and Brown—were merely going through the motions, waiting for the playoffs, waiting for him to return and shoulder the major part of the load. And he was more correct than not.

Over in the Atlanta locker room, meanwhile, Doc Rivers was trying to describe a play during which Hawks guard Rumeal Robinson drove

the lane and threw a shot high over the outstretched arms of
Vrankovic. ". . . then Rumeal threw it up over . . . over . . . damn, just
can't remember his name," said Rivers.

Jon Koncak leaned over from a nearby locker and said, "You mean
Weird Al Yankovic?"

After the game, the entire Celtics family—players, coaches, execs,
broadcasters, wives, girlfriends, children—drove over to Hellenic College for the traditional end-of-the-season picnic, which was moved
inside because of rain. The mood was somewhat rainy too—four
straight defeats by an average margin of 18 points dominating the
emotional weather pattern. Kleine came armed with his videocam to
record a few final impressions of the regular season. At one point he
zoomed in on Johnny Most who was, incredibly, lighting up a cigarette
even though he was attached to an oxygen tank that helped him
breathe. "I gotta get this on tape," whispered Kleine. "I could be
recording history. Hellenic College blows up with all the Celtics in it."
Doing his best Fellini, Kleine aimed his zoom lens at the no-smoking
warning on the machine.

"It's no problem, babe," Most rasped through the breathing device.
"Ya can smoke. Just gotta be careful."

Immediately after the two-hour affair, Ford, Casey, and Jennings
gathered up the leftover cookies and cake and headed for Ford's house
to establish the game plan for the first round of the playoffs. "We
drowned our sorrows in junk food and the Pacers," said Jennings.
Kathy Ford, who had lived through two straight first-round elimina-
tions, studied the agitation, the nervous energy, and the preoccupation
woven into the faces of her husband and his assistants, and offered this
assessment of the playoffs: "It's a whole new wave of terror."

If nothing else, the Celtics' poor finish carried with it the possibility
of a formidable rationalization—in the previous season under Rodgers,
Boston had played some of its best ball late in the season, winning
eleven of its last thirteen games, yet still went belly-up in the playoffs
against the Knicks. Perhaps the disastrous finish was just what the
Celtics needed to awaken from their stupor and realize exactly how
much better they had to play to win a championship. Perhaps. Perhaps.
Perhaps.

In the NBA world, four full days of practice preparation was a
godsend, so Ford decided that he had the time to go back to basics.
When the team gathered at Hellenic on Monday morning, April 22, the
day after the final-game loss to Atlanta, they found waiting for them a
host of drills they hadn't run since training camp, drills that stressed

conditioning and fundamental defensive principles, like sliding, keeping the hands up, and keeping the butt low. "We recreated training camp" was the way Jennings put it. Peter May called it something else in the *Globe:* "Gulag II Playoff Preparedness Camp." The staff felt that the Celtics' biggest problem was a lack of defensive tenacity on the perimeter, that Shaw, Lewis, and Brown had been far too complacent in allowing their opposing backcourtmen to penetrate and either drive to the basket or dish off; this was particularly important since the Pacers were a "drive-and-kick team." Much had been made of Parish's poor defensive play over the final few weeks of the season, but the coaches believed that he had been ineffective only because he was forced to spend too much time picking up penetrators who had shed their Celtics defenders.

On the other end, Indiana was a team that did not match up well inside with LarryKevinandRobert, and was not particularly fond of playing defense in any case. Ford decided to concentrate on the Celtics' "three-out-two-under offense," thus giving the three big men room to operate underneath. And after all the weeks and months of Ford's hollering "RUN!" the staff wanted the Celtics to slow down the tempo slightly, fast-breaking if the opportunity was clearly there, but concentrating more on taking fourteen to eighteen seconds off the shot clock and pounding the ball inside. A track meet against a young team like Indiana had disastrous possibilities.

X's and o's aside, the staff's bigger problem was reviving the enthusiasm, confidence, and killer instinct that had all but disappeared in April. Privately, the coaches felt that a lack of maturity was the root cause, augmented by the fact that Bird hadn't been around to supply that maturity. What the coaches sensed from the young guys was mental complacency. *Well, we beat every team in the league at least once. We beat Chicago at Chicago and we took care of Detroit when we had to, and, beyond that, we even beat Portland and the Lakers on the road. So we can relax a little and still win the East, particularly because Larry will be there for the playoffs.* What they should've been doing was planning for the worst, trying to elevate their own level of play and aggression should Bird not be available. Coaches didn't like to admit it, but some teams, like the Pistons of 1989–90 or, for that matter, the Celtics of 1985–86, were mature enough to coast for a while, then turn it on when they had to. But the Celtics, dependent upon Shaw, Gamble, and Brown, players untested in playoff situations, were probably not one of those teams.

Auerbach deemed the crisis of spirit so crucial that he showed up at Hellenic on the first day of postseason practice, sent the coaches to their small office, and talked to the team alone. He mentioned

toughness, the importance of setting a physical tone, and the long
tradition of postseason excellence. Nobody smiled, nobody snickered,
not when the old man was that serious. Gradually, the team seemed to
get the message and their practices became much more enthusiastic
and fruitful than they had been over the final weeks of the season. Bird
did not do much of anything at Hellenic except ride the stationary
bicycle, and besides a few reluctant "How's Larry?" queries from the
press, no one talked much about him. Casey theorized that the atmosphere was similar to that around the White House when the President
had a health problem—everyone thought about it but no one wanted to
mention it. Each day the coaches, players, and press watched Bird ride
and ride and ride—McHale joked that he was a full-fledged member of
"The Hellenic Health Club"—and every night the staff mentally pen-
ciled in "Bird" when they discussed strategy. "That isn't fair to Larry,"
said Jennings at midweek, "but it's the way it is."

   The larger question was this: Even with Bird, were the Celtics good
enough to win a championship? Some observers said yes, most said
no. But M. L. Carr, the eternal cheerleader, knew how the Celtics
should've been answering that question in their own minds.

   "There's been all this talk about 'the youngsters' and 'the new blood'
and all that," said Carr. "But what these young guys should do is get
together and think to themselves: 'We may *never* have a better chance
to win a championship than we do this year. No matter how much
better we get, we'll never be here again with players like Larry Bird,
Kevin McHale, and Robert Parish.'"

CHAPTER 10

Unfinished Business

THE PLAYOFFS

The roster of the Indiana Pacers was replete with NBA "almosts." Their best player was shooting guard Reggie Miller, who was almost a perennial All-Star. Young Michael Williams had almost turned himself into a potent point guard after a slow start. Detlef Schrempf had almost lived up to his reputation as one of the league's most versatile players and had just been voted the NBA's best Sixth Man. LaSalle Thompson, who had spent three seasons on the same Sacramento merry-go-round as Joe Kleine, was almost a legitimate NBA power forward. Between the awkward muscle provided by Greg Dreiling and the surprising finesse of the seven-foot-four Rik Smits, the Pacers almost had one legitimate NBA center. Bob Hill, who had taken over midway through the season after Dick Versace was fired, had almost become an established NBA coach. And the Pacers' most interesting ingredient, small forward Chuck Person, was almost a certified . . . what? Flake? No, he was beyond "almost" in that category. Jump-shooter? No, he was beyond "almost" there, too. In fact, Chuck Connors Person was, at times, the most devastating jump-shooter in the league, a player who sometimes lived up to his namesake, the actor who played a TV character known as "The Rifleman," through his knack of squeezing off accurate, long-range jump shots in rapid fashion.

But Person had several basic failures as a player. He was incredibly inconsistent, even given the general inconsistency of long-range jump-shooters. He relied on his jumper almost exclusively, eschewing drives to the basket that would give the Pacers more free throws and Person more clout as an all-around player. The Celtics considered him not merely a poor defensive player but an atrocious one. Person had the

211

reputation for being somewhat of a divisive force too, a man who expended more energy touting his own ability and taunting the opposition than focusing on team goals.

Person took particular delight in taunting Bird. In any real sense, he had no business doing so, for Person's NBA achievements, such as they were, did not begin to measure up to Bird's. But Person fashioned himself as somewhat of an Ali-in-the-making and figured he would garner maximum attention by challenging the gods. He figured correctly. In the days before Game 1, Person said that he was sorry Bird was in pain but added: "I'm hoping to inflict a little pain on him myself. I'm hoping when I'm done with him, he's gonna want to soak in that Jacuzzi all night long." Person came across like a pug trying to hype a fight with lines scripted by a promoter, except that these lines came from Person himself; the Pacers, as an organization, much preferred a silent Rifleman.

Bird's back was hurting—there was no doubt about that. The pain was etched in his face even when he walked around the locker room, but he communicated it most emphatically by his silence. He described the pain to Kleine and other close friends as sometimes being "excruciating," but he never talked about it publicly. Infrequently now did he bust his teammates or joke with the "brain trust." When reporters approached, he measured them warily, prepared to dodge any and all questions about backs, pain, stiffness, tenderness, and postseason surgery. For the most part, his teammates left him alone. The general feeling was that, first, his presence was needed on the floor, even if he were only 75 or 80 percent effective, and, second, that he would play as long as humanly possible. His high threshold of pain was legendary around Boston. M. L. Carr remembered an occasion early in Bird's career when he sat in the training room as Bird prepared to get an incision between his small toe and the fourth toe. "The doctor said he couldn't see well enough, so Larry reached over, grabbed a light, and stood there holding it while he got cut," said Carr. "Now, if it would've been Cedric Maxwell on that table, he would've been asking to be put to sleep." Before Game 1, Bird was in fact worried not so much about his ability to play in pain, but more about his jump shot. He had missed four full days of practice, and throughout his career he had depended upon off-day shooting sessions to keep him sharp.

That worry was justified, considering the way he played in the first half of Game 1. He missed his first six shots, and, moreover, seemed to be totally out of the flow of the game. Even when he dared to lurch his body into traffic to get off a shot, he couldn't get a favorable whistle. After one noncall, he turned to referee Bernie Fryar and asked, "Bernie, can I do that down there on defense?" Fryar nodded his head. "You sure?" said Bird. "Okay, then." And he went down and clubbed Thompson. No call. Ford, too, felt the necessity to work referee Mike Mathis after Mathis whistled Lewis for a foul on Reggie Miller. "Mike!" hollered Ford, "watch out for the World B. Free move now. Remember him?" Mathis turned and looked at him. "Yes, Chris, I remember him." Free was a legendary NBA gunner known for drawing fouls by kicking out his legs when he shot and drawing a tripping call. For the most part, though, Lewis was all over Miller without fouling him in the first half, holding the Pacers ace without a field goal, while scoring 17 himself. Bird was only 3-of-13 from the field and the Celtics halftime lead was an uncomfortable 61–56.

Ford sent the carnivorous Derek Smith into the fray in the third period. For Smith, it was clearly Show Time, a chance to demonstrate that he was still a player with NBA skills; and for the Celtics, it was time to turn Smith loose (somewhat) and try to get a return on that aggressiveness and spirit for which they had paid big bucks back in December. During the previous two weeks of practice, Smith had committed hard fouls against McHale and Michael Smith, moving someone to suggest that he suffered from a testosterone imbalance. Smith wasn't in the game twenty seconds when he dove for a loose ball and, somehow, drew a foul on Smits. The crowd promptly gave him a standing ovation. Still, the Pacers hung around and finally tied the game at 110–110 with 4:58 remaining. The intensity of the game was incredible. Bird and Person, paired off at small forward some of the time, traded insults; at one point, Bird pantomimed throwing the ball at Person during a deadball situation. McHale made matters worse late in the game when he strode up to Person and gave him a little shove, drawing a technical foul, and driving Ford crazy on the bench. McHale is known for his reluctance to get into real fights when punches are actually thrown.

But then the Celtics got hot, and the Pacers, true to their reputation as an "almost" team, got cold. Lewis and Shaw hit consecutive baskets, and then Bird stepped back and hit a jump shot over Schrempf to make it 116–110. As Michael Williams brought the ball upcourt, Bird went chest-to-chest with Person, staring right at him and saying, "Wadn't that shot a bitch, Chuck? Huh? Wadn't it a bitch?" With 2:14 left, Person made a rare drive to the basket and Bird switched off on him and literally ripped the ball out of his hands without fouling him, securing the game. At the other end, Person committed his sixth foul, and walked off the parquet as all of Boston Garden hooted at him.

"What would you call it?" said Casey after the 127–120 victory. "A game of reaffirmation? Is that a word, 'reaffirmation'? I'm getting fancy now. I don't say 'store' anymore. I say 'delicatessen.'"

Bird looked tired, but more at ease than he had been in a while, which was understandable. He had made just 6 of 20 shots from the floor but nevertheless finished with a triple-double—21 points, 10 rebounds, and 12 assists. "Early in the game I was just shootin' to warm up for the fourth quarter because I knew it was going to be a close one," he said. "I'm happy with the 6-for-20 game. I wouldn't a been during the season, but I am tonight. In this league it's tough to get the job done without practicin'."

Over in the Pacers' locker room, Person, The Mouth That Scored, as someone dubbed him, said he didn't feel at all like a loser. He had scored 23 points and even picked up 8 rebounds and 7 assists, above-average totals for him. Typically, he had made 3 of 6 three-point shots but didn't get a single free-throw attempt; Reggie Miller, by contrast, scored 12 of his team-high 24 points from the line, although he had been outplayed by Lewis, who scored 28 points.

"Bird made some big plays at the end," said Person. "But for most of the game we were able to exploit him fairly well." Actually, Person was more correct than not. Bird had defensive success only when he was matched against the none-too-quick LaSalle Thompson, known as Tank; both Person and Schrempf were far too agile and fast for him. But no one could deny that Bird's overall performance was spectacular, considering the circumstances. When the game was over, M. L. Carr turned to his son, Michael, and said, "You know, it was Larry's greatest game ever." Michael looked at him incredulously and shook his head. "I'm serious, Michael," said Carr. "You've got to realize that the man did that without a back, do you understand what that's like?"

Ninety minutes after the game, public relations director Jeff Twiss was frantically trying to locate all of the Celtics beat reporters, even those who were winding down at Fours, the bar across the street from the Garden. The medical staff had decided that Bird, who had played 41 eventful minutes, should spend the night at New England Baptist Hospital. In traction. Bird checked out of the hospital in the morning, stopped home for something to eat, and showed up at Hellenic College, right on time, for an early-afternoon practice. "Hello, asshole," was his greeting to Casey. Casey watched him walk away. "Well, he must be feeling all right," concluded the coach. The press figured that Bird would not talk, but after the brief practice session he wandered over to the sidelines as a favor to Vrankovic, who had arranged for him to be interviewed by a Yugoslavian television station. And when that interview was over, Bird found himself ringed by at least a dozen reporters. He looked wary.

"How was your stay in the hospital?" someone asked him.

"Rather not talk about it," said Bird. "Just questions about the game."

Someone tried another approach.

"Ever been in traction before, Larry?"

Bird pursed his lips. "I don't want to talk about it," he said. Then he smiled briefly. "Just in sexual acts." The crowd broke up laughing. It was another small victory for Hoosier-style public relations.

If Bird's back was bothering him, he didn't play like it—by the midway point of the second period in Game 2 at the Garden on April 28, he had been on the floor at least five times. Person was playing his game, too, raising his arms to give the three-point signal each time he released one of his long-range bombs. The Celtics seemed to be a step late getting everywhere, getting to rebounds, getting into defensive position, getting up to defend Person on the outside. Early in the second period, McHale arrived late and fouled Williams just after the point guard had made a lay-up. That led to a three-point play and brought Derek Smith off the bench. "One or the other, but not both," he shouted to McHale. "Either knock him down or let him have it. Not both." The master of mayhem himself was finally called into action midway through the third period and he immediately draped himself onto Person and forced The Rifleman to shoot an airball, one of the few times he was off target all night. But the Celtics fell behind, and Ford could not afford to leave Smith in the game for too long because he needed scoring. He never did get enough of it, and the Celtics lost 130–118. Person finished with 39 points on 16-of-24 shooting, including 7-of-10 from three-point range, one of the best displays of long-distance shooting in playoff history.

As the Celtics headed for the locker room, one fan yelled at Ford: "Better get more than two minutes out of Derek next game." Smith stopped for a minute and shook his head in agreement.

Surrounded by reporters, Person was enjoying perhaps his finest moment ever.

"I love it," he said. "I love it. National TV. Parquet floor. Fuckin' banners. All trying to stop me. But no one can."

It might've grated on the Celtics, but, on this night at least, The Rifleman was absolutely correct. With games 3 and 4 moving to Indiana, another first-round elimination did not seem out of the question.

After the game Jan Volk and several of the Celtics beat writers found themselves together at a benefit dinner at a local Jewish Community Center. The writers decided to pledge $50 in exchange for Volk's singing "Feelings." Redfaced but game, Volk staggered through an off-tune rendition probably earning more points from the press than he

had in the previous decade. At the very least, everyone agreed that his
warbling was no worse than the Celtics' defense had been on Person a
few hours earlier.

On the bus ride from the airport to the Westin Hotel in Indianapolis
two nights later, Bird and Vrankovic got to talking about the Yugoslav's
hero and tutor, Dave Cowens. Bird offhandedly mentioned the fact that
Cowens once drove a cab as a part-time job while he was one of the
outstanding centers in the NBA. Unless one knew the Dave Cowens of
fifteen years ago, "a hardwood Thoreau," as Dan Shaughnessy once
described him, the story did seem farfetched, and Vrankovic had trouble comprehending it.

"Dave drove cab?" Stojko asked.

"Sure did," said Bird.

"A cab?" said Stojko.

Bird assured him the story was true, and, gradually, Vrankovic saw
the humor in it. The joke about Cowens was that he'd turn around and
tell his passenger, "That'll be four bucks for the fare and two-fifty for
the tip." Whenever they would pass a cab after that, Stojko would poke
Bird and say, "Lazlo, is that Dave?"

Back in Boston, Johnny Most was in what was best described as a
confused state. In his rambling pregame show that aired on WEEI—
that was the bone tossed to Most when he was let go—he told his
listeners that the key for the Celtics was stopping "that Chuck Dril-
ling," thereby combining Person's first name with Dreiling's last name
and mispronouncing the latter to boot. Presumably he meant Person,
and, on that count, Most was absolutely correct.

Bird's physical condition continued to be the number-one topic of
conversation that no one conversed about. As he stepped gingerly off
the team bus before Game 3, he pronounced his condition as, "Not too
good, not too bad." Once in the locker room, a Pacers representative
stopped in to invite Parish to pregame chapel. "Make sure you tell Cap
about it," Parish told the man. "I'm serious. Very serious. Number 33."
The man nodded, but Bird did not attend. Michael Smith looked on, his
mood as somber as Parish's. "I know the whole Mormon community is
praying for Larry," he said. "He needs our prayers." The atmosphere
was so heavy the room threatened to sink.

Ted Green of the now-defunct *National* asked Smith about the
Celtics' mental state. As he paused to form his usual thoughtful and
intelligent answer, Derek Smith jumped in.

"No, Michael," said Derek, "you going for that thoughtful stuff. You
wanna be all-interview in this league, you just gotta let that shit flow.

Don't be thinking too much." Derek knew of what he spoke. If there was anyone who let the shit flow, it was Derek, who liked nothing, the Celtics came to realize, more than the sound of his own voice. A few weeks earlier, during the road trip to Orlando, Smith showed up at poolside wearing his Celtics warm-up outfit, a definite signal that he was not in search of anonymity. Celtics fans, the infamous Green People who congregate at every hotel and arena where the Celtics happen to be, poured out the doors to talk to Derek. It started to rain a little while later, but Derek was still talking and a group of fans were still listening. Eventually, they hunched together under an umbrella as Derek continued to talk. One of the players noticed the poolside convention and called another player, who called another player, who called another player. Pretty soon everyone was watching from their windows as Derek talked and the rain continued, on and on, deep into the afternoon.

The Pacers did their best to get the crowd into the game from the outset by choosing that evening to recognize Detlef Schrempf—or "Deltlif" as Bird called him—for winning the Sixth Man Award, an understandable ploy. The Pacers had castigated their fans in the past for showing favoritism toward the Celtics; after a Pacers victory over Boston at Market Square Arena two seasons ago, Indiana guard Vern Fleming deadpanned: "It was so nice to come away with a win at Boston Garden." The message seemed to get through, and on this night the home fans booed all of the Celtics, their beloved Hoosier native included, during the pregame introductions. Curiously, though, the Pacers came out tight and tentative; after the game several of them mentioned that the excitement level of the crowd left them too keyed-up to play well, surely one of the great rationalizations of all time.

Actually, the Pacers probably had no chance from the outset; in the locker room before the game McHale announced that he was feeling particularly good, and, as had been the case since that fateful February night in Seattle, as went McHale's physical condition, so went his performance. He was feeling so loose, in fact, that early in the second period he stepped back behind the three-point line as if to unleash a bomb, then smiled at the bench and took a normal two-pointer that swished. He caught Ford's eye and laughed as he trotted back upcourt. In the third period, McHale again played the role of "enforcer," although in a much more McHale-like fashion. Gamble and Miller were trading words when Tank Thompson came in to intercede and pushed Gamble, drawing a technical. McHale charged up to the pack again, but this time succeeded in goading Thompson into shoving him. Thompson was ejected, and McHale sealed a 112–105 victory with a big block on Schrempf late in the game.

Boston's box score was a coach's dream. Six players scored between 13 and 22 points, and no one took more than 13 shots. The Celtics outrebounded, outassisted, and outhustled the Pacers. Lewis had once again won the battle of the Reggies, containing Miller by forcing him to his left, as the scouting report had insisted he must do. All that, and Person's tongue was tied by an exceptionally poor performance (2-of-8 from the field for 6 points). As Ford talked to the media outside the locker room, McHale shouted from the rear: "Hey, Ford, why don't you let McHale shoot more three-pointers?"

The Celtics led the series 2–1, but Brian Shaw was upset. At the practice session between Games 3 and 4 he suddenly announced he was not talking to the Boston media and wouldn't say why. When pressed by Bulpett, he finally mumbled something about "backstabbing, and I'm not just talking about what's been written." Shaw refused to elaborate in the days that followed, but, obviously, his anger had something to do with the Shaw-or-Brown point-guard debate, which had never subsided. Contrary to what Shaw thought, however, most members of the press, not to mention those whose opinion really mattered (the coaches), felt that Shaw should be the starter and Brown the off-the-bench reserve. The general public missed several points in its eagerness to embrace the new kid in town. First, a team didn't suddenly change its quarterback, certainly not in the middle of the postseason; that would send the wrong message, a message of panic to the team. Secondly, part of Brown's success stemmed from the very fact that he *was* a reserve and therefore spent much of his playing time matched up against other reserves. Brown had clearly turned into one of the better backup point guards in the NBA, but that did not necessarily translate to his being a better starting guard than Shaw. Finally, the players' respective temperaments were better suited to the roles in which Ford had placed them, Shaw the (outwardly) calm signal-caller, Brown the more mercurial element who could come in and change a game around; even Brown repeatedly referred to himself as a "spark plug." In truth, the Celtics' staff felt that Shaw had done a decent enough job in the first three games of the playoff—the tentative play of Gamble was another matter—and had no intention of making a change. Shaw should've ignored the criticism, implicit and otherwise, but, by getting himself into a funk over it, he might have hurt his performance in the playoff games that followed, a self-fulfilling prophecy of sorts.

A reporter from *The Indianapolis News*, meanwhile, came in search of the classic off-day feature story: What did the visitors do in our city between games? In point of fact, the Celtics did next to nothing outside of hitting the malls, lounging around their rooms, going out to eat, and visiting the Indianapolis Speedway. Kleine had run into a man who asked him to judge a bikini contest, however, and McHale obligingly gave that information to the reporter.

"Well, I'm not doing much of anything, but Joe's going to judge a bikini contest," McHale told the reporter.

"Ah, don't print that," said Kleine. "I'm not gonna do that." The moment the story hit the paper, Kleine said, the wife of Pacers Randy Wittman, a close friend, would Fed-Ex it to Dana back in Boston.

Sure enough, though, the following day's editions reported Kleine's invitation, followed by his plea not to print it. "Those things have a way of getting back to your wife," Kleine was quoted as saying. The moment Kleine arrived at Market Square Arena for Game 4, he picked up a courtside phone, called his wife, and explained the situation. "You know who Kevin's like?" said Kleine. "That character on 'Andy Griffith' who's always stirring up trouble, Ernest T. Bass. He's a six-foot-eleven Ernest T. Bass." In the locker room, Ernest once again pronounced himself ready and even offered instructions on how to get a call from a referee. It was McHale's theory that refs occasionally blew the whistle but had no idea who they were going to call the foul on. "Sometimes if you whirl immediately and look at the ref with a disbelieving look in your eye, he'll call it on someone else," said McHale.

Facing the prospect of elimination in their own building, the Pacers came out with unusual fire, and the game was intense from the outset. In the first period, Person lurched toward the scorer's table for a loose ball, which Tommy Heinsohn, broadcasting the game back to Boston for SportsChannel, grabbed and held for a moment.

"Gimme the ball!" Person shouted at him.

"Fuck you!" said Heinsohn, not into the microphone, before he finally tossed the ball to a referee.

Jeff Twiss, standing nearby, surveyed the scene and concluded: "Johnny Most would've been proud."

Bird and Person continued their personal battle. At one point when Bird was out of the game and lying on his towel in front of the bench, he reached over and untied Person's shoelaces as the Pacer waited for a free throw at the other end. Even when the Celtics built an 84–71 lead midway through the third period, Bird seemed to apprehend, when his teammates did not, that the game was not over. He was extremely animated in time-out huddles, slapping hands and encouraging everyone to remain aggressive. Perhaps he sensed the importance of clinching the series on that night because it would give him at least four days of rest before the second-round series began. Sure enough, Bird's fears

were justified. Indiana came roaring back over the final fifteen minutes with Person hitting one improbable shot after another. "Nobody
can guard me!" he hollered as he ran upcourt after a three-pointer.
"I'm a bad man! A BAD MAN!" Person scored 12 straight Pacers points
in the final five minutes, including a three-point shot with 2:06 left
that all but clinched Indy's 116–113 win. And the primary victim,
much to Person's joy, was Bird, who couldn't check Person on the
defensive end and even threw a misguided pass that Person stole just
prior to his clinching three-pointer.

The gloom in the locker room was palpable—the Celtics had blown
one and they knew it. There was some grumbling, and not just from
Derek Smith himself, that Ford should've used Smith (who played just
six minutes) to contain Person down the stretch. But in place of
whom? Parish, who was needed for rebounding? McHale, whose scoring (24 points) led the Celtics? Bird, who throughout his career has
rarely, if ever, been on the bench in crunch time? And if he gave Smith
big minutes by playing him consistently at small forward, Ford ran the
risk of losing Gamble for good. No Celtic was affected by the presence
of Smith more than Gamble, who was not a terribly confident and
secure individual to begin with. His head bowed slightly every time
Ford replaced him with Smith, and Gamble had to be thinking: "Hey,
no one shouted *my* name at Boston Garden this season." Gamble had
been a valuable member of the team from mid-November to the playoffs and, sooner or later, Ford knew he would need Gamble's jump
shots instead of Smith's guerrilla warfare . . . even if "later" meant next
season.

Much joy and chest-thumping, not surprisingly, filled the Pacers'
locker room. The longer the series went, believed the Pacers, the better
their chances of prevailing because of their youth and boundless energy. And the series was now going the max. Person could not be
turned off—had there been a reporter willing to spend the night, The
Rifleman would've stayed, too, rambling on and on about his play. A
sampling:

"Larry knew I was in his ear, and now I'm gonna be in his dreams."

"I knew when Larry and McHale got on me the shots were going in.
It's like I was out there for target practice, shooting H-O-R-S-E by
myself."

"Unless they come up with something different, then we're going to
go tear some of that parquet up in Boston."

Curiously, though, the one Celtic who might've been expected to be
down in the dumps after the defeat was animated, even exhilarated.
Bird challenged the Boston Garden crowd to be every bit as loud and
enthusiastic as Indiana's had been, and while he praised the play of

Person, he indicated that the situation would be much more difficult for The Rifleman on a Sunday afternoon in Boston. When a reporter related some of Person's nonstop commentary from the other locker room, Bird feigned terror. "Oh, I'm scared to death," he said. "As a matter of fact I'm so scared I'm going to jog home right now and not even wait for the plane." Had Person been able to gauge Bird's mood, even he might've held his tongue somewhat, for Bird had carved his signature into many a clutch playoff game on many a spring afternoon.

Sunday, May 5 began badly for Don Casey. He left his home at the normal time for the twelve-minute drive to Boston Garden but suddenly found himself in a massive traffic jam because of the annual Walk For Hunger. Ignoring the advice of his wife, Dwynne, he made a few other wrong turns and was suddenly lost on unfamiliar city streets. (Driving with "Casey," as his wife always called him, could be an adventure. A few weeks earlier they were en route to a game during a driving rainstorm when they had a flat tire. Casey was already running late, so he flagged down a cab, leaving his wife with the car and promising to call her on the car phone from the Garden. But he forgot the number of the phone and couldn't get in touch with her to find out if everything was all right.) Finally, Case made it to the North End of town, from where Boston Garden was visible but not immediately approachable. "Look, just drop me off at Paul Revere's house," said Casey to Dwynne, "and the hell with it." When the Caseys finally arrived, it was twelve-ten P.M., twenty minutes after the starting time for his pregame meeting with Ford and Jennings.

"Well, I guess if we don't know what we're doing now," said Casey, "we're all in big trouble."

Owner Alan Cohen, meanwhile, was breathing easier—Blades and Boards, the club in Boston Garden where many of the team executives gather before games, was serving cheese blintzes. A year earlier blintzes had been mistakenly left off the pregame menu, and the Celtics went out and lost their infamous Game 5 to the Knicks. The superstitious Cohen was positive there was some kind of cause-and-effect relationship between the blintz omission and the loss and let his feelings be known on the subject, to the point that McHale referred to that dark afternoon as "The Blintz Game."

In situations such as the one the Celtics faced on that Sunday afternoon, Bird and McHale sometimes reversed roles. McHale became the nasty Celtic, brushing aside reporters and snapping that he would only talk after the game; at the Celtics practice at Hellenic the day before the game, in fact, he almost bowled over a network cameraman who was filming him walking up the sidewalk. Bird, on the other hand, often opened up before a big game, either because he was honestly unable to hide his excitement or because he felt that conveying his enthusiasm publicly would be intimidating to the opposition. Now, one would not exactly describe his mood before Game 5 as "convivial," but he seemed more relaxed and eager than at any time in the past few weeks.

As he laced up his sneakers, NBC, which was televising the game that day, showed a clip of Person stepping off the Pacers bus outside of Boston Garden. It was brought to Bird's attention.

"There he is," said Bird, glancing ever so briefly at the screen, "the best basketball player in the world."

Ford seemed to be removing himself from center stage, not that he ever sought it to begin with. He and his tub of popcorn sat quietly in front of Derek Smith's locker in one corner of the locker room. He was asked if it was harder to be a player or a coach at such moments.

"Much harder now," said Ford. "When you're a player, you're only worried about one guy."

Tod Rosensweig came by to chat for a moment and clapped Ford on the back as he left. "Good luck," said Rosensweig, "I know you're gonna win today."

"I know it, too," said Ford.

Did he really? Dozens of times over the past months he had seen his team falter in crucial situations, fail to rise to the challenge, fail to finish off a lesser team they should've beaten. On the other hand, Ford had presided over some of the best basketball that had been played in the NBA that season. All things being equal, there was no way that Chuck Person, Reggie Miller, and the rest of the Indiana Pacers were better than LarryKevinandRobert, not to mention ReggieBrianand-Dee. Certainly not at Boston Garden in a nationally televised game that the Celtics had to win. But all things were not equal. Back pain could get to Bird. Ankle pain could get to McHale. And playoff pressure could get to anyone, the way it had already gotten to Gamble and, to a lesser extent, Shaw. And if the Celtics lost, Ford, for all of his successes as a rookie coach, would be, like Jimmy Rodgers before him, merely a guy who couldn't get the Celtics out of the first round. That thought was not pleasant.

Ford had decided that Derek Smith would get meaningful minutes and he went to him in the first period, earlier than usual. The Garden hummed with excitement and Smith promptly tried to remove Reggie Miller's head from his neck as Miller took a jump shot. But even plays like that, and the presence of a hostile Garden crowd, did not upset the Pacers. The Celtics led by only 48–46 with about four minutes left in the first half when the Pacers' Mike Sanders batted the ball away from Bird and touched off a chain-reaction of events that ultimately produced Bird's finest moments since his legendary fourth-period performance against Atlanta in the 1988 playoffs.

As soon as Sanders made the steal, Bird instinctively dove to recover it. (Though the Celtics did not keep statistics on it, Bird's dive was either his seventh or eighth of the series.) His head struck the floor hard and he remained there for several seconds, a horrifying sight for the home fans, who included his wife, Dinah. Finally, he dragged himself to his feet and walked slowly toward the bench. Ford headed him off and guided him toward the locker room, Eddie Lacerte in close pursuit. The half ended at 58–58.

NBC cameras and various members of the press camped outside the Celtics locker room, along with the Pacers' general manager Donnie Walsh, who was nervously chain-smoking.

"He'll be back," Walsh said. "It'll be a late entry for the crowd. I'll bet on it." Walsh took a long drag, then realized he didn't want his words to be misunderstood. "You know what? I hope he does come back. It'd only be right."

Inside the Celtics' locker room, while Ford discussed intensifying the defensive effort, Bird sat in the trainer's room just off the locker room. Arnie Scheller and Lacerte applied ice to his zygomatic arch (the bone directly under the right eye) to control the swelling and, according to what they said later, "evaluated him for neurological damage." In other words, *Larry, do you know what sport you're playing?* Having had much practice in the exercise, the Celtics didn't speak Bird's name at halftime, nor did they even catch a glimpse of him—the door to the training room was closed. Everyone knew that unless he was talking in tongues, he would be back.

The first five minutes of the third period were played before an audience paying divided attention, 15,000 right eyes watching the game, 15,000 left eyes scanning the ramp that led from the locker room to the court for a glimpse of number 33. With 6:51 left in the period, Bird appeared suddenly on the runway during a time-out. Bob Hill had warned his team during halftime that Bird would probably make a dramatic return—ironically, that meant they talked about the injury more than the Celtics did—but that didn't stop most of them from staring at the scene, probably with some sense of dread. Ford barely glanced at Bird when he arrived at the huddle. He figured that if Bird was back, Bird could play, for that was his MO; he rarely showed up to cheerlead. When the huddle broke, Ford nodded to him, and Bird stripped off his warmup jacket. He wiggled his left hand at the scorer's table, hollered to Parish, "I got Deltlif," rubbed his hands together, and walked back onto the court. The ovation that began when he appeared on the ramp continued as the ball was inbounded. His face was noticeably swollen.

To what could Bird's performance over the ensuing eleven minutes be attributed? His iron will? His ability to perform in the clutch, or, conversely, the Pacers' cracking under the weight of his legend? Serendipity? Celtics mystique? Coincidence? The law of averages, since he had not turned in a spectacular playoff performance to that point? All of them? Who knows? But from that point until Ford took him out of the game with 7:02 remaining, Bird played the game of basketball about as well as it could be played by anyone, never mind a thirty-four-year-old with an aching back and a mouse above his eye. He rebounded a Pacers miss and threw an outlet pass to Reggie Lewis for a basket. He assisted Lewis on a short jumper. He hit a nineteen-foot jumper from the left side. He rebounded and threw a long baseball pass to Lewis for a dunk. ("The best over-the-first-wave passer in history," Casey once said of Bird.) He drove the right side and lifted a shot high off the glass for a field goal. He drove under the basket for a reverse lay-up, drew a foul, and made the free throw. He posted up Sanders, drew contact, took a fallaway jumper from the corner and sank to his knees, like a triumphant craps player, as the ball went through; he made the foul shot for another three-point play. He found Brown for a basket on the break. He made two free throws. He took a perfect pass from Parish for a lay-up. The Celtics led by 110–96, and Ford felt it was safe to give him a rest.

It wasn't, and, as was the case in Game 4 less than forty-eight hours earlier, Bird sensed it. He didn't want to sit down and frowned when Ford told him to take a breather. He knew that the one thing the Pacers had gained during the series—heart—was the one thing that could bring them back. That, and a trapping defense to which the prone-to-panic Celtics were vulnerable. And back the Pacers came. When Bird was finally hustled back into the game, the lead had shrunk to 116–107, and even his supply of magic was exhausted. The Celtics, all of them, handled the ball uncertainly, going into the NBA version of the prevent defense by trying to hang onto a lead rather than build on it. It was clearly the time for the team quarterback to step forward and take charge, but that area was problematical. Just who *was* the quarterback in such situations? Bird, or the point guard, in this case Shaw? One could blame Shaw for not taking charge, but it is no easy matter to take the reins away from Larry Bird at Boston Garden. Since 1979, the Lakers have enjoyed an advantage over the rest of the league in such situations because the quarterbacking duties were clearly defined, i.e., when Magic Johnson is in the game, he is the boss.

With twenty-two seconds left, Boston led by only 120–118. "If they blow this," said *Herald* columnist Michael Gee at the press table, "it'll be the most discouraging playoff loss in the history of the franchise." The Pacers had the ball, and the ball, everyone knew, was going to Person. Derek Smith was quickly dispatched to cover him, which left Bird on the much fleeter-of-foot Fleming. Nevertheless, Fleming, who probably could've beaten Bird to the basket with a drive, twice passed up shot opportunities and eventually passed the ball to Person, who desperately tried to carve out a post-up position on Smith. Smith, as everyone knew, did not carve easily, and when Person finally got the shot, he was beyond the three-point line. He missed, and Shaw, after being fouled, made both free throws to give Boston a 122–118 lead.

Person promptly rumbled downcourt and swished a shot from at least thirty-five feet to make it 122–121. Whether that shot was improbable or routine no one knew by that point. Shaw was fouled again with 1.5 seconds left, and, as he waited at the free-throw line, the Pacers milled about and talked to the officials, trying to delay the game and upset Shaw. When Ford came to investigate, Person lurched at him, trying, as he admitted later, to goad either the coach or the ever-ready-to-rumble Derek Smith into a technical. It almost worked, but Ford got himself under control. Shaw hit both free throws and they were the final points in a memorable 124–121 win.

Person finished with 32 points, and, after much conversation with reporters, wandered into the Celtics locker room to congratulate Bird. Surely, Person must've been thinking, he now had the enduring respect of the Celtics legend, and, by extension, the respect of a league that hadn't really made up its mind about him. But by the time Person arrived, Bird was gone. He didn't have nearly as much to say as Person did, and, besides, there was a lot more work to be done.

Was he up to the task? Could he pull off another miracle? Who knew what Bird was thinking? But as the ensuing Detroit series progressed, it became more and more obvious that Bird's supply of guts and bravado was all but exhausted. Only his closest friends knew how badly he wanted to beat Indiana, so he would be able to summer as usual back in French Lick without the hauntingly derisive voice of Chuck Person in his ear. Lose to the home-state Pacers? That thought was poison to Bird. And over the next twelve days it became obvious that Sunday, May 5, was Larry Bird's championship game.

At practice the day before the Celtics' second-round playoff opener against the Pistons, Ford announced that game-day shootaround at Boston Garden would be "10 to 11." Pinckney and Kleine, who lived in the same apartment building in Brookline and often drove to practice together, somehow interpreted that as "10 minutes to 11" and showed up at that time. "Now, has anyone in the history of the world," wondered Jon Jennings, "ever begun a shootaround at 10:50?"

Pistons assistant coach Brendan Suhr sought out Ford before the game. "Boy, you really messed up Chuck's mind with that day-glo tie you wore in Game 1," Suhr told him. "He was out shopping for four hours trying to match it." Pistons coach Chuck Daly's reputation as a clothes horse was not unearned and was, in fact, one story line that was definitely not overblown by the media. Early in the season, *GQ* declared Mike Dunleavy, the Lakers' rookie head coach, as the best-dressed coach in the NBA, which was ridiculous. "Hey, anybody can look good for seven, eight games," complained Daly good-naturedly but sincerely. "Just try looking good for seven, eight years, night after night." The story went that he dispatched the Pistons' second assistant, Brendan Malone, on a scouting mission to L.A. specifically to report on what Dunleavy was wearing. Somehow, though, Daly's fascination with looking good never came across as pure vanity. It was a full-time hobby, an avocation, and he never tried to hide it. He was the perfect NBA coach, a man who cared deeply about winning but rarely to the point of obsessiveness. Daly could in one moment preside over an intense time-out huddle, shouting instructions and motivation, and, in the next, turn to the press table, straighten his tie and say, "Think they bought it?" Coaches like Chuck Daly were the reason that the NBA had an element of fun and looseness to it, that the militaristic NFL and the overly serious "national pastime" could never match.

The Pistons were in relatively the same state as the Celtics—they, too, had been extended to five games in the first round before turning back the Hawks. Their veteran players, championship experience, and defensive ability made them formidable, but Isiah's injury, like Bird's, also made them vulnerable. Some observers felt they could still win a championship, and were probably a better bet than the Celtics, but the prevailing opinion was that, even if they beat Boston, they would not get by the Bulls for their fourth straight appearance in the Finals.

"Well, I got us by the first round," said Daly, smiling in the locker room. "It's out of my hands now."

Laimbeer was the man the press went to before a Celtics game. He reveled in the rivalry and was much more liable to say something interesting than Thomas, who, having never forgotten his grand faux pas of 1987 ("If he was black he'd be just another good guy"), talked about the Celtics with something approaching paranoia. Laimbeer had a bruise around his eye—he generally had a bruise somewhere—and someone asked him about it.

"Oh this?" said Laimbeer. "It's a bruise to my—let's see, what's it called now?—oh, yes, my zygomatic arch. Now, it didn't get quite as much attention as when it happened to Larry." Laimbeer went on a mild but nevertheless heartfelt tantrum about what he perceived as the publicity overkill on the Bird story two days earlier. A reporter protested mildly that it was legitimate news.

"Are you telling me that a bump on the head, on anyone else, would've gotten THAT much attention?" said Laimbeer.

It was an interesting question and the answer was: With the exception of Jordan, probably not. But it didn't follow that it was not a legitimate story. The tradition of scintillating playoff games in Boston Garden, first of all, was a long-standing one that guaranteed maximum media attention. Part of the interest was negative too, since the Celtics stood to be eliminated in the first round by a lowly team and for the third straight year. So, all eyes, figuratively speaking, were on Boston Garden. The bottom line was, Bird did produce, and produce magnificently, in a situation that was almost impossibly dramatic. More to the point, he produced at a point when his very *ability* to produce was in serious question. He seemed to reach back in time during that eleven-minute streak, and his performance had an almost mystical element to it. Was the story line overblown? Not the right question. Was it irresistible? Absolutely.

"Well, you better get out of here now," Laimbeer said to a reporter. "Dave Gavitt's having a press conference, and you know what that means."

Gavitt's first words as he gathered the press around him at six-forty-five P.M., forty-five minutes before game time, were: "You know it's not good news if you see me, right?" On the preceding morning, the day after Game 5 of the Indiana series, Bird had begun experiencing severe back spasms that continued to bother him into the following day. They may have been, ironically, a legacy of Person, who, during the fourth period action in Game 5, plowed his forearms directly into Bird's lower back while setting a pick. But Bird's back problems were so much a part of his regular routine by then that nothing specific could be pinpointed as the cause. And neither, of course, could the probability of his return for Game 2 be predicted. Every Celtic knew that their chances of beating Detroit without Bird were next to nil—the Pistons were a cocky enough bunch without removing the opposition's cockiest player from their thoughts.

Considering the expenditure of emotion needed to beat Indiana, the Celtics might've suffered a letdown even with Bird in the lineup; without him, they were nearly bereft of emotion and no match for Detroit's stifling defense. The biggest cliché in sports was also the most unimpeachable: A team's offense might slump for extended periods of time, but a good defense, which is largely the result of desire and determination, could pull it through. Lewis scored 16 points in the first half but was stifled almost completely in the second, finishing with 20. In place of Bird, Ford decided to start McHale instead of Pinckney, but even the low-post genius couldn't do much against the swarming double-teams and finished with only 13 points. The Celtics didn't even score back-to-back baskets until the third period, and, early in the fourth, they surrendered 4 straight rebounds at the defensive end, watching helplessly as the Pistons ran the twenty-four-second clock down after every one. The most obvious place where Bird was missed was registered in the assist column—the Celtics had only 10 and none over the final fourteen minutes of the game. A chorus of halfhearted "Der-RICK!" cheers began in the fourth, and Ford finally called him off the bench. He promptly blocked a Joe Dumars shot, then exchanged angry words with reserve Scott Hastings as he chased down a loose ball near the Pistons bench. Smith later claimed that Hastings tripped him and sent him sprawling. Hastings admitted that he stuck out his leg but at the same time reached out to grab him before he fell.

"The one counteracted the other—it was kind of like eating a hamburger with lettuce on it," said Hastings, whose mind worked in stranger ways than McHale's.

As the seconds ticked down on Detroit's 86–75 victory, scattered boos drifted down to the floor, evidence of how quickly even a Celtics crowd could forget.

"We both sucked," was McHale's summation. "We just sucked worse."

During the Indiana series a news-side columnist for the *Herald* had, for reasons known only to her, printed the home addresses of Dee Brown and Reggie Lewis. Lewis's home was promptly burglarized. And Brown began to receive ugly, racially oriented letters at his home. After practice at Boston Garden between Games 1 and 2 of the Detroit series, he sat courtside and pondered the many and varied ways that his life had changed since he arrived in town some nine months earlier. Indeed, did anyone in the NBA have more reason to be bewildered than Brown, who had gone from obscurity to symbol of racial prejudice to slam-dunk poster boy to part-time playoff quarterback?

"My family is down in Florida thinking about how great my life is, but, well, I don't know," said Brown, dribbling a ball at his side. "I guess it is, and I'm certainly not going to complain about it, but, man, it's happened awful fast. I can't go shopping like I used to. I can't eat out in public like I used to. It's been harder on Jill than on me, too. As an athlete, I'm used to some attention, but she certainly isn't. You're eating dinner and somebody comes up and says, 'Sorry to interrupt you, but . . .' Well, if you're sorry to interrupt us, then don't interrupt us.

"The letters? Well, I'd say we get dozens and dozens. The difference now is that since our address was printed we can get them sent directly to our house. Great, right? They're addressed to both Jill and me. The white people ask how she can be married to a black man, and the black people ask how I can go with a white girl. It goes both ways. If the Wellesley incident hadn't happened, I don't think the letters would've come, either. Sure, I think about them. Some of them are threatening. 'We know where you live.' 'We know when you're at the game.' Stuff like that. What are you going to do, believe them? Live in fear?

"Around town, I see police officers all the time, some who were there that day, and now they're overly nice. They're so nice that I feel kind of funny about it. I wish they wouldn't act that way and just treat me normal, the way they treat anyone else.

"The slam-dunk contest? The only word I can use is 'astounded.' I'm astounded at the attention I got for winning it. I try to reason it out myself. Is it because I'm a rookie? Is it because I'm a different guy on the scene? Is it because of the shoes? Is it because I'm a Celtic? Is it because I look like a little kid? I kind of think that's a big reason. People see Dominique Wilkins and can't relate to his height, but they see me at 170 pounds and they think, 'Hey, I can do that too.' It's had a negative side too. I'm trying to become known as a *player*, yet I've always got this dunking thing. Sometimes in a game when I'm going baseline I wonder if I should dunk it or just do a fundamentally sound lay-up. The way it's been going, in practice I go for the slam, but in games I go for the lay-up.

"The response to the contest by the team was great. Not just the players but people like Mr. Cohen and Mr. Gavitt. They really seemed to appreciate it and talk about how it changed the image of the team, pushed some of those old images out the door.

"It's opened up a lot of things off the court. My agent tells me, 'You can talk well, you can relate to young people.' It could be phenomenal. I've just got to weigh everything after the season and see which direction I want to go."

Listening to Brown, for whom fame and promise and money lie behind each door of his life, one could only hope that in the coming years he chooses wisely.

* * *

A couple of hours before Game 2 on May 9, Ford, Auerbach, and a few players were gathered in front of the TV watching an episode of "The Sally Jesse Raphael Show" that held particular interest to male millionaires. It centered on the complaints of men who felt their wives spent too much money. Parish ambled by and looked at the screen for a few seconds. "I should go on that show," he said. "At one time, anyway." It was widely known that Parish, who had spent nearly one million dollars trying to launch his ex-wife's ill-fated singing career a few years ago, was a much happier man since his divorce. He had not remarried.

At precisely eleven-fifty A.M., Bird walked through the door, carrying his Celtics bag. That meant he was going to play. He was wearing his no-nonsense, don't talk-to-me expression. That meant his back was feeling lousy but he was going to play anyway. Neither coaches nor teammates had known he was coming until twenty minutes before he walked in; that's when Arnie Scheller called the locker room and said, "He's on his way." Bird had spent the morning getting treatment from Dan Dyrek and didn't make a decision until about eleven-fifteen. News from the other locker room, meanwhile, was bad. Isiah Thomas, who had sprained his foot badly in the fourth period of Game 1, would not play, the continuation of a season of frustration for the defending champions and their captain.

For a variety of reasons, Game 2 was being played on a Thursday afternoon, a happenstance that kept thousands of ticket-holders who also happened to have a job from seeing the game. The normal schedule, obviously, would've put Game 2 on Thursday evening. But the Bruins, who own the building, were playing the Pittsburgh Penguins in Game 5 of the Wales Conference playoffs at that time. The Celtics could've elected to play Game 2 on the previous evening, Wednesday, but at the time the decision was made (before the conclusion of the Pacers series) they did not want to play the night after Game 1 for fear that Bird, and possibly McHale, would not be able to suit up on back-to-back games. And Game 2 couldn't be moved to Friday night, May 10, because The Tour of World Figure Skating Champions was booked for the Garden on that evening. Theoretically, the Bruins could have made matters even more complicated by demanding to practice on Thursday afternoon since their agreement with the Garden gives them control of game-day ice. The fact that Ford and Bruins coach Mike Millbury, who lives in Lynnfield and whose daughter takes piano lessons from Kathy Ford, are friendly might've been the only reason the Bruins waived that privilege.

Among the spectators was Zeke Mowatt, the Patriots tight end involved in the Lisa Olson incident. He wore a lovely matching Bermuda shorts-and-shirt ensemble and had a prominent seat near courtside.

Olson still kept her public appearances at a minimum. She had been assigned to the Bruins beat, at least partly because the press area at Boston Garden for NHL games is high above the floor, out of view and heckling range of most spectators.

"That's the height of irony, isn't it?" said Steve Bulpett. "Zeke Mowatt can come to the game and Lisa Olson can't."

Before the game a fan walked behind the row of chairs that serves as the Celtics bench and stared at Dave Popson, who was not on the playoff roster and had long since faded from the memories of many fans. Nevertheless, Popson sat on or near the bench at every game, neatly dressed in a sportcoat or sweater, cheering on his mates.

"Who ARE you?" the fan asked finally, curiosity having gotten the best of him.

Popson looked up, slights and anonymity being part of his lot as a Celtics reserve. "No," he said, "who are YOU?"

Bird was the player everyone expected. The stiffness in his back once again got him off to a slow shooting start—he missed his first three, including one airball—but he grabbed four early rebounds and started to get untracked in the second period. But even when the Celtics started rolling, Bird's pain was obvious. He didn't shake his fist or point his finger or jaw at Dumars and Laimbeer; he even declined high-fives from his teammates, saving the exertion for when he really needed it, as he knew he would. Boston had a 60–58 halftime lead, but the Pistons suddenly took control early in the third period and led by 66–61 with 5:08 left in the quarter. That's when the pigeon arrived.

The bird had been flying around the building for several moments before he landed near midcourt as Parish stood at the line for two free throws. He stayed for a good fifteen seconds and the crowd began to chant: "La-REE! La-REE!" (An even more humorous Bird/bird moment occurred when the Celtics participated in the McDonald's Open in Madrid in October of 1988. The NBA had hired The Famous Chicken, "El Pollo Famoso" for the Spaniards, to entertain the crowd. Most of them did not understand the concept—perhaps that is to their credit—and thought that it was Bird's personal mascot.) Finally, referee Paul Mihalik rolled the ball toward the pigeon and it flew off for a moment, only to alight again.

"Hey, Mike," Kleine shouted at referee Mike Mathis, "cover your head. He's coming after you."

John Salley later suggested that perhaps the pigeon was being operated by Auerbach's remote control. And Daly deadpanned: "Should've been a technical. Too many Birds on the court." To credit the pigeon for the Celtics' inspired play over the remaining seventeen minutes of the game was ridiculous, of course, but the fact remained that the extended stoppage of play worked in Boston's favor. "It was like an extra time-out when they needed it the most," said Laimbeer. The Celtics outscored the Pistons 10–4 from the appearance of the pigeon to the end of the period and never lost that 71–70 lead. Everyone played well, but the real hero was Dee Brown, who became the first Celtic in the playoffs, other than Bird, to step forward and consistently nail outside jumpers when the big men were double-teamed. Brown scored 15 points and had 3 assists in the fourth period and was un-doubtedly the Celtics' player of the game in a 109–103 victory. The number of crucial foul calls the Celtics got down the stretch was also a factor. The biggest whistle occurred with 2:34 left when Detroit's defensive master, Dennis Rodman, was called for his sixth foul on a loose ball situation. It was truly a horrible call, and as Rodman walked off the court, Daly stood at the sidelines with his arms folded and a smirk on his face that seemed to say: "Exactly the kind of call I'd *expect* to be made against us at Boston Garden." Daly was in more subtle, but no less rare, form after the game when someone asked him his opinion of the officiating. He looked quizzical, as if—Holy smoke!—he'd never even considered that the referees might have been a factor.

"Hmm, let's see," said Daly, studying the final box score. "We got six more points off field goals than they did. I like that. But, then, they had fourteen more free-throw attempts, thirty-six to twenty-two, than we did. Well, strange things happen." One of the most significant lessons an NBA coach can learn is how to plant a dagger without collecting huge fines from the league office, and Daly did it as well as anyone.

The Celtics were obviously relieved that the series was even, but their mood was sober, possibly because the thought of playing Games 3 and 4 at The Palace of Auburn Hills was not pleasant. Derek Smith was one of the few Celtics to hang around and talk. "Dee was great, unbelievable," he said. "I'll tell you one thing—there's a lot of guards in this league thinking, 'Oh, how many more years of this guy?' " Detroit was just glad to be going home that afternoon—the game was over by four P.M. and they could get out of town without disturbing the control tower at Logan Airport. "The home games are what's critical for us," Laimbeer said, "because if we win them, we win the series."

The headline in the *Globe* the day after Game 2 read: "Bird(s) help Celtics fly."

Before the start of Game 3 at The Palace on May 11, a Saturday afternoon, there was a palpable deadness of spirit about the Pistons. "You could tell when we got in the lay-up line that we were in trouble," said John Salley after the game. Thomas, who returned to the lineup but was not 100 percent, detected the ennui and gathered the troops together just before tip-off to rally them, but it was no use. The Celtics seemed to instinctively sense the Pistons' torpor and demolished the home team right away. The lead reached 36 points in the fourth period before Boston settled for an unbelievable 115–83 victory. Not only did the Pistons make just 33 percent of their field-goal attempts, but they also converted only 47.2 percent of their free throws, a bad percentage for a bad high school team. "I've never seen anything like it," said Detroit's Mark Aguirre. "Twelve guys playing badly. All twelve."

And almost all twelve played well for the Celtics, who seemed themselves almost bewildered by what was either their own resurrection or the Pistons' collective suicide. Parish played on a sore right ankle but contributed 13 points and 11 rebounds. Shaw turned in his first good game in a while with 19 points, 8 rebounds, 5 assists, and, most importantly, a lot of offensive assertiveness; perhaps he sensed that element was needed since Bird struggled with just 4 field goals on 11 shots. At one point, he and Bird even combined on the old no-look, backdoor play that D. J. and Bird used to run. And when Shaw wasn't running the show, Brown, who had 13 points, was equally effective. Lewis led the scoring with 21 points and easily shed Dumars, one of the top defensive guards in the league.

Most gratifying perhaps was the inspired play of Pinckney. The coaching staff had been ragging him since the beginning of the series about Rodman, the maniacal defensive specialist. "This guy's going to tear you up," they'd tell him. Or: "It's a disgrace that this guy with his limited ability turns himself into an All-Star, and you, with all that natural talent, are a bench warmer." Pinckney took it with his normal good humor, but his performance suggested that some of the message might've gotten through. Early in the game after Pinckney entered to give Gamble a rest, Rodman tried to goad him into a fight with some pushing and shoving, to which Pinckney retaliated only slightly, not backing down but not accelerating the confrontation, either. Steve Javie, who most NBA coaches believed would not be working playoff games except for his close relationship with Darell Garretson, the league's supervisor of officials, promptly blew his whistle and called a double technical foul on Rodman and Pinckney. The double-technical, the ultimate cop-out call, has unfortunately become increasingly prevalent. The NBA seems to believe that *all* confrontations are started by two players when, in fact, they are often the fault of one man, who should receive singular blame. The Rodman-Pinckney double-T illustrated the call at its most absurd, nailing as it did one of the league's most passive players right along with one of the league's most aggressive. The call got the crowd into the game but Pinckney didn't back down. Over the next two minutes he blocked a shot, caught a difficult pass from Bird and dunked over his head, and grabbed a key offensive rebound that led to a basket.

The game no doubt secretly pleased more than a few of the well-heeled Pistons fans who take up space in their suburban pleasure Palace, many of whom leave games early to beat the traffic or get to the country club on time. They could've departed halfway through Game 3 and had a pitcher of martinis down before the curtain closed on the Pistons. Emptying an opponent's arena early is something the Celtics had done rarely over the last few seasons, and the feeling was a good one.

One fan who sat through it all, however, was Leon the Barber, the sharp-witted, acid-tongued old gentleman who has made life miserable for many an NBA team over the years. Most teams have a grudging respect for Leon, because he knows the game and the players and he's funny. After the Nuggets were called for a twenty-four-second violation during a Detroit-Denver game a few seasons ago, Leon suddenly appeared near the team huddle, waved his watch inches in front of Nugget guard Fat Lever, and shouted, "Hey, Lever! You need this?" Dennis Johnson would frequently place a towel over his face so no one could see him laughing when Leon started in on the Celtics. Anyway, as the final seconds of Game 3 clicked off, Casey turned around and said, "Leon, you're awful quiet today."

"What the hell would I say?" asked the Barber. "There's nothing to say."

"I turned around a couple times just to make sure you were there," added McHale, smiling.

Ford's task between Games 3 and 4 was obvious: He had to convince his young players that the series was not over just because the Celtics had climbed back on top. It was not going to be easy. The Celtics had routed the Pistons by 32 points even with Isiah in the lineup, and there were reports that his throbbing foot would keep him out of Game 4 at The Palace on May 13, a Monday night. Ford had some facts and figures at his disposal and he brought them to the attention of the team at practice the day after the rout. In the 1982 Eastern Conference final, the Celtics beat the 76ers by 121–81 in Game 1 at Boston, then lost to the same team three days later, also at the Garden; Philly went on to win that series with a Game 7 victory in Boston. And following the Celtics' most celebrated postseason rout, the 148–114 "Memorial Day Massacre" over the Lakers in Game 1 of the Finals in 1985, the Celtics were defeated by 109–102 and also ultimately lost that series at home. And there was more recent history to point to also. Boston beat the Knicks by 157–128 in Game 2 of the infamous 1990 first-round series, then lost Games 3, 4, and 5. After his presentation, Ford called on LarryKevinandRobert, who had been around for all of those famed foldaramas, and they, too, emphasized the need to think about what still had to be done, not what was already accomplished.

Actually, the mere presence of Bird, who had not been in attendance at an offday practice in almost a month, was a cause for minor celebration. Considering the collective physical condition of LarryKevinandRobert, Ford did not make the session a strenuous one and Bird was there, he said, mostly to work on his free-throw shooting. He was in a good mood, too, still reluctant to provide specifics about his back, but loose and funny and analytical in a Bird sort of way.

"I'm worried about my free throws," Bird said after practice. "I'm not sure at all that I'm going to make them and I don't want to be fouled late in the game and go to the line without some practice. That concerns me the most. I've lost my touch." Indeed, he had made only one of three free throws in Game 3.

Someone asked him how his presence affected the team; he had made just 42 percent of his shots through the first three games, but it had been proven time after time throughout the season that the Celtics were still a lot better club with him than without him.

"Sometimes I hurt 'em, sometimes I help 'em," said Bird. "But I'm paid to perform. That's what I do. If I don't play, then I feel I'm lettin' someone down. Tickets aren't cheap and if you buy one expectin' someone to perform and he doesn't, it's a letdown. It'd be easy for me to sit back and say, 'To hell with the rest of the year,' and jist git healthy. But I can't do that." Bird was then asked if he felt humbled by the fact that he sometimes could not do what used to come so easily to him. "It's how much can you take. And are you willing to sacrifice your ego because you know you can't play the way you're used to playin'? If you can let your ego go and withstand the pain, then you should play." That's about as close as one could ever get to hearing Bird explicate his code.

Bird felt so good after the game-day shootaround the following morning that he and Kleine took a twenty-minute jog in 90-degree heat when the bus pulled back into the hotel. Nobody advised him against it because Bird's biggest worry, no matter how much he talked about his free-throw touch, was his conditioning. He always believed that he excelled in the late stages of the game not just because of his mental toughness, but because he had tuned his body for the long haul. That was no longer true. All the game-time minutes and all the postpractice sprints up and down the Hellenic College floor he had missed had reduced his aerobic capacity, and that was a major concern.

Still, he felt confident and looked confident. The degree to which the Game 3 rout had changed the complexion of the series, at least to the outside observer, was phenomenal. Conventional thinking now said that all the Celtics had to do was come out strong, crush Detroit in the early stages of Game 4, coast to another easy win, then capture the series back in Boston. And if that was underestimating the mental toughness of the defending champions, then the point was made that *these* Pistons weren't the champions, not without a healthy Thomas.

Perhaps anticipating a one-on-one fashion duel with Daly, Ford showed up for Game 4 in an unusual rust-colored suit that attracted a lot of attention. "Hey, Chris," Ordway shouted at him when Ford walked out before the game, "I remember when you had a leisure suit that color." Before long, though, the color of Ford's face was more noticeable than the color of his suit. It turned crimson red, as he pleaded and shouted for the Celtics to increase their defensive effort. They didn't look bad on offense, but they couldn't stop the Pistons, even without Thomas. In the second period, Dumars and Mark Aguirre were the only Detroit players to score, yet Boston's advantage over those twelve minutes was only three points and the half ended in a 53–53 tie. That type of scoring imbalance, though, typified the Detroit offense. Daly, like Golden State's Don Nelson, was known to go with his hot hands, clearing the floor and calling only plays for the man or men who were scoring at the time. And if those Pistons stayed hot, it made it extremely tough for a defense. The Celtics could not preplan to double-team Dumars, for example, lest someone else get hot, Vinnie Johnson, James Edwards, Aguirre, Laimbeer, or, obviously, Thomas, if he was playing. A team could not design a special defense for Detroit as they could for Chicago and Michael Jordan because no one had any idea who was going to be the main man on any given evening; all a coach could do was hope his team played tough, basic man-to-man defense. The Celtics were not equal to that task in Game 4. Ford must've really known he was in trouble, however, when Daly put the seldom-used Hastings on Bird for seven full minutes in the second period without Bird doing much damage. Hastings frequently used Bird as part of his self-deprecating humor. "I always hear my name mentioned in connection with Larry Bird's," Hastings would say. "People are always saying, 'That Scott Hastings, he's sure no Larry Bird.'" But, frighteningly for the Celtics, in the first half of Game 4 there was little to choose between them.

In the third period McHale was unstoppable, but so was the man he was guarding. Aguirre was one of the least popular players in the league, a talented but extremely enigmatic individual who was known as "Buffet" for his prodigious accomplishments in the chow line. It

drove Ford to distraction that a player like Aguirre was beating the
Celtics almost single-handedly. "Let's see you do something at *this*
end," Ford shouted at McHale as he trotted downcourt after making a
basket. Boston still trailed by just 82–79 early in the fourth period
when Aguirre's baseline jumper began a 12–4 Pistons run that iced
the game. Near the end an obviously frustrated McHale shoved Rodman into the Celtics bench, the kind of bush-league move for which
the Pistons had a reputation. It was even more annoying to the Celtics
that Rodman didn't even bother to respond; he just gave McHale a
brief look, then strutted to the foul line. The final score was 104–97.

"We were physically outplayed, and we weren't mentally ready," said
Parish in a locker room that was almost deathly quiet.

It was an explanation that explained nothing. "Physically outplayed"
was understandable, given the conditions of LarryKevinandRobert,
but not being "mentally ready" seemed incomprehensible—the
Celtics had their opponents all but floored after the Game 3 debacle
and could've completed the process with a strong effort in Game 4.
How could they not have been "mentally ready"? The only reasonable
explanation lay in the forty-four minutes played by Bird. As hurting as
he was, the Celtics still looked to Bird for leadership, for that spark that
would get them started, and their captain was simply unable to provide
it. His lack of scoring (13 points on only 4 field goals) was not that
important—the Celtics had seen that before—but his inability to have
any effect on the game was significant. It was almost as if he wasn't
there, and that is not like Bird. He had 6 rebounds and 4 assists, but
those are just numbers, and not great ones at that. Rodman took
exactly one shot the entire night (he made it), but had 18 rebounds, 5
at the offensive end. John Salley tried only one field goal (he missed it),
but blocked three Celtic shots. Even Aguirre, a player for whom Bird
has absolutely no respect, had 6 rebounds to go with his 34 points.
Game 4 was played somewhere beyond Bird's sphere of influence, and
that was an extremely discomfiting thought for the Celtics.

Ford and his assistants had marveled all season at the unpredictability
of the Celtics' mood, so they were really not surprised that the team
seemed loose and confident in the locker room before Game 5 on May
15 at Boston Garden. Casey was still taking his share of abuse for an
incident that happened a couple nights earlier in Detroit. He had
received a phone call in his hotel room from one "Nancy Lieberman
Kleine," who wanted to interview him on a radio show from Dallas.
Most coaches would've recognized "Nancy Lieberman" as one of the
greatest women players in the history of basketball, but Case had no

idea who she was. "I agreed to go on because when I heard 'Kleine,' I thought she had something to do with Joe Kleine," he explained. The interview went well and after a while, Casey said to her, "Boy, you really know your stuff. You should be a coach or something."

The color of Ford's Game 4 suit had not been forgotten, either.

"I don't think it was that unusual," said Ford. "Rust. It was rust. I guess it was kind of clay-colored, too."

"Oh, I think it was mauve," said McHale in an affected voice.

"Here it is," said Dee Brown, who was stretching on the floor. He held up a manila envelope from his fan mail. "It was manila. Chris wore the first manila suit in history."

M. L. Carr was a pregame visitor and he and McHale began to talk about the old, championship days, as Brown listened in from his customary position on the floor.

"Dee, I've got a question for you," said McHale. "How long's it take to make a baby?"

"Nine months," said Brown, playing along.

"Well, that's how long it took for me to get my first ring," said McHale. "Here in October, ring in June." Carr cracked up.

"This doesn't look much like a Bill Fitch playoff team, does it?" said Bob Ryan, noting the atmosphere.

"No," said McHale, "but after all these years, the desire is in here." He pounded his chest.

Despite having Isiah for only part-time duty, however, the Pistons were the more inspired team for the better part of three quarters and led by 88–75 entering the fourth. It didn't help the Celtics that Parish, who had been the one veteran to escape serious injury all season, went down in the second period with a badly sprained ankle. But, suddenly, the Celtics woke up. Bird's jumper began falling, Lewis stepped up to make some big shots and Brown was nearly unstoppable; he and Pinckney played most of the key minutes while Shaw and Gamble watched from the bench. As Boston crept closer and closer, Ford gestured to his bench to get up and join the screaming crowd; he shouldn't have had to do it. Bird's jumper over Rodman finally tied the score at 100–100 and it seesawed for a couple minutes after that, the Pistons going up by two, the Celtics tying the score. McHale's jump hook over Salley's outstretched hand tied the game at 106–106 with less than a minute left, and Lewis turned in a big defensive play at the other end, cleanly blocking Dumars's shot out of bounds. That gave the Pistons just six seconds on the twenty-four-second clock. They called time-out to set up a play and, as Bird turned to go back onto the court, Ford said to him, "Get up on Laimbeer." But Bird didn't get up close enough. Laimbeer slid out near the three-point line, took the inbounds pass, and buried a long shot over Bird to put the Pistons back on top, 108–106, with thirty-nine seconds left. Bird missed a three-point attempt, but Lewis grabbed the offensive rebound, drove to the basket and gathered himself for a shot. Whistle. Offensive foul. Pistons' ball. Replays showed the call to be marginal at best. After another time-out, Thomas stood at sidecourt for a throw-in.

"Let's see, how does this go now?" mused the *Herald*'s Michael Gee, conjuring up the famed Game 5 from 1987. "Bird steals the ball, right? From Isiah, right?" Oddly enough, Dee Brown was thinking the same thing out on the court. "That play flashed through my mind," said Brown. "Remember, I know all that history." Brown did get his eager hands on the inbounds pass too, but he couldn't quite come up with it, and McHale was eventually forced to foul Aguirre, who made both free throws to make it 110–106. Now in the desperation mode, Brown drove to the basket and flattened Dumars. This time the offensive foul call was obvious, and Dumars made both free throws to put the game out of reach. The final was 116–111.

There was a sense not of outright defeat, but possibly of inevitability in the Celtics locker room. Down 3–2 with the series returning to Detroit for Game 6, what more could they do? Could Bird turn it up a notch? Didn't look likely. Could McHale? Probably not. Could Shaw (who had only four points and just one assist in twenty lethargic minutes) be counted on in the clutch? No. Could anything be done to stop the steel-eyed nervelessness of Dumars, who had 32 points in Game 5? Didn't seem so. Could Parish somehow recover and come back out to harass Laimbeer, who had 24 big points? It would be a minor miracle. Could the Celtics play any more courageously on the road than they did in the fourth period of Game 5 at home, when they *still* came up empty? That was the big question. And the answer to that seemed to be a resounding "no."

Casey arrived at home following Game 5 to find his answering machine working overtime. Being part of the network of NBA and college coaches who talk endlessly on the telephone, Casey had received several messages from coaches all over the country offering advice on how to defense the Pistons' vaunted pick-and-roll, the play with which Dumars and Laimbeer had hurt them. Most of the advice was sound and well intentioned but ultimately meaningless. In point of fact, a successful pick-and-roll like Detroit's was extremely hard to stop. The Pistons had guards, Dumars, Vinnie Johnson, and Thomas, who could shoot from distance or take it to the basket, and they had a pick-setting big man, Laimbeer, who could flare off, get the return pass, and shoot a long jump shot. An "ABC team" was Casey's description of the Pistons. "You defense A, they run B," said Casey. "You defense B, they run C. It's simple but they do it well. That's why they won two championships." What the Celtics needed, most of all, was to aggressively double-team the ball far out on the floor, i.e., to put such pressure on the guards that they could not easily shoot, drive, or make the simple pass to Laimbeer. The problem was that one of the double-teamers had to be Bird, McHale, or Parish, none of whom guarded players out on the floor very well.

Practice the following day at Hellenic looked normal enough; if anyone stopped and pondered the fact that it might be the last one of the season, he did not mention it. Gamble worked hard on the stationary bike, trying to compensate, he said, for the exercise he was suddenly not getting during games. "It's between you and Larry to see who has the yellow jersey," Gavitt hollered up to him, making a joke about the Tour de France that Gamble didn't get.

Kleine and McHale played a brief revival of their one-on-one game, though far less spiritedly than their matchups in the winter. When McHale came to the sidelines, someone brought up the inevitable subject of injuries.

"Who wants to hear about a guy who makes a million dollars pissing and moaning about injuries?" said McHale. "Think a guy who makes six-fifty an hour laying cement wants to hear athletes pissing and moaning? I don't." Mentioning the common man was a favorite theme of McHale's, as well as a good way to wriggle out of commenting on a subject of which he was dreadfully tired. Just then Parish hobbled by in street clothes; his ankle had kept him from practicing that day and he was listed as questionable for Game 6 in Detroit the following evening.

"How would you rate Robert?" a reporter asked McHale, hoping to get a hint on whether or not the Chief would play.

"Hmm," said McHale. "Sandals, shorts, matching tank top. I'd rate him very highly. I have no idea if he'll play, though."

He didn't. Chief moved through the visiting locker room like walking silk, disappearing into the "players only" section. Most of his teammates were in there with him, Bird included. The word was, his back felt bad, and he was not planning on being around to confirm it. It was six-thirty P.M. on May 17, an hour before what would be the Celtics' last game of the season. Ford, Dee Brown, and Derek Smith idly watched a videotape of Game 5. They talked about the phone calls some of the Celtics had received at seven o'clock that morning from a Detroit radio station. Ford answered the phone and hung up when he realized who it was. Parish did the same. Brown talked for a few minutes, and later had no idea what he said. Ford munched on popcorn and looked nervous. When he talked to Dee, he knew he was talking to the best point guard on his team at that moment. Except for Game 3, when everyone played well, Shaw had not done the job, while Brown had clearly elevated his level of play. More and more out-of-town reporters had been asking the coaches if there was any thought to starting Brown—the local writers knew better—and the staff would always stand firmly behind Shaw. "As far as I'm concerned, Brian Shaw is our starting point guard until he retires," Jennings had said a few days earlier, obviously overstating the case. Deep inside, Ford knew he'd like to get forty minutes out of Brown, but he couldn't take a chance on making so radical a change. He could only hope that Bird's back and McHale's ankle held up reasonably well, and that Kleine could somehow do a respectable impersonation of a first-string center in Parish's stead, and that Gamble would come out of his offensive lethargy, and that either Pinckney or Derek Smith could make a statement off the bench, and that . . . And if all of those things happened, maybe, just maybe, the Celtics could bring the series back to Boston for another magical Sunday afternoon.

The Pistons streaked to a 7–0 lead, however, and any thought that Shaw's confidence and gamesmanship would return were crushed by Dumars's domination of him early in the game. The Celtics were frustrated by the youth and athleticism of the Pistons. Bird was called for a flagrant foul for decking Salley in the second period, and McHale and Salley squared off—somewhat comically, for neither is a fighter—a few minutes later. Detroit led by 56–50 at halftime and by 80–63 with 3:30 left in the third period. The Celtics would go down, it seemed, not with a bang but with a whimper.

But suddenly, improbably, they came back. It wasn't one player or two, it was everyone. Lewis, who would finish a disastrous 9-of-27 from the floor, hit a few jumpers. McHale, who would lead all scorers with 34 points, was unstoppable. Pinckney was a terror on the boards. Bird, in obvious pain, played the role of decoy to perfection, calling for the ball, drawing an extra defender, and working it around to the open man. And Brown breathed new life into the team as soon as he hit the floor. That was Ford's five—Bird, McHale, Pinckney, Lewis, and Brown. Gamble and Shaw watched from the bench. The Pistons lead shrunk to 82–75 after three periods, to 92–89 with seven minutes left, and to 99–98 after Brown made a sensational block of a Dumars drive, and Bird hit a turnaround jumper over Rodman with 2:57 left. Was it possible?

Laimbeer missed a jumper, and Bird was fouled in a scramble for the ball. He made both free throws and the Celtics were up by 100–99,

their first lead of the game. James Edwards made two foul shots at the
other end but Lewis took a pass inside from McHale, turned and made
a lay-up, was fouled by Laimbeer, and made the free throw for a three-
point play and a 103–101 lead. Dumars tied the game with a running
jump shot, but McHale cleanly tapped in a Lewis miss with fifty-eight
seconds left to give Boston an apparent 105–103 advantage. But veteran official Jack Madden waved off the basket for offensive goaltending and awarded the ball to the Pistons. It seemed to be a bad call right
away and replays showed it was, in fact, an atrocious call—the only
possible explanation was that Madden saw how wide-open McHale
was when he tapped the ball and instinctively reasoned that he *must've*
pushed the ball back in when it was still in the cylinder directly above
the basket. McHale leaped and yelped and pointed but to no avail. No
basket and the score was still 103–103. Brown, doubling down on
James Edwards, committed a foul and Edwards made both free throws
for a 105–103 Pistons lead. At the other end, Brown worked the ball to
Lewis, who missed a shot. But Pinckney kept it alive on the backboard
and Lewis made a followup shot to make it 105–105 with twenty
seconds left.

Though Dumars had been the main man for the Pistons throughout
the series, the designated game winner was Thomas, never mind the
bad wrist and the bad foot. He drove toward the basket with Brown all
over him and spun into the lane to find McHale looming in front of
him. He lost the ball as the buzzer sounded, sending the game into
overtime.

The stat sheet from the final five minutes of the Celtics season is
revealing for more than its log of baskets and free throws. It lists 14
distinct substitutions made by Chuck Daly, who sent players through a
constant revolving door, getting Rodman in the game, for example, to
defense Bird, then replacing him with Aguirre, a superior offensive
player. Ford started the extra period with Bird, McHale, Pinckney,
Lewis, and Brown, and, with the exception of a desperation substitu-
tion with twenty-five seconds left, that's how he finished. He had lost
confidence in both Gamble and Shaw, and saw nothing to gain by
using Kleine or either of the Smiths.

Still, the tired Celtics took a 109–105 lead on a Lewis jumper and a
Pinckney dunk. Edwards scored on a jumper over McHale and, after a
McHale miss, Thomas hit a three-pointer, the ball banking uninten-
tionally off the backboard as the shot clock wore down. The Pistons'
captain had a history of making big, clutch shots, but never, he admitted later, had he made one that was so utterly lucky. "I was basically
just trying to get the ball up on the rim, and God picked up the ball and
put it in," he said in the locker room. Professional athletes often make

the miscalculation that God is watching sporting events, but they are entitled to their opinion. The three-pointer gave Detroit a 110–109 lead.

Dee Brown, suddenly a twenty-two-year-old Mr. Clutch, hit a jump shot to give the lead back to the Celtics, but Thomas matched him at the other end for a 112–111 Detroit lead with 1:41 left. Brown then missed a jumper, and after McHale fouled Salley trying for the rebound, Laimbeer made a jumper to make it 114–111. With forty-three seconds left, Thomas finally did something that the Pistons had been counting on him doing all series long—he made Brown look like a rookie. First, Thomas forced Brown into a travel call with intense defensive pressure. Then he came hard off a pick set by Laimbeer, juked Brown with a crossover dribble, pulled up and stuck a jump shot from twenty feet for a 116–111 lead. It ended soon after, 117–113.

Suddenly, the season was over. Celtics equipment manager Joe Qatato shook hands with Pistons reserve Gerald Henderson, a former Celtic. Daly reflexively tightened the knot in his tie and headed for the locker room, relief written in his face. Aguirre held his fist aloft, mugging for the fans. Ford shook hands with Salley and tried to smile. Michael Smith shook his head as he walked slowly toward the locker room. "I'm convinced God doesn't intervene in basketball games," he said, "because I said too many prayers to him during this one." Perhaps that settled the issue, then. Isiah caught up to McHale and told him what an honor it was to compete against LarryKevinandRobert.

Later, in the Pistons locker room, even Laimbeer had something positive to say about the Celtics.

"They are the Boston Celtics," said Laimbeer. "They have a lot of pride and they are outstanding competitors. They don't quit and we have a lot of respect for them."

Had he heard them, the words would've meant nothing to Bird. He knew they had pride, and he knew they were competitors, and he knew that they had given their all. But what he knew, most of all, as he bolted out of the locker room and made a determined beeline for the bus, was that a long, painful, and ultimately frustrating season was over. And not a moment too soon to suit him.

Epilogue

Two weeks after their victory over the Celtics, the Pistons were eliminated in the Eastern Conference Finals. They were swept in four games by the Chicago Bulls. They compounded the defeat by walking off the court before the final buzzer had sounded in Game 4. The Celtics would probably not have furnished any stiffer opposition than the Pistons, but they would have certainly been more honorable losers. The Bulls then proved to be unstoppable in the Finals, beating the Lakers in five games.

Less than four months later, on the morning of Friday, October 4, the Celtics convened at Hellenic College for the traditional media session that opened the 1991–92 season. The first Celtic to appear was Dennis Johnson, who had been hired as a West Coast scout. He was glad to be back and everyone was glad to see him. For the first time in anyone's memory, Johnny Most was not around, however. True to the prediction of many, the Celtics legend was severely burned a few weeks after the season ended when he stuck a lit cigarette under his oxygen mask and it ignited. He was home from the hospital but in extremely poor health. Lisa Olson was nowhere around, either, having left for Australia and a newspaper job in Sydney. A suit she had filed against the Patriots for sexual harassment was due to go to trial in March of 1992.

Dave Gavitt was working actively to land free-agent and ex-Piston Vinnie Johnson, but nothing had been worked out by the first day of camp. And so the Celtics of 1991–92 appeared to be much like the Celtics of 1990–91. Only two of the twelve players who had been on last season's final active roster were not in attendance—Kevin Gamble, who was home in Springfield, Illinois, and Derek Smith, who was home in Louisville, Kentucky. Both were free agents battling the Celtics for more money through their representative, Ron Grinker. Of the assorted rookies and free agents in camp, only two figured to have any chance to make the club. They were number one draft pick Rick Fox, and a 6-foot-9 forward named Steve Scheffler, who, despite an extremely muscular 250-pound frame, had a Muppetlike face. Should Scheffler make the team, McHale will have some fun with that.

The first player to amble onto the court was Stojko Vrankovic, who had spent part of the summer back in his native Yugoslavia. His hometown is not close to the fighting that was tearing his country apart, but the civil war weighed heavy on his mind when he and his wife, Lola, and their two daughters boarded a plane to return to America. "I worry about them much," he said of his mother and sister who are still back in the homeland. Chris Ford's working plan was to get substantial minutes for Vrankovic early in the season to determine once and for all if he was going to be an NBA player.

That was bad news for Joe Kleine, but nothing he didn't expect. He had played for the Celtics in the Los Angeles Summer League in August specifically to showcase his talents for other teams. Aside from that, he spent most of his free time in Arkansas, cheered by the birth of a daughter, Courtney Frances, as well as frequent reruns of "The Andy Griffith Show." "They even review them every day in the local paper," said Kleine.

His good buddy, Eddie Pinckney, had a quiet summer with his wife and children. They spent a lot of time with Pinckney's parents, who now live in the relatively wide-open spaces of Westchester County, New York. "We felt it was important for them to get to know their grandchildren," he said. Pinckney didn't cough once during the two-hour session.

The highlight of Brian Shaw's summer was his second-annual fishing trip to Alaska, where he and his father hauled in salmon and cod eight hours a day for a solid week. Not surprisingly, Shaw's name had surfaced in trade rumors as soon as the 1990–91 season ended, and, even in October, no one could be sure that he would not be dealt, with the starting point-guard role then going to Dee Brown. "People keep asking me if all the trade rumors made it a tough summer," said Shaw. "They've got to be kidding. Now last summer, when I was in court and in the newspapers every single day, *that* was tough."

Brown spent much of his offseason giving clinics, visiting camps (one of them in Spain), and judging slam-dunk contests in malls, the latter a Reebok promotion. He also filmed several local commercials, including one for Dunkin' Donuts. He had worked out with weights to bulk up his skinny frame too, and he looked good.

So did Michael Smith, who pronounced: "I'm in the best shape of my life." Like Kleine, however, there was talk that he would not be a Celtic for long. There were even reports that if the club couldn't work out a trade for Smith, it would buy out his contract, worth about $1.3 million over the next two years. "If it happens, it happens," said Smith, "but this is where I want to be."

Reggie Lewis was where he wanted to be in the summer—back at Northeastern working toward his B.A. in criminal justice. He took two courses, "Criminal Research" and "Legal Aspects of Security Management." "It kind of shocked some people when they looked around and there I was," said Lewis. In July, he married his fiancée, Donna Harris.

Jon Jennings's summer plans did not work out nearly as well. The day before he was scheduled to fly to London for a vacation and an intellectual rendezvous with his hero, Winston Churchill, he was taken ill and hospitalized. The diagnosis was two perforated ulcers brought on by severe esophagus problems. Don Casey, meanwhile, went on a fast and lost twenty-one pounds immediately after the season. He looked great but had received some bad news the day before camp opened when a routine checkup revealed an irregular heartbeat. "All that trouble to get in the best shape of my life, and I've got to hear that," said Casey. "Tough world, isn't it?"

Chris Ford's summer got off to a great start when he learned that the *Daily News Record,* the voice of the men's clothing industry, had named him one of its Best Dressed Men. (Perhaps the magazine missed the night that he wore the manila-colored suit.) And the rest of his summer was fairly peaceful, much more so, obviously, than the summer of 1990. "The Jersey shore," said Ford, "was beautiful."

The highlight of Dave Gavitt's summer was a week-long golfing vacation in Scotland. The highlight of Jan Volk's summer was, he said, "just staying out of court." And the highlight of Auerbach's? "Christ, I didn't do nothing different," he said. "Played some racquetball, took care of myself. At my age, what the hell can you do different?"

About twenty minutes after the session began, LarryKevin-andRobert emerged together. Parish, who would be the oldest player in the league for the second straight year, looked terrific. "And I feel good," he said. He spent the summer keeping in shape through daily ninety-minute sessions with weights, exercise, and martial-arts instruction. There was no talk, as there had been in October 1990, of trading him. McHale looked about the same too. He talked about retirement for a short while after the season ended but eventually signed a contract extension that should keep him a Celtic through the 1992–93 season. He had surgery on his left foot and ankle on July 17, after which he escaped to his summer home in northern Minnesota to spend time with family and friends, and, as his old battle cry went, "to drink beer with impunity." During one fishing excursion to Canada with Ordway, McHale's boat ran over a submerged rock, splitting the engine in two and plunging them into the lake. They didn't see anyone for an hour until, finally, a lone fisherman happened by and picked them up. McHale said that his feet and ankles were coming along, but he doubted that he'd be able to begin the season at full strength. "I'm already tired of people asking me how I'm feeling," said McHale, "so I always just say, 'I'm feeling fine.'"

Just then a reporter joined the group and asked McHale how he was feeling.

"Gee, I don't know," said McHale. "Fine, I guess."

As for Bird, he underwent his back surgery on June 7, left the hospital on June 8, was walking 10 miles a day by June 15, and reported to camp at least 10 pounds lighter than he had been a year ago. He lost the weight with an exercise program and a reduction in his caloric intake. Even on those quiet Hoosier mornings while he waited for the bass to bite on Patoka Lake in French Lick, he did not indulge in any wedding cake, not even a single slice. In August he accepted an invitation to be on the 1992 United States Olympic team, the first that would include professional players. Though he would never admit it, his 1991–92 season would be, on one level, a campaign to show he was worthy of the honor.

And all that wasn't even the biggest news of the summer. He and Dinah also adopted an infant son, Connor.

It was incredible, really, that LarryKevinandRobert were still together on that sunny morning in October. There had been talk of breaking up the trio years ago, even before they had begun to break down physically. Yet there they were, back together again, in as good a physical condition as humanly possible considering the thousands of hours of pain and several surgeries logged among them. Did they honestly believe, deep in their stubborn hearts, that one more championship was possible? Did they think that they could once again conjure up their ancient magic?

"None of us would be here if we *didn't* think it was possible," said McHale.

One final note: Tod Rosensweig said that the club was considering playing rock music from time to time at Boston Garden instead of letting Ron Harry's organ carry the entire load.

"But the sound system's so bad," said Rosensweig, "we probably won't be able to do it."

Index